Flesh and Blood

REAY TANNAHILL

FLESH
AND BLOOD

*A History of the
Cannibal Complex*

STEIN AND DAY/*Publishers*/New York

First published in the United States of America in 1975
Copyright © 1975 by Reay Tannahill
All rights reserved
Printed in the United States of America
Stein and Day/*Publishers*/Scarborough House,
Briarcliff Manor, N.Y. 10510

Library of Congress Cataloging in Publication Data
Tannahill, Reay.
Flesh and blood.

Bibliography: p.
Includes index.
1.   Cannibalism.   2.   Blood (in religion, folk-lore,
etc.)   I.   Title.
GN409.T36 1975   394'.9   74-26943
ISBN 0-8128-1756-7

CONTENTS

ILLUSTRATIONS

Between pages 134 and 135

13 A Cranach woodcut, early sixteenth century, of a wild man making off with a baby.

14 The werewolf of Gévaudan. An engraving made in 1764.

15 A witches' sabbat, from the Abbé Laurent Bordelon: *L'Histoire des Imaginations Extravagantes de Monsieur Oufle.* Amsterdam, 1710.

16 'Faim, Folie, Crime.' An oil painting, dated 1853, by Antoine Wiertz. Musée Wiertz, Brussels.

Between pages 166 and 167

17 One of Géricault's rejected studies for 'The Raft of the Medusa'. From Gobin: *Dessins, aquarelles et gouaches par Géricault, chez Maurice Gobin.* Paris, 1935.

18 The 'lady vampire' in 1974. Pauline Peart in the Hammer Films production *The Satanic Rites of Dracula.*

19 Transfusion for a vampire, from Luis Murschetz: *Draculas Ende, 28 Zeichnungen.* Zurich, 1969.

20 Strip cartoon 'The Wizard of Id', from the Elmira *Star Gazette*, New York, May, 1973.

ACKNOWLEDGEMENTS

The author wishes to express her thanks to the following.

To Dr A. I. G. McLaughlin whose medical expertise, generously given, was invaluable in the section on vampires—though the use made of that expertise is in no way his responsibility.

For permission to reproduce illustrations, to A.C.L., Brussels, 16; the Bibliothèque Nationale, Paris, 5, 14; Diogenes Verlag, Zurich, 19; Gannett Tripp Group, New York, 20; Mansell Collection, London, 3; Phaidon Press Ltd, London, 17; Thames and Hudson Ltd, London, 1; Trustees of the British Museum, London, 2, 8, 9, 15; Warner Bros, 18.

For copyright material quoted in the text, to Professor William Arrowsmith and the University of Michigan Press for an extract from *The Satyricon* of Petronius; Mrs George Bambridge, Macmillan of London and Basingstoke, and Macmillan Co. of Canada, for 'The White Man's Burden', from *The Five Nations* by Rudyard Kipling; Professor A. L. Basham for his translations of 'The Hymn of Primeval Man' from the *Rig Veda*, and of Dandin's *Dasakumaracarita*; the Division of Christian Education of the National Council of the Churches of Christ in the U.S.A. for Scripture quotations from the Revised Standard Version, *Common Bible*, copyright © 1973; and Penguin Books Ltd, for J. M. Cohen's translation of *The Conquest of New Spain* by Bernal Diaz, and Aubrey de Sélincourt's translation of *The Histories* of Herodotus, copyright © the Estate of Aubrey de Sélincourt, 1954.

Flesh and Blood

Flesh, Blood and Spirit

'I M A D E its walls gleam like the sun,' boasted Nebuchadnezzar. 'With shining gold . . . with lapis lazuli and alabaster I clothed the inside of the temple. . . . The best of my cedars, which I brought from Lebanon, the noble forest, I sought out for the roofing of the shrine.'[1]

It was at this richly endowed shrine of Marduk that the people of Babylon, every spring, began a re-enactment of the great cosmic struggle that ended in the creation of the world and of mankind.

For seven days there were rituals within the temple while wailing and mourning, anarchy and chaos ruled in the streets. But on the eighth day the glittering image of the god was brought forth to go in cavalcade through the city. Past the great ziggurat—the Tower of Babel—and north along the Processional Way, with incense perfuming the air, music resounding from the walls, and the faithful kneeling in awe and adoration. On, past the royal palace and the green terraces and tinkling waters of the Hanging Gardens of Babylon, to a covered avenue ablaze with blue and crimson, alive with bas-reliefs of dragons and bulls. Finally, through the Ishtar Gate to a garden temple beyond the city for the ceremonies symbolising the creation of the universe.[2]

Despite the material wealth and magnificence that made Babylon in the sixth century B.C. one of the most advanced and envied cities of the age, these ceremonies enshrined ideas that were almost as old as man himself and as stark as the world about him when he first became capable of speculative thought.

Briefly, the Babylonians held that 'in the beginning were the gods', some of them timid, some brash, some statesman-like, others warlike. There was dissension in heaven. When

1

the day of reckoning came, the divine Marduk—armed with lightning, hurricane and flame as well as more conventional weapons—advanced alone in his storm chariot against the primeval goddess Tiamat and her husband Kingu, with their attendant horde of demons, scorpions and centaurs.

Marduk was victorious. Dramatically, he slew Tiamat, split her down the middle 'like a shellfish', and began his creation of a world order by setting up half her body to make the sky. When all was ready, he beheaded Kingu and from his flowing blood fashioned the human race.[3] As the Old Testament has it: 'The blood is the life.'[4]

This conviction that the world itself had been created from the flesh and blood of the gods reflected early man's belief in the magical properties of the elements that constituted his own being. From almost the first moment when he formulated the question 'why?'—the question that marked his final, irrevocable divergence from the family tree of the apes—he had begun to shape ideas about the association between life and death, flesh, blood and spirit, that were to remain embedded in the human subconscious throughout all succeeding centuries. Sometimes they were to be expressed in the rituals of cannibalism, blood-drinking, and headhunting, sometimes in the clearcut shape of werewolves and vampires. Sometimes they were absorbed into bland religious observances. Always they were implicit in everyday speech. The attitudes, the practices, and the responses to them form the themes of the present book.

There is little enough unequivocal evidence about man at the dawn of his existence, more about his death than his life, perhaps, nothing at all about his thought processes. Nevertheless, it is worth recapitulating what is known because it was out of the human situation hundreds of thousands of years ago that there grew, as naturally as a plant from a rock fissure, mankind's view of the meaning of flesh, blood and spirit.

In the million years that ended in 10,000 B.C., when the New Stone Age can be said to have begun, roughly 35,000 million people were born, lived, and died.[5] So far, the remains of only a few hundred of these have been dug up—a sampling that would produce a frenzy of disclaimers from the modern opinion pollster. To make matters worse, the human bones found at 'habitation sites' almost certainly represent the exceptions rather than the rule. In his early days, man did not clutter his caves or refuse dumps with the bodies of the dead, but carried them off to some distant spot and abandoned them. Human bones found in or near the caves, therefore, usually belonged to people killed and buried by some natural calamity such as a rockfall, or to bodies brought back for some specific purpose—to be eaten or, at a later stage in human development, worshipped. The fact that many of the skeletal remains found in Stone Age caves show signs of cannibal attention does not, by any stretch, mean that for hundreds of thousands of years *every* man finished up in someone else's stomach.

A few of Peking man's contemporaries certainly did, however. *Pithecanthropus pekinensis*, or *Sinanthropus*, or Peking man, was the marginally subhuman predecessor of *homo sapiens* who lived from about 500,000 B.C. onwards in the caves of Dragon Bone Hill, thirty miles south-west of modern Peking. His brain was two-thirds of the size of the average modern brain. He still lived, anthropologists believe, in much the same way as the gibbon—in single-family groups where the mother chased away the daughters and the father the sons as soon as an incestuous gleam began to show in the other parent's eye.[6]

The domestic debris of Peking man's caves consists mainly of the broken-up bones of the animals he hunted for food, but there are also a number of human bones, fractured in much the same way, some of them split to give access to one of early man's favourite delicacies, the marrow.[7] This implies not only that he was prepared to eat his fellows when the hunting was poor, but that he ate them without much more compunction than he ate deer, otter, or wild sheep.

What the archaeologist turns up much more frequently than bones, however, are skulls—skulls in which the *foramen magnum*, the gap through which the spinal cord connects with the brain, has been artificially enlarged after death. The purpose was probably to make it easy to get at the brain which, to the hungry realist, was just as good eating as the marrow. Anthropologists, however, mystified by the fact that none of the appropriate vertebrae (evidence of on-the-spot butchering) have been found on Dragon Bone Hill, have come up with the theory that these skulls were not dealt with immediately on the demise of their owners, but brought back to the cave only after the flesh had withered away, so that the brain could be extracted and eaten according to some undiscovered Stone Age ritual.[8] It seems legitimate to wonder just how much brain would be left, for ritual or other eating, after a body had been exposed to the mild damp of northern China for a few weeks or months.

On the whole, and particularly since there is no other evidence that Peking man had developed either ideology or ritual, it is more reasonable to assume that he treated human game just like any other game. Until very recently, hunters in some parts of the world were accustomed, after they had killed their prey, to have a snack of its more perishable parts (the heart, liver, brains, and the fat behind the eyeballs) before they got down to the task of carving up the carcase into pieces that could be easily transported back to the cave. This would account for the absence of vertebrae on Dragon Bone Hill.

But in that case, why bring the skulls back to the cave at all? There was a very practical reason. Until pottery was invented around 6,000 B.C., Stone Age man had to make use of whatever nature provided when he wanted cooking pots or drinking cups. The possibilities were limited. Near the sea, large scallop shells might be used. In the tropics there were probably wild coconuts, much smaller than the modern cultivated variety. In some regions there were gourds. But wherever man was to be found, there were skulls whose upper, cranial section made an excellent and almost indestructible cup. Broken skulls such as those found in the caves of Nyandong in Java (see illustration 1) were almost certainly used for this purpose. And long after Peking man's day, the nomad Scythians still made cups from the skulls of people they particularly disliked. 'They saw off the part below the eyebrows,' reported Herodotus, 'and after cleaning out what remains stretch a piece of rawhide round it on the outside. If a man is poor he is content with that, but a rich man goes further and gilds the inside of the skull as well. In either case the skull is then used to drink from. . . . When important visitors arrive, these skulls are passed round and the host tells the story of them.'[9]

Although Peking man may not have evolved any rituals, it seems probable that he had begun to formulate certain ideas about life and death. When he went hunting for his food he often had to confront savage foes—the rhinoceros, wild boar, and tiger among them. Against the horns, tusks and claws of his quarry he could pit only his developing wits and his simple stone weapons.

He knew that life was uncertain and sometimes short,* that death was inevitable and sometimes abrupt. Every time he set out for the hunt he was aware that some day, perhaps today, the end would come with a slash and an outpouring of blood. It is not difficult to understand why, when he embarked on his first tentative exercises in logical thought, he should have come to the conclusion not merely that blood was essential to life, but that it was the essence of life itself.

The same kind of logic probably taught him to equate flesh with strength. What we would now recognise as vitamin deficiencies, seasonal malnutrition, slow-acting plant poisons, and organic diseases took their toll. The flesh of an ailing child or a sick woman visibly wasted away, and as it did so the sufferer became frail and feeble. If loss of flesh meant weakness, then flesh itself must be strength.

These basic observations about the positive, intrinsic power of blood and flesh may have developed quite rapidly, and it is impossible to know how long they persisted in their first, rudimentary form. Because of the nature of the subject, there can be no direct evidence from the paleolithic era. To discover how, in fact, they evolved into the extremely complex pattern of symbolic practices and beliefs that had taken shape by the beginning of recorded history it is necessary to resort to mind-reading, to an attempt to co-ordinate archaeological facts with a projection back from the thought-patterns of primitive peoples who have survived into modern times.

---

* In modern terms, very short indeed. It has been estimated that pre-historic man was fortunate if he survived to the age of twenty.[10]

The first firm foothold in a quagmire of speculation is provided by the long-surviving belief that, if flesh and blood had independent potency, they could be regarded as transferable assets. In the few thousand years preceding the neolithic era, even cave paintings became more efficacious if the pigment used was blood. But it was in relations between man and man—and, later, man and god—that flesh and blood were to have their most significant role to play. For one man to absorb the blood of another (living or dead) was equivalent to absorbing part of his essence, his force, his nature.

There are references to that most solemn of contracts, the blood covenant with the living, all the way through recorded history, from God's covenant with Abraham (see p. 28), to the Catiline conspiracy against the Roman republic, to the Triad fellowship of seventeenth-century China.[11] The nineteenth-century Anglo-American explorer Henry Morton Stanley exchanged his life essence with so many tribal chiefs that, as one contemporary commentator put it, 'the blood of a fair proportion of all the first families of Equatorial Africa now courses in Stanley's veins'.[12] The usual method of sealing such a covenant was for the participants to drink a few drops of each other's blood, but sometimes they made shallow cuts in their arms and mingled the blood that welled out. The nineteenth-century Kayans of Borneo mixed blood with tobacco, rolled it into a cigar, and smoked their covenants.[13]

Blood covenants with the living appear comparatively innocuous to modern eyes. Not so covenants with the dead. Yet there is a fundamental logic in the idea of absorbing back into a tribe the life essence represented by the flesh and blood of those of its members who have died. The wise man's genius is not lost, nor the warrior's strength, nor the cheerful man's humour (though historians still cannot decide whether paleolithic man *was* capable of seeing the funny side of things).

An example of this kind of covenant may be evidenced by the hundred-thousand-year-old remains of what is generally taken to have been a cannibal feast at Krapina in Yugoslavia. The bones of thirteen adults and six or seven children were found, broken into numerous fragments, some of the bones showing cutting marks which suggest that the meat had been scraped off, some of them scorched and mixed with scorched animal bones.[14] The presence of animal bones implies that hunger was not the only motive for cannibalism on this occasion. By this date, some kind of rites may have been developed similar to those attributed to the Issedones of central Asia in the fifth century B.C. 'When a man's father dies, his kinsmen bring sheep to his house as a sacrificial offering; the sheep and the body of the dead man are cut into joints and sliced up, and the two sorts of meat, mixed together, are served and eaten. The dead man's head, however, they gild . . . and then preserve it as a sort of sacred image.'[15] Four hundred years later Strabo reported that the Irish, too, reverently ate their dead parents,[16] and in twentieth-century eastern Peru the Amahuaca still grind up the teeth and bones of their dead and make them into a potion to be drunk by the bereaved. However, as a nineteenth-century Mayoruna cannibal remarked to a European visitor: 'When you die would you not rather be eaten by your own kinsmen than by maggots?'[17]

In fact, despite the indiscriminate accusations of cannibalism levelled at prehistoric man in all periods, people-eating can never have been a regular feature of the diet. Even after Peking man's day, when the single-family unit expanded into a larger clan group, a man might be acquainted in his whole lifetime with no more than forty people, mostly related. It has been estimated that to feed forty humans adequately, especially during the climatic conditions of the Ice Ages when vegetable food was scarce, around 150 lb liveweight of meat was needed every day—the equivalent, per week, of at least one or possibly two adolescent wild cattle, or just over eight fully grown humans.[18] At this rate, killing and eating the family would have wiped it off the map in no time at all. And with the neighbours scattered at a density of only four people to every sixty square miles,[19] dining out would present insuperable problems.

There was, however, greater potential by about 70,000 B.C., when many regions of Europe, Africa and Asia began to fill up. Instead of ranging round their caves as far as they wished in the search for meat and wild plants, the clans began to find that they had to compete for territory. As skirmishing with neighbouring tribes became more common, the death rate soared. So, in compensation, did the birth rate. Naturally, there was a preference for boy rather than girl children. But women in primitive societies have much to do besides raising children—their food-gathering role is just as important—and raising *too many* children not only distracts them from their other tasks but places a burden on food resources.

Among the Yanomamo Indians of the Brazil–Venezuela border today, a census of twenty-six villages has shown a sex ratio, below the age of fifteen, of 141 boys to 100 girls—a desirable ratio in tribes constantly engaged in feuds and wars, but hardly a natural one. In fact, the preponderance of boys is a result of systematic female infanticide.[20] In paleolithic times the evidence of skeletal remains suggests that the sex ratio was as high as 148 males to 100 females.

The practice of infanticide, usually female, as a method of selective population control has been common all through the centuries, though not always associated with cannibalism. Certain Polynesians are said to have killed as many as two-thirds of their children, and the Jagas—warrior nomads of Angola—are recorded as having put *all* theirs to death, so that the women should not be encumbered with them on the march; to maintain tribal strength they simply adopted thirteen- or fourteen-year-old boys and girls, whose parents they first killed and ate.[21] In nineteenth-century western Australia there was a tribe that ate every tenth baby born, so as 'to keep the population from increasing beyond the carrying capacity of the territory'.[22] Population control is by no means a new idea.

But though serious warfare requires a clan to have a high proportion of sons, it also ensures that many of those sons die in battle. Though there are 141 Yanomamo boys to 100 girls below the age of fifteen, the proportion between adults is only 105 to 100. If the same was true in paleolithic times, as seems probable, early man may have had to make a serious re-appraisal of his relationships with the dead.

Every body represented not only a formerly living being, or even a potential source of food. It was also a powerhouse of blood, or life-essence, and of flesh, or strength.

Even if a tribe did not, except when the hunting was poor, make a habit of reabsorbing the qualities of the dead back into itself, it could certainly not permit enemies to do so.

Burial of the dead, a practice which began to emerge in Neanderthal times (around 75,000 B.C.), may initially have been a method of concealment.

Regular feuding, too, may have led to the first clear-cut distinction between endophagy and exophagy—in other words, between eating *only* friends and eating *only* enemies. When a man killed an enemy, it was believed that he could take complete possession of his life-essence and vitality by the simple process of swallowing some of him. The soldiers of pre-dynastic Egypt did it; the Scythians of the Black Sea did it; in China, the chiefs of the Ch'in armies did it.[23] During the wars preceding the establishment of the Han dynasty in 202 B.C., one of the main contenders threatened to do it. The general Hsiang Yü had captured the father of his rival Liu Pang. He would boil the old man alive, he said, if Liu Pang did not surrender. But Liu Pang affably replied: 'Hsiang Yü and I were formerly brothers in arms, my father is thus his father too. If he absolutely insists on boiling *our* father, let him not forget to save me a cup of the soup!' Curiously enough, Hsiang Yü instantly released his prisoner.[24]

Reports of enemy-eating occur all the way through the centuries. The aborigines of Australia, the Maoris of New Zealand, the Hurons and Iroquois of America, the Ashanti of Africa, the Uscochi of the Balkans are only a few of the many peoples who have absorbed strength from their enemies through the media of blood, flesh, heart or broth.[25] Generally, the cannibal's aim was to increase his own power, but in a number of instances this was transmuted into a desire for total vengeance, an ultimate demonstration of hatred or scorn. As late as 1971, a member of the Black September organisation accused of assassinating Wasfi Tal, prime minister of Jordan, said: 'I am satisfied now. I drank from Tal's blood.' Eye-witnesses confirmed that he was speaking literally.[26]

Blood covenants with the living, with the dead, and—once they had been invented—with the gods. An inscription from the tomb of Seti I of Egypt relates an ancient legend about a rebellion of mankind against the gods, who decreed destruction for the whole human race. But harmony was restored with a brew of human blood and mandrake juice; the gods drank some of it, and gave some back to man by pouring it over the earth. The world came to life again. And this, says the legend, was the beginning of sacrifice.[27]

There seems little doubt that, in the early days of most religions, sacrifice was a blood covenant designed to ratify an alliance with the gods. If it were to make sense, it had to be human sacrifice, an idea that fills the modern mind with revulsion—although, as at least one commentator on the contemporary American scene has pointed out, twentieth-century warfare is no more than a mass perversion of it, a multiple echo of an ancient ritual.[28] In the beginning, however, sacrifice did not have the modern connotation of giving *up*, but simply of giving, and the destruction of the victim was no more than incidental to the process of releasing life-essence and vitality to add to the power of the gods. Only as the purpose of sacrifice changed (see p. 25) did a human victim become less necessary.

At some time in the dark void before 100,000 B.C., already preoccupied by his belief in the mystical powers of flesh and blood, man also discovered his immortal soul—though it was, then, by no means such an abstract concept.

In so far as it is possible to judge from the beliefs of primitive peoples today, the idea of the soul first emerged as a means of explaining the two different, related states of disengagement which fell within man's everyday knowledge—death and sleep. He knew, or thought he knew, what caused death. But what *was* death? He knew he slept, but what *was* sleep?

A man died and his body became dry bones, but an ethereal image, a transparent portrait of him still appeared in the dreams of the living. Or a man slept, and though his physical substance did not stir from the floor of the cave, he dreamed Stone Age dreams and awoke convinced that he had been up and active. It seemed that there must be some quintessential spirit capable not only of detaching itself from the body but even of wandering off on its own.

There was one problem about this idea of the peripatetic soul that was to trouble man for thousands of years. Not only was it liable to get into mischief when it was out alone,* but—

* If it were waylaid and injured by an enemy, for example, its owner, deprived of it, would sicken and die.[29]

since it does not appear to have been credited with any high degree of intelligence—it was perfectly capable of returning to the wrong body. This helped, of course, to explain why people sometimes behaved quite uncharacteristically, but it could be much more serious than that at a time when all the different elements in creation were also believed to have souls. Where the modern town-dweller sees the rest of the world as 'it', to primitive man the river and the sea, the birds and the fish, the earth, animals and plants were all indisputably 'thou'.[30] The nearest the twentieth century comes to this way of thinking is in recognising that inanimate objects may sometimes be possessed by a kind of active malevolence.* The intimate I-thou relationship between early man and his world, however, meant that there was always the possibility of a man's soul returning, not to him nor even to another man, but to a sheep, for example, or a wolf. Or vice versa. In this belief may well lie the origins not only of the sophisticated doctrine of transmigration of souls, but of that fearsome monster of later mythology, the werewolf (see pp. 108–20).

Another problem was that souls which had been beneficent in life sometimes became actively baleful just after death. Since Freud was not around to explain about guilt complexes, prehistoric man had to work it out for himself. He seems to have concluded that there were two possibilities. Firstly, that the unfortunate shade wished to get back into its earthly body again, but could not find it. To this idea the world owes the superb portrait statues and wall paintings of Egyptian tomb art, which were designed to ensure that the *ka* and *ba* souls would have no difficulty in recognising their proper home. Alternatively, the soul might be feeling uncharitable because something—incompetence on the part of the mourners, perhaps—had impeded what should have been its smooth progress to the other world. Gradually, the most complex funeral rites were developed to help it on its way, but the ill-disposed spectre was never to be entirely banished, and still lingers in folklore in the form of 'ghosts and ghouls and long-leggèd beasties, and things that go bump in the night'.[32]

* A phenomenon popularly known as Sod's Law, briefly defined as 'the force in nature that always makes the phone ring just as you have stepped into the bath'.[31]

This first, ingenuous view of the soul as a kind of colour transparency of the body was in time superseded, perhaps because the increasingly inquisitive mind of man began to wonder where precisely it hid itself during waking life. Some nineteenth-century primitives located the soul in the shadow, an idea which may well go back into the paleolithic era. The Quiché, Arawak, Tasmanian and Zulu languages, among others, all use the same word for shadow and spirit, and in many regions it is believed that harm to the shadow means harm to the body. The Basutos used to be wary of walking on the river bank in case a crocodile should drag the shadow down into the water.[33] In China, when the coffin lid was about to be closed, mourners were inclined to draw back a little lest their shadows should be shut in, while grave-diggers tied *their* shadows firmly round their waists with a strip of cloth.[34] To have a shadow was equivalent to living; he who had no shadow had no life. The dead in Purgatory recognised that Dante was alive when they saw that his figure, unlike theirs, cast a shadow on the ground, while the sinister image of the man who casts *no* shadow was for long a popular literary device, guaranteed to raise a shudder even as late as the nineteenth century.* The shadowless man was like the zombie of voodoo—a body without a soul.

But many peoples during paleolithic times were well-informed and expert anatomists. For thousands of years they had been observing and dissecting animals, and had learned in the process not only about animals but about man.[35] When they began seriously to set about deciding on the location of the soul, they knew too much—and not quite enough. Was it in the heart, or the liver, or the gall-bladder? Was it in the breath? Was it in the steam that rose when hot blood was spilled? Was it in the inert, slippery mass that filled the cranial cavity—the brain? Was it in the moisture that plumped out youthful flesh but gradually dissipated with age and vanished altogether when the flesh withered from the bones? Very nearly all these possibilities were ingeniously incorporated into early Greek views of the soul.

By Homer's day there had been a spiritual division of labour. Man was believed to have two souls, the *thymos* and

* In, for example, von Chamisso's tale of Peter Schlemihl.

the *psyche*.* The *thymos* was a kind of portmanteau containing the consciousness, breath, blood-steam, and also, upon occasion, emotions fed to it from the liver. The relationship between breath and mind, or consciousness, seems to have derived from an identification of thoughts with the words that expressed them, and of the words themselves with the breath that uttered them—a throw-back to days before writing was invented.[37] The concept of the soul as breath can be traced in the beliefs of many nations. The *atman*—the 'world soul' of the Hindus—comes from the word meaning 'to breathe'; the Slav *duch*, from 'breath' has come to mean 'soul' or 'spirit'; the English 'ghost' and German *Geist* are similarly derived.[38]

The *thymos* was what might be called the working soul. The *psyche*, in contrast, was quiescent during life, fulfilling its function by its presence alone. It was a life-principle, but a curiously anonymous one, with nothing much to distinguish it except a tendency to gibber when it left the body after death and floated phantom-like down to Hádes to become one of Homer's 'witless shades'.† Very occasionally, some activity *was* attributed to it. If a man sneezed, it usually meant that his *psyche* was uneasy—so where the bystander today might exclaim 'Bless you!' or 'Gesundheit!', the ancient Greek cried 'Zeus save me!' A sneeze could, however, be taken as prophetic (though not of a cold in the head). No maternal solicitude distracted Penelope when her son sneezed violently; she merely took it as a sign that her amiable plan to massacre her suitors would prosper.[40] In later times it was believed that a sneeze meant not just the disturbance but the departure of

---

* Other civilisations had the same idea. In Egypt there were the *ba* and *ka*, in China the *p'o* and *hun*. The Hebrews had *nephesh* and *ruach*; in Zoroastrianism there were the *daēnā* and the *urvan*; and in Islam, a late creed influenced by Judaism and Christianity, the *rūh* and the *nafs*. Loosely speaking—very loosely in some cases, as the area is fertile with confusion—the first of these was the animating or activating soul, which usually perished with the body, while the second was the indestructible life principle that survived in the other world.[36]

† According to a passage in the *Odyssey*, it was only when the *psyche* was given a taste of blood and so reunited with its blood/breath/consciousness *thymos* (the meeting of two souls) that it became capable of utterance and aware of what was going on around it.[39]

the soul. Rabbinic tradition had it that a man sneezed only once, and that his soul left him in that instant.[41]

The *thymos*, because of its links with breath and blood, was believed to be situated in the lungs. But the *psyche* resided in the head and could not be released to flutter down to Hades until all the life-moisture in the flesh had completely dried up, a process hastened in Greek times by the practice of cremation.[42] 'This is the way with mortals when one dies,' explained Odysseus' mother. 'For no longer do the sinews hold the flesh and the bones, but the mighty energy of burning fire overcomes these . . . and the *psyche* like a dream-phantom flies away hovering.'*[43]

The Greeks were not alone in believing that the soul made its home in the head. It is, after all, a reasonable enough assumption if the soul is regarded as a personalised life-essence; no other part of the body is as recognisably personal as the head, or as expressive of vitality. In much later times, the Karens of Burma considered that the *tso*, or life-principle, resided in the top of the skull, a position also inhabited by the manikin who represented the soul to the Nootka of British Columbia. In Borneo, the soul was an invisible balloon contained in the head and full of a vaporous magic essence. In Wales until the nineteenth century it appeared as a candle flame that quitted the head just before death and preceded the corpse on its way to the grave.[44] All over the world, in fact, the firefly souls of the dead still flicker by night in country churchyards.

Nor were the Greeks alone in believing that the soul needed assistance in leaving for the other world. The Chinese used to make a hole in the roof to let the soul out at death, and until very recently it was the custom in some parts of France, Britain and Germany to open a window in any room where a corpse lay so that the soul might find its passage clear.[45]

Such ideas as these, combined with a belief that the soul possessed a life-essence as transferable as blood, help to illuminate both the practice of headhunting and the cult of skulls which was so widely diffused throughout the pre-historic world.

* After Homer's time the separate images of the *psyche* and *thymos* began to coalesce, the *psyche* absorbing the other's attributes.

Although Peking man had no inhibitions about eating brains and drinking from skulls, it seems probable that his successors—once they had decided that the soul lived in the head—became hesitant about treating the skull quite so cavalierly, especially one that had belonged to someone whose personality, in life, had been powerful. The new practice of burial would reinforce such doubts; the very act of burial—requiring time and labour, and haunted by the formidable presence of the corpse—must have exerted strong psychological pressures. By Neanderthal times (which began around 75,000 B.C.), certain skulls were being treated with, at the very least, deference if not actually worship. Brought back to the cave, they were propped up in a niche or jammed into a fissure to make a kind of memorial shrine—a paleolithic prototype of the mantelshelf bust of John Fitzgerald Kennedy or Winston Spencer Churchill.

A number of skull shrines have been excavated, one of the most-studied being that at Monte Circeo on the Italian coast about sixty miles north-west of Naples. It is dated at approximately 55,000 B.C. The skull, centred in a circle of stones in a chamber of the cave clearly set apart from the living quarters, belonged to a man who was forty-five years old at death—a centenarian (and more) in Neanderthal terms. He had died as the result of one or more violent blows to the temple. The *foramen magnum* had been considerably enlarged.[46]

There are two possible interpretations of these facts. It may have been a case of the mercy-killing of an old and respected member of the tribe, the *foramen magnum* being enlarged either to enable the soul to fly free, or to allow the skull to be cleaned out so that it could be set up in state to preside symbolically over future clan councils, or used as a drinking cup when some solemn pact was agreed.

The more frequently canvassed interpretation, however, is that ritual murder and ceremonial brain-eating were involved. This theory is based on the customs of certain primitive tribes that have survived into modern times, without—it is claimed—their traditions ever having been distorted by contact with people or knowledge from the outside world. In some areas of New Guinea, for example, it is incumbent on the father of a newborn child to kill a man who is known to him by name. The victim's brain is extracted through the enlarged *foramen magnum*, then cooked—with sago!—and ceremonially eaten. Thereafter, the new child takes the dead man's name. When the Dutch colonial government tried to put a stop to this singularly un-Christian mode of christening, the tribes would have none of it. How otherwise, they demanded, could they name their children?[47]

In the absence of evidence to the contrary, either theory is tenable, the first more so, perhaps, as Neanderthal man is known to have cared for the sick and aged—and may (with perfect accuracy) have looked on euthanasia as the ultimate pain-killer. The second theory raises almost as many questions as it answers, especially since the brain was not recognised as playing an active role in the human system until early Egyptian times. It is still possible, however, that prehistoric man, convinced that the soul resided in the head and anxious to absorb it, ate the only part of the skull's contents that he did not already know to have some *other* function. The fact that he had long regarded the brain as a gastronomic delicacy is not necessarily irrelevant.

Whether or not early man believed that the brain contained the soul, an atmosphere of life-essence clung firmly to the head and continued to do so. In such caves as those of Ofnet in the Jura and Grimaldi, on the Riviera frontier between France and Italy, skulls have been found tinted with ochre (magical substitute for blood), while at Jericho, in the seventh millennium B.C., they were made into stylised portraits of their owners by moulding the features in plaster and setting in shells to represent the eyes.[48] The Baganda of Africa are known to have preserved the skulls of their kings for as much as a thousand years, and in Aztec Mexico the skull of a human sacrifice was overlaid with turquoise and obsidian to make an image of a god.[49] In many countries, realistic-looking death masks were made to simulate the living head and perpetuate its life-essence; while in some of the secret places of the world today men still go on headhunting raids to steal the life-essence needed to supply the children they hope to beget.*[50]

* As representational art developed, the naked skull gave way (except for horrific purposes) to the portrait image. Nevertheless, the

Neanderthal man treated some bodies, like some skulls, with special reverence. The more loved or feared members of the community were laid most carefully to rest, their bodies arranged often as if in sleep, and sometimes decorated with red ochre or shells or even strewn with flowers.[51] But the new sensitivity in areas where burial was practised does not seem to have led to any feeling that eating people was necessarily wrong. That cannibalism was a continuing, if occasional, practice is shown by excavations at Předmost in Moravia, where a mammoth-hunters' camp (dated at about 25,000 B.C.) revealed a number of successive, unsuspicious burials, but also one skeleton broken into many pieces and revealing the cut-marks which betray cannibal attentions.[52]

For as long as man remained a hunter and plant-gatherer, with only limited control over his food supply, he was sometimes of necessity a part-time cannibal. But when some men learned to cultivate the soil, settled down, and became farmers, and others turned into pastoral nomads, driving their herds of domesticated animals over vast tracts of country, the need for supplementary food began to diminish. Nomads still gave its full symbolic significance to human blood, but human flesh in a society where there were plenty of alternatives came to be reserved for occasions of the most solemn ceremonial. Settled farmers were in a rather more difficult position. Living mainly on grain foods and the dairy products supplied by their comparatively small flocks, they were usually short of meat.* But since they had chosen to live in communities they were bound by the very rules that made community living possible. The basically practical ban on killing and eating the family had to be extended. The circumscribed world of the village ruled out enemy-eating, too; the insult to a neighbour would have been too apparent, the

full-fleshed—if detached—head held its own in terms of magic symbolism. Consider, for example, the legends concerning the heads of Osiris, Odysseus, Medusa, and John the Baptist.

* In some regions (usually islands, or isolated areas deep in the continental interior) livestock suitable for domestication were entirely lacking. Farmers could raise nothing but starchy foods, and it was, in fact, the resultant craving for meat that turned such peoples as the Caribs and the Papuans into the great cannibals of the post-mediaeval world.

consequences too destructive. As law and religion developed and became institutionalised, they began to erect a scaffolding of morality and rectitude, and gradually there grew up a climate of opinion that was opposed to the casual eating of human flesh.

But not, for many centuries—in some societies, never—to its sacramental eating. There was still to be a long period when the gods demanded human sacrifice—and permitted man to share it with them.

CHAPTER ONE

Eating People is Wrong

UNTIL MAN discovered that he had a soul, he must have felt—like Harry S. Truman—that the buck stopped here. Although his capacity for awe had probably long ago been stimulated by such commanding figures of the animal world as the great wild bull or the sleek and menacing tiger, it was only when he developed the idea of an afterworld and peopled it with gods of his own kind—human enough to understand his problems and superhuman enough to overcome them—that it became possible for him to shuffle off some of the burden of responsibility.

The traditions of his tribe supplied the gods. As the centuries passed, the soul of one great man in tribal history would merge imperceptibly with that of another, until he-who-could-always-find-shelter fused with he-who-could-read-the-sky into a single weather god, and she-who-had-many-children with she-who-gathered-most-plants into an ancestral goddess of fertility. Gods of air, earth and water, friendly deities who brought sun and rain at the appointed times, and unfriendly ones who called down flood or drought, pestilence or plague, not only took over some responsibility for the direction of events but also provided a framework for myths that helped to explain the inexplicable—the universe.

The early gods were, however, intensely human and by no means infallible. They needed—and expected—both help and encouragement from mortals, as well as an occasional *douceur* to ensure the continuance of friendly relations. Their requirements were met by the system of sacrifice. The candles and incense and small change of today's church offerings echo the blood (that was life) and the flesh (that was strength) which were presented to his gods by primitive man.

By the beginning of recorded history, woven tightly into

the fabric of all religious beliefs were two dominant myths, one that explained the annual death and rebirth of the soil, and the other the creation of the world. Despite the fertility figurines that survive from the late Stone Age, there is no indication as to which of these myths came first. But in later times it was usually the creation myth that preoccupied hunting peoples and nomadic herdsmen, while settled farmers (dependent on the produce of their fields) were, not unnaturally, more concerned with the subject of resurrection. To both groups, the past was an integral part of both present and future. The creation of the world was no single irrevocable act, nor was the establishment of an annual pattern of death and rebirth for the soil. If the world and the seasons were to continue, the original dramas had to be re-enacted every year by the gods, with the aid of man.

Although he had been aware of the progress of the seasons since the very earliest times, it was only when man became a farmer that he found himself deeply dependent on them for his food, and his life. Now, during the long months between one year's harvest and the next year's spring, he waited in doubt and uncertainty. The green sprouts of new grain did not depend on sowing and ploughing, feeding and irrigating—of which, in the beginning, he knew almost nothing—but on whether the fertility deity was successful in overcoming the forces that were determined to prevent her from returning to earth after a temporary sojourn in the underworld. Until she returned, the soil would remain barren.* To aid her in her struggle, the farmer contributed power and strength in the form of human sacrifice.

It was human sacrifice offered in the most literal terms. The method is clearly indicated in the Egyptian legend of Osiris, the grain god who was credited with having weaned the Egyptians from cannibalism and introduced them to agriculture. When Osiris was murdered by his brother Set, his wife Isis found the body and carried it home. Set followed, hacked

---

* This is the essence of the resurrection myth contained in the literature of Sumer, the earliest in recorded history (*c.* 3500 B.C.). The fertility deity was a goddess, Inanna, but her role was taken over in later times and other lands by male deities—for example, Tammuz in Babylon, Baal in Canaan, and Adonis in Greece.

it in pieces, and scattered these all over the countryside, but Isis perseveringly gathered them all together again and succeeded in reassembling her husband and restoring him to life. At this point the fertility chapter in the Osiris myth ends.* The significant element in it is the dispersal of fragments of the divine corpse around the landscape.

Egyptologists are agreed that the legend, as it has come down through the ages, is a literary sublimation of the ancient —and, in some parts of the world, modern—practice of burying the dissected parts of a human sacrifice in the fields to give flesh, blood and power to the resurrection god. Because of the nature of the sacrifice, solid archaeological proof is lacking, and literary sources provide only oblique references based on oral tradition. But the use of human beings as symbolic fertilisers is well attested, at much later periods of history, among peoples whose social development remained at a level not much more advanced than that of prehistoric Egypt. In the mid-nineteenth century, for example, the American Pawnees ritually killed a girl of the Sioux and sprinkled her blood on the seeds; her heart was eaten by the chief sacrificer. The tribal Gonds of India kidnapped and sacrificed boys of the brahmin caste and sprinkled their blood over the fields; the flesh was eaten. Another group of tribals had a sacrificial custom known as *meriah*. The victim was usually purchased from outside the tribe and kept in luxury for some years; thereafter, sacrifices were 'generally so arranged . . . that each head of a family was enabled, at least once a year, to procure a shred of flesh for his fields, generally about the time when his chief crop was laid down'.[1]

The cannibal elements that intrude into some of these basically power-giving sacrifices may have evolved in one of two ways. Most probably, the participants believed that, by eating a portion of the sacrifice, they identified themselves directly with what was being offered to the god. Some authorities, however, argue that in certain cases the resurrection myth had been infiltrated by a creation-myth belief that from one god, purposefully immolated, had grown man's essential

---

* In more ways than one, since a piece of the reconstructed god proved to be missing—his genitalia, which had unfortunately been devoured by the oxyrhynchus fish!

food plants. If so, the human sacrifice would symbolise the plant god himself, and those who ate part of the sacrificial victim would in fact be eating the god and absorbing the divine.[2]

Because the history of the last ten thousand years has encouraged settled farming at the expense of cattle-herding economies—land put down to grain can feed far more people than the same land devoted to livestock—it is virtually impossible to isolate early nomadic beliefs in their 'pure' form. All have absorbed at least some elements from agricultural mythology. But it seems clear that nomads were less single-minded than farmers about the purpose of sacrifice. Blood might be offered to the rain god when drought withered the pastures or to the fertility god when the cattle were barren, but ordinary everyday sacrifice was commonly designed to maintain amicable relations with ordinary everyday gods, who were prepared to descend to the sacrificial field, eat and drink with their worshippers, and duly reward them—on a *quid pro quo* basis—with success in war and prolific wives and cows. When the gods came to dine, they took pot luck—boiled beef, or grilled horse kebabs, or perhaps, on special occasions, roast hump of camel.

It was a different matter on days of important ceremonial when the story of the creation was relived. Unless the correct sacrificial formula was strictly adhered to, all cosmic processes would fail and chaos would come again. The formula necessarily involved a death ritual, because it was from death that life had come.

The Babylonian creation myth, a late version carried into city life by former nomads, has already been summarised (see p.2). Another variant is to be found in the *Rig Veda*, the earliest literary source for the religion of the nomadic Indo-Europeans (or Aryans) who settled in India in the second millennium B.C. Prajapati, 'the Lord of Beings', was the primeval man who existed before the foundation of the universe. The gods were his children, and they, at an appointed moment, sacrificed Prajapati to himself. From his body the universe was created. . . .

From it he made the animals
of air and wood and village.

From that all-embracing sacrifice
　were born the hymns and chants,
from that the metres were born,
　from that the sacrificial spells were born.

Thence were born horses,
　and all beings with two rows of teeth.
Thence were born cattle,
　and thence goats and sheep. . . .

From his navel came the air,
　from his head there came the sky,
from his feet the earth, the four quarters from his ear,
　thus they fashioned the worlds. . . .[3]

What form the ritual re-enactment of this myth actually took remains obscure, but that there was a mystical identification of god, victim and sacrificer is clear from the *Rig Veda*. The likelihood is that, as in the case of resurrection rites, this identification was brought about by the sacrificer consuming part of the sacrificial victim.* The probability is reinforced by what is known of the later Orphic mysteries of Greece, which were associated with Dionysos. He, it was said, was the son of Zeus and Persephone and while still a child was lured away by the Titans, who tore him in pieces and devoured his smoking flesh. Their grisly banquet, however, was interrupted by Athene who salvaged the child's heart so that he might be begotten and born again. Zeus, it need hardly be added, blasted the cannibal Titans with his thunderbolt, and it was from their smouldering remains that the human race was born. This myth was dramatised by the Orphic priests in a

---

* Plain statements of fact are scarcely to be expected in religious texts based on oral tradition, as the priestly hands that transcribe them only too often moderate the originals to suit the tone of later doctrine. In India, in any case, a note of doubt about the creation was soon to creep in: 'Whence all creation had its origin . . . he, who surveys it all from highest heaven, he knows—or maybe even he does not know.'[4] Preoccupation with the creation myth and its rituals was superseded in a matter of only two or three centuries by a belief in transmigration of souls, which had no place for the sacrifice of human beings and was opposed even to that of animals.

mystery play witnessed only by neophytes and initiates. The substitute Dionysos was torn in pieces and eaten (raw) by the devotees, who believed that they thus participated in the divine nature of the god. By the end of the third century B.C., said Pliny, 'it was regarded as a supreme act of religion to slay a man and as a most salutary act to eat his body',[5] and it had become necessary to pass the famous *De Bacchanalibus* edict to ban such rites from the Italian peninsula. It should perhaps be noted that no Orphic who had eaten the flesh of his god ever again touched meat of any kind![6]

What is particularly interesting about the creation myth of the *Rig Veda*, however, is that the universe was created not from the body of a god but from that of the very *first man*. It is probable, therefore, that the formula for re-enactment required the human sacrifice to be of a *first-born* son. This would, in part, explain the recurring emphasis on sacrifice of the first-born in, for example, the Old Testament—which is not only holy scripture but a history of those Hebrew tribes who began to drift into the settled Near East in the second millennium B.C. and were, historians believe, related to the Indo-Europeans who took the *Rig Veda* and its beliefs to India. God's covenant with Israel stated: 'The first-born of your sons you shall give to me'—which might have implied nothing more (past or present) than spiritual dedication, had it not been for what immediately followed. 'You shall do likewise with your oxen and with your sheep.'[7] In fact the belief that the gods, or God, placed a particular value on the first-born was to die hard. Instead of being suffocated by the stolid routine of agricultural life, it was strengthened by the rituals of the first-fruits in the Near East and Egypt, where what had once been human sacrifices, in spring, were now softened into a vicarious sacrifice of newborn lambs and sheafs of green corn.

As far as re-enactment of the creation myth is concerned, by Biblical times the only unequivocal testament to any such former custom was enshrined in the commandment: 'Six days shall you labour and do all your work; but the seventh day is a sabbath to the Lord your God. . . . For in six days the Lord made heaven and earth, the sea, and all that is in them, and rested the seventh day.'[8] But theologians see traces of rites that may once have involved human sacrifice in the weird events of that night commemorated as the Passover. The Biblical narrative is such a tangled web of historical fact and mythological fantasy that it takes an industrious theologian indeed to disentangle it into its component strands, but sacrifice of the first-born and of the first-fruits both have a place in it.

The Passover was originally a Near Eastern spring festival on to which the immigrant Hebrews grafted historical meaning. Ostensibly, it now commemorates the events preceding the flight of the Israelites from Egypt. Instructed by Yahweh, the Lord, the Israelites sacrificed a lamb in each household, marked the doorposts and lintel with its blood, then roasted it and ate it with bitter herbs and unleavened bread. That same night, 'the Lord smote all the first-born in the land of Egypt, from the first-born of the Pharaoh who sat on his throne to the first-born of the captive who was in the dungeon, and all the first-born of the cattle'.[9] But not the first-born of the Israelites. (The eating of the lambs represents the first-fruits element in the story; the slaughter of the first-born is regarded as echoing an ancestral memory of some great sacrificial massacre.[10]) Horrified, Pharaoh bade Moses and Aaron to take their people and their flocks and be gone, and 'the people took their dough before it was leavened' and departed forthwith.*[11]

Because the Old Testament has been more microscopically studied than any other work in the whole of world history, much has been done to correlate the actual wording of the narrative, its attitudes, and its laws, with the known chronology of historical development. This makes it possible to trace the different stages of sacrificial practice and, more informatively, of attitudes to them, with a clarity not always possible in the case of other early religions, though—because the Bible was not written down until after human sacrifice had ceased—there are of course only hints of what happened in pre-scriptural times.

As in the majority of civilised areas, by the beginning of the

* This convincing touch of realism derives from ordinary farm custom. In early spring everyone ate unraised bread for a few days while fresh leaven was prepared—the idea being to avoid transferring ill or

first millennium B.C. human sacrifice had been commuted into animal sacrifice. This change is signalised in the story of Abraham's sacrifice of his son Isaac. 'When they came to the place of which God had told him, Abraham built an altar there, and laid the wood in order, and bound Isaac his son, and laid him on the altar, upon the wood. Then Abraham put forth his hand and took the knife to slay his son. But the angel of the Lord called to him from heaven and said . . . "Do not lay your hand on the lad or do anything to him; for now I know that you fear God, seeing you have not withheld your son, your only son, from me." And Abraham lifted up his eyes and looked, and behold, behind him was a ram, caught in a thicket by his horns; and Abraham went and took the ram, and offered it up as a burnt offering instead of his son.'[13] It must be understood, of course, that all that was burnt in the case of a 'burnt offering'—and this was true of many countries, not just of the Hebrews—was the fat, liver and kidneys. The meat itself fell to the portion of the priests, who were even advised by the Lord on how to avoid food poisoning: 'If the sacrifice of his offering is a votive offering or a freewill offering, it shall be eaten on the day that he offers his sacrifice, and on the morrow what remains of it shall be eaten, but what remains of the flesh of the sacrifice on the third day shall be burned with fire.'[14]

As life became urbanised, the people of Israel were no longer required to sacrifice even an animal in place of their children. Their salvation—and the priests' sustenance—was catered for by permission to redeem their progeny for a fixed sum of money, ranging from fifty shekels of silver for an adult male (thirty for a female) down to five and three shekels respectively for children under five.[15] This idea of monetary redemption was partly a product of the changed attitude to sacrifice which had come about in the sixth century B.C., when the Temple at Jerusalem was destroyed and the children of Israel were sent into exile for almost fifty years. During this time they rejected the idea of offering living sacrifices anywhere other than at Jerusalem. But the results of the exile went deeper than this. Deprived of the Temple, the symbol of their unity, they

evil from the old to the new year by using old sour-dough with new grain.[12]

learned under the guidance of Ezekiel to look instead to a transfigured God—a new, all-powerful God, a being of transcendent greatness and holiness who demanded from every individual a life of active and beneficent virtue in place of the former passive obedience to a myriad of divine commandments.[16]

This not only encouraged the stirrings of a sense of sin, but showed clearly that it was absurd to offer sacrifices designed to augment the power of One who was already all-powerful, or to ward off the evil that must in effect be an aspect of the Almighty's justice. This view was succinctly stated in one of the Psalms. Saith the Lord:

> I will accept no bull from your house,
>   nor he-goat from your folds.
> For every beast of the forest is mine,
>   the cattle on a thousand hills. . . .
> If I were hungry, I would not tell you;
>   for the world and all that is in it is mine.
> Do I eat the flesh of bulls,
>   or drink the blood of goats?[17]

Although sacrifice was resumed after the return to Jerusalem and the building of a new Temple, it had lost its innate meaning and become purely a symbol of contrition. When the Temple was once again destroyed in A.D. 70, it was finally accepted that prayer and fasting would suffice instead. Yet the old ideas still lingered. As the prayer of Rabbi Sheshet put it: 'Lord of the world, when the Temple was standing, one who sinned offered a sacrifice, of which only the fat and blood were taken, and thereby his sins were forgiven. I have fasted today, and through this fasting my blood and my fat have been decreased. Deign to look upon the part of my blood and my fat which I have lost through my fasting as if I had offered it to Thee, and forgive my sins in return.'[18] It was not only an interesting piece of reasoning, but a symbolic return to the human sacrifice which men still secretly believed was the sacrifice most acceptable to the gods.

The Biblical pattern of sacrifice—from probable human, through animal, through monetary, to its symbolic form of fasting and prayer—follows much the same sequence in other countries and other religions. But something else that is clear from the Bible, and is equally true of other countries, is that however much attitudes to flesh-and-blood sacrifices changed, attitudes to blood itself did not.

All through the rituals set out in such exhaustive detail in the early books of the Old Testament there is a recurring accent on blood. 'The life of the flesh is in the blood . . . it is the blood that makes atonement by reason of the life . . . the life of every creature is in the blood of it . . . you shall not eat the blood of any creature, for the life of every creature is its blood.'[19]

The early Hebrews were a nomadic people, tied to no particular place, and laying considerable emphasis on kinship and the relationship between god and man. Blood was the suspension fluid of social life, the substance that enveloped and united the clan. Strangers who wished to join a primitive Semitic tribe had to be inducted by means of a blood ritual,[20] while blood feuds and an attitude to blood guilt that visited the father's sins upon the children unto the third and fourth generation figure in the Old Testament with some frequency. Blood was even regarded as having human attributes; it was, for example, the *blood* of Abel the herdsman, not his spirit, that cried out for vengeance against his brother Cain, the farmer.[21]

It was hardly surprising, therefore, that all sacrificial ritual should involve the sprinkling of blood on and around the 'mercy seat', a return to God of the life-essence he had given. Nor was it surprising that the three rocks on which Judaism was built—God's covenant with Abraham, the Passover, and the covenant with Moses—should have been drenched with blood symbolism.

'And God said to Abraham . . . "This is my covenant, which you shall keep, between me and you and your descendants after you: Every male among you shall be circumcised. You shall be circumcised in the flesh of your foreskins, and it shall be a sign of the covenant between me and you." '[22]

Some historians believe that this was merely a translation of hygiene into doctrine, others that circumcision was a tribal recognition symbol (though scarcely, it might be thought, a very convenient one). The subject has also been a source of perennial fascination for psychoanalysts, in whose works initiation rites and castration complexes jostle for precedence with theories of phallic primacy and female preference.[23] In the majority of areas where circumcision is, or was, practised— in Egypt, by some African and Polynesian peoples, in Peru, by the Aztecs, the Maya, and certain American Indian tribes— it was a rite performed at puberty, marking a boy's entry into the adult world. But the Bible enjoined that the descendants of Abraham should undergo the operation when they were only eight days old. Clearly, circumcision in this case was not a puberty rite but a blood covenant, admitting the 'signatory' into an immediate special relationship and therefore to be performed at the earliest practicable moment.

When blood was shed as part of a covenant between men, it was usually taken from whichever limb was most convenient. But God's covenant was not with Abraham alone. 'You shall keep my covenant, you and your descendants after you throughout their generations.'[24] For the covenant to take on its full meaning, the blood had to come from Abraham's reproductive organs. Although modern sources are reticent about the circumcision ritual today, one nineteenth-century authority says specifically that the religious official who carried out the operation sucked the blood from the wound— ostensibly, so that it might 'congeal more quickly'—and then spat it into a glass of red wine.[25] This has strong undertones of a very ancient tradition, identifying God (through the agency of his representative) with the human participant in the covenant.

In the Passover story, the most striking elements are the sacrifice of the lamb, the massacre of the first-born, and the stress on unleavened bread. But the blood signs on the doors and lintels are no less important. The blood was the life-essence that reiterated the covenant with God, while simultaneously protecting the Israelites from the lethal attentions of the avenging angel. The specific form of the signs seems to have owed something to the custom of 'baptising' new buildings with blood in order to ensure that the gods would protect them, or to pacify demons who might be disturbed during the work of construction. According to one somewhat debatable theory, early man carried his view of the creation myth into every aspect of life. 'Since the gods had to slay and dismember a marine monster or a primordial being in order to create the world from it, man in his turn must imitate them when he builds his own world, his city or his house. . . . If a "construction" is to endure (be it house, temple, tool, etc.), it must be animated, that is, it must receive life and a soul. The transfer of the soul is possible only through a blood sacrifice. . . . The house is not an object, a "machine to live in"; it is the universe that man constructs for himself by imitating the paradigmatic creation of the gods, the cosmogony.'[26]

Whatever the interpretation, man persisted with his building sacrifices until very recent times. Joshua cursed the man who would rebuild Jericho: 'At the cost of his first-born shall he lay its foundation, and at the cost of his youngest son shall he set up its gates.'[27] When Hiel of Bethel carried out the task: 'He laid its foundation at the cost of Abiram his first-born, and set up its gates at the cost of his youngest son Segub, according to the word of the Lord.'[28] In mediaeval Europe, the master mason's unfortunate wife is said to have been sacrificed during the building of Scutari, in Yugoslavia, and there are similar traditions relating to other towns. In Burma, many cities had invisible Guardians of the Gates—the spirits of human sacrifices immured in the foundations. In nineteenth-century Arabia, one traveller reported, 'I asked wherefore the corner of this new building had been sprinkled with gore? They wondered to hear me question them thus . . . they thought I should have known that it was the blood of a goat which had been sacrificed to the *jân* [spirit] for the safety of the workmen.' Even when work began on the railroad line between Beirut and Damascus, a blood sacrifice was still felt to be necessary.[29]

The third and pivotal event of scriptural history was the covenant at the foot of Sinai. After God had declared his ordinances, Moses built an altar and had sacrificial offerings prepared. Then he 'took half of the blood and put it in basins, and half of the blood he threw against the altar', so identifying God with the covenant. Next 'he took the book of the covenant, and read it in the hearing of the people; and they said.

"All that the Lord has spoken we will do, and we will be obedient." And Moses took the blood and threw it upon the people, and said, "Behold the blood of the covenant which the Lord has made with you. . . ." '[30] So the people, too, were identified with the covenant.

It was a primitive rite suited to a still primitive religion, to a covenant in which the Lord undertook that if the children of Israel obeyed his voice they should be set high above all the nations of the earth, but if they failed to observe his commandments, 'cursed shall you be in the city, and cursed shall you be in the field'.[31] The curses were precise, and well within the people's understanding. 'You shall eat the offspring of your own body, the flesh of your sons and daughters. . . . The man who is the most tender and delicately bred among you will grudge food to his brother, to the wife of his bosom, and to the last of the children who remain to him; so that he will not give to any of them any of the flesh of his children whom he is eating. . . . The most tender and delicately bred woman among you . . . will grudge to the husband of her bosom, to her son and to her daughter, her afterbirth that comes out from between her feet and her children whom she bears, because she will eat them secretly, for want of all things.'[32]

The covenant at Sinai required from the people of Israel negative obedience rather than positive morality. It was only during the exile from Jerusalem in the sixth century B.C. that a more constructive attitude towards good and evil began to develop, and not until the second century B.C. that there emerged ideas of heaven and hell, of *personal* reward or damnation, of death not as an end but as a beginning.[33]

For the Jews, and the Christians who followed them, this was the point of no return in relation to human sacrifice—and cannibalism. Three thousand years of civilisation in the Near East had instilled into man's mind the beliefs that sharing a human sacrifice with the gods was occasionally advisable; that eating people for revenge was understandable (if a trifle *farouche*); and that eating them for food was, on the whole, uncalled for. What brought the Jews into absolute conflict with this view was their newly adopted belief that a man still needed his body after death, so that he might rise again on the

Judgement Day. Just how literally this belief was held can be seen, for example, from the last will and testament of the fourth-century Rabbi Jeremiah, who instructed that he be buried in a white-bordered linen cloak, wearing fine socks and slippers, and clasping a staff in his hand, so that he would be ready to rise at a moment's notice when the call came.[34] There was, at first, an escape clause which meant that Jews had no need to be particular about what happened to the bodies of gentiles—whoever disbelieved in the resurrection of the dead would himself have no share in the world to come.[35] But ultimately the importance placed on the body led Jews and Christians to view human sacrifice and cannibalism with a fundamentally disproportionate horror that has no real parallel in any other of the world's great religions.

Most other religions, then and now, regarded the fate of the body as more or less irrelevant. Though the Etruscans, for example, despatched their dead carefully to the underworld and even believed that they ascended again to earth on certain days, they viewed the afterlife as a state of unrelieved gloom, presided over by the hideous figure of Charun, with his horse's ears, beaked nose, and body the colour of decaying flesh—the embodiment of the grave. The Etruscans' morbid preoccupation with pain and death found nothing remarkable in cannibalism or human sacrifice. To the Greeks, the corpse was a pollution, and an extraneous one, at that. They believed in fact that death was not complete until the flesh had been destroyed, by whatever method. As the Bronze Age swallowed up the country's timber, cremation became difficult and expensive, so the body was immured instead in a sarcophagus (often painted red inside to simulate fire); the word 'sarcophagus' means 'flesh-eating'. In Mesopotamia, the afterlife had always been viewed as grim and desolate. As a belief in justice developed in the early second millennium B.C., death came to be seen as the ultimate injustice; since the spirit was doomed without reason or reprieve, what happened to the corpse was of no importance.

Far to the east, in *Vedic* India, a man was born in impurity and died in impurity. As with the Greeks, Zoroastrians, and the later Hebrew tribes, the corpse was a pollution. It had to be cremated as soon as possible and there was a period of mourning lasting for several days during which time the soul of the departed was believed to hover uneasily around its mortal remains, without realising the fact of death. 'For a few days he continues to converse with his former associates and is surprised that nobody answers his questions or notices his presence.'[36] Only when all the mourning rites had been fulfilled was the departed truly dead. (This belief that death was not an instantaneous but a protracted experience was common to many early peoples.) Errors in the correct funeral procedure—and cannibalism instead of cremation *could* be regarded as such an error—prevented the spirit from acquiring its new 'subtle body' and proceeding on its other-worldly way. Because of this sensitivity, in fact, the Indian countryside is still today thickly populated with uneasy ghosts.

For Buddhists in India and China, the body was but a material envelope, discarded as soon as the spirit returned to the Wheel and of no possible value in the scheme of things. In Iran, however, the Zoroastrianism that followed closely on the chronological heels of Buddhism in India was to have an influence on the Hebrew view of the afterlife, despite the fact that Zoroastrians regarded burial as a defilement of the earth. Until timber ran short, they cremated their dead; later, they exposed them to birds of prey—a return to prehistoric practice. Nevertheless, they like the Hebrews believed in resurrection. It was just that they were more logical. If their god was, as they believed, genuinely omnipotent and had created the world single-handed, then a small matter like reconstituting the dead on Judgement Day presented no problems. 'Zoroaster asked Ohrmazd, "From whence can the body which the wind has carried off and the water swept away be put together again; and how will the raising of the dead come to pass?" And Ohrmazd made answer and said: "When [I established] the sky without pillar . . . and when I created the earth . . . and when I created grain on earth and . . . plants and . . . the embryo in its mother's womb, and gave it nourishment . . . when I created each one of these things, each was more difficult than the raising of the dead . . . Behold! If I created what had not been, why should it be impossible for me to recreate what once was? For at that time I shall demand from the Spirit of the Earth the bones, from the water the blood, from the plants the hair, from the wind the spirit, even as they received them at the primal creation. . . . And each man will arise in the place where his spirit left him or where he first fell to the ground." '37

Only in Egypt, and later in Islam, was there a preoccupation with the corpse which approached that of the Hebrews. On the Judgement Day, a man's heart was weighed in the scales against the balance of truth. In Egypt his body, statues of his body, portraits of his body, were all preserved with passionate care. That the Egyptians did not, like the Hebrews, translate this care for the body into a pathological hatred for human sacrifice and cannibalism may be attributed to the complexity of their religion and the number of their special-purpose gods. In Egypt there was no single deity with the power to place a total ban on human sacrifice. In the case of Islam, deeply influenced by Judaism and Christianity, corpses were buried facing Mecca so that all would be well on the Judgement Day when the true believer would rise and go to Paradise—the most delightful and sensuous afterlife in the whole gamut of the world's religions. But it was only Muslims who could go there, and only Muslim bodies that mattered. In fact, some of the more ferocious tribes of Islam were to seek merit for themselves by destroying the bodies of the infidel with a crudity that was designed to prevent them from finding their way to their own Christian or Jewish heaven.

Most modern states are built on social contract and compromise and a few hundred years' observance of the curious composite of beliefs we choose to call religion. But though, almost everywhere, human attitudes and divine commands alike forbid murder *for whatever purpose*, it is fundamentally only Jews and Christians who are dedicated to the proposition that eating the dead is worse than murder. On those rare occasions when instances of cannibalism are reported in the modern world, there is always talk of breaking 'man's oldest tabu'. Yet the tabu on eating human flesh is by no means the oldest tabu in the world—just one of those most deeply ingrained in the religions which have shaped the societies and the attitudes of the richer nations of the western hemisphere today.

CHAPTER TWO

The Centuries of Hunger

To MAKE tincture of mummy, says an ancient Egyptian medical prescription, 'select the cadaver of a red, uninjured, fresh, unspotted malefactor, twenty-four years old, and killed by hanging, broken on the wheel, or impaled, upon which the moon and the sun have shone once: cut it in pieces, sprinkle with myrrh and aloes; then marinate it for a few days, and pour on spirits'.[1] A case, it may be felt, of the remedy being worse than the disease—whatever the disease may have been. The papyrus does not say.

A few hundred years later, one Shih Hu, who ruled the Huns of northern China between A.D. 334 and 349, from time to time 'used to have one of the girls of his harem beheaded, cooked and served to his guests, while the uncooked head was passed round on a platter to prove that he had not sacrificed the least beautiful'.[2]

But medical practice and exhibitionist hospitality cannot be numbered among the more commonplace stimulants of cannibalism in the first thousand years or so of the Christian era. The recurring theme of the period was to be dearth, hunger, famine. Harsh realities also gave continuing currency to the age-old beliefs that blood-drinking gave strength and enemy-eating the satisfaction of ultimate vengeance. Mythology still reflected the grislier customs of an earlier world, and in some religions blood and human sacrifice played an integral part.

It is the strength and vengeance motif that provides the most colourful stories, some of them certainly apocryphal but nonetheless informative.

In A.D. 625 there occurred one of the better-authenticated cases. The prophet Muhammad, having fled from Mecca to Medina, was at war with the Quraysh of Mecca. He had won

35

a notable battle at Badr in 624, but the situation was reversed at Uhud in the following year. The prophet himself was wounded and many of his followers killed, including his uncle, Hamza. At the earlier battle of Badr, Hamza had been responsible for the death of one of the Quraysh who had a fearsome daughter called Hind. She was present at Uhud, beating a drum and screaming encouragement to the Quraysh army, and would herself have been killed except that one of Muhammad's followers—a true male chauvinist—'had too much respect for the sword of the apostle to kill a woman with it'. This was a mistake. After the battle 'the infidel woman, Hind, and her companions mutilated the bodies of the Muslims slain that day; they cut off the ears and noses, and Hind made necklaces, bracelets and earrings from them. Also she cut off a piece of Hamza's liver and chewed it but could not swallow it, so she spat it out again. Then she climbed a high rock and shouted the Quraysh victory from it.'[3]

A Muslim was also the victim in an incident in Spain in A.D. 890. Arab troops led by a commander known as Sauwar (which means 'horseman') had inflicted a resounding defeat on the Spanish army outside Elvira, to the north-east of Granada. 'Of a truth Sauwar brandished that day a right good sword which severed heads as only a blade of fine temper can! It was by his arm that Allah slew the unbelievers.'[4] Twelve thousand Spaniards were said to have been killed on that day, and thousands more in a subsequent battle. But, not long after, Sauwar fell into an ambush and was slain by the inhabitants of Elvira. 'When his corpse was borne into the town the air rang with shouts of joy. Drunk with vengeance, the women glared like beasts of prey at the body of him who had bereft them of brothers, husbands, and children, and then with yells of rage cut it into morsels—and devoured it!'[5]

Sometimes such tales have a crude ring of truth about them. According to Geraldus Cambrensis, when Dermot, prince of Leinster in Ireland, was presented with the head of a personal enemy, he 'tore the nostrils and lips with his teeth in a most savage and inhuman manner'.[6] Sometimes they are told with a cheerful zest that almost defeats the laws of historical probability. During the third Crusade, *did* Richard the Lionheart dine in the presence of Saladin's ambassadors on curried head of Saracen?

'soden [boiled] full hastily
With powder and with spysory [spices],
And with saffron of good colour.'[7]

The first great historian of the Crusades, a scholar and rationalist, Guibert de Nogent, relates that the armies of the first Crusade had, as auxiliary, a cannibal troop of professional beggars, who went barefoot and carried no arms. 'A Norman who, according to all accounts, was of noble birth, but who, having lost his horse, continued to follow as a foot soldier, took the strange resolution of putting himself at the head of this race of vagabonds, who willingly received him for their king. Among the Saracens these men became well known under the name of Thafurs [which Guibert translates as *Trudentes*], and were held in great horror from the general persuasion that they fed on the dead bodies of their enemies; a report which was occasionally justified, and which the king of the Thafurs took care to encourage. . . . This troop, so far from being cumbersome to the army, was infinitely serviceable, carrying burdens, bringing in forage, provisions, and tribute, working the machines in the sieges, and above all, spreading consternation amongst the Turks, who feared death from the lances of the knights less than that further consummation they heard of, under the teeth of the Thafurs.'[8]

Strength rather than the desire for vengeance was what, according to the great German epic, the *Nibelungenlied*, led the Burgundians to drink the blood of the fallen during a great battle in the burning hall of the Huns. The supposed date of this event was A.D. 437, but the epic appears to have been compiled in the twelfth or thirteenth century. The translation belongs to 1901, and McGonagall would have been proud of it.*

'We all are lost together,' each to his neighbour cried,
'It had been far better we had in battle died.

* William McGonagall (1830–1902), arguably the greatest Awful Poet in the history of Western literature.

Now God have mercy on us! woe for this fiery pain!
Ah! what a monstrous vengeance the bloody queen has
    ta'en!'

Then faintly said another, 'Needs must we here fall dead!
What boots us now the greeting, to us by Etzel [Attila]
    sped?
Ah me! I'm so tormented by thirst from burning heat,
That in this horrid anguish my life must quickly fleet.'

Thereat outspake Sir Hagan, the noble knight and good,
'Let each, by thirst torment'd, take here a draught of
    blood.
In such a heat, believe me, 'tis better far than wine.
Naught's for the time so fitting; such counsel, friends, is
    mine.'

With that straight went a warrior, where a warm corpse
    he found.
On the dead down knelt he; his helmet he unbound;
Then greedily began he to drink the flowing blood.
However unaccustom'd, it seem'd him passing good.

'Now God requite thee, Hagan,' the weary warrior cried,
'For such refreshing beverage by your advice supplied.
It has been my lot but seldom to drink of better wine.
For life am I thy servant for this fair hint of thine.'

When th' others heard and witness'd with what delight
    he quaff'd,
Yet many more among them drank too the bloody
    draught,
It strung again their sinews, and failing strength renew'd.
This in her lover's person many a fair lady rued. [9]

In the thirteenth century, the Mongols—usually, at that
time, called Tartars—acquired a not wholly unjustified reputation for bloodthirstiness. This was probably founded on
the political holocausts in which Genghis Khan had indulged
as his armies swept across central Asia from China to the Near

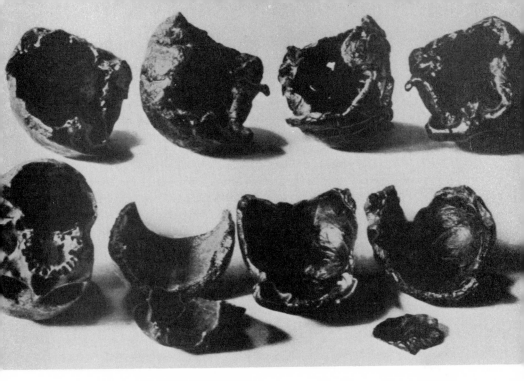

1. Prehistoric skulls from Java. Their cup shape is in sharp contrast to that of the modern Dyak headhunting trophy, lower left.

2. A human skull encrusted with turquoise and obsidian to make the image of the Aztec god Texcatlipoca.

3. Goya's painting of Cronus swallowing his children.

4. A twelfth-century mosaic in the Palatine Chapel, Palermo, showing Abraham preparing to sacrifice Isaac.

5. Mediaeval travellers were convinced that ritual cannibalism flourished in the Andaman Isles in the Indian Ocean. This illustration is from the *Livre des Merveilles* in the Bibliothèque Nationale, Paris.

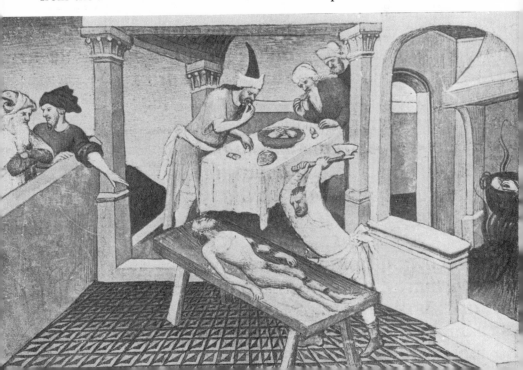

6. A 1477 woodcut showing the wafers of the Host being bought and tortured by the Jews at Passover; and the penalties they paid.

East. There is a particular story told about Genghis's great-grandson, Abaga, Ilkhan of Persia, which may well be true, as it appears in the works of two intelligent and usually reliable contemporaries—the Armenian prince, Hayton (Hethoum of Corycus), and the European friar, Ricold. Apparently a Turkish nobleman had been found guilty of treason against Abaga and was condemned to death. According to Hayton, 'he was taken and cut in two, and orders were issued that in all the food eaten by Abaga there should be put a portion of the traitor's flesh. Of this Abaga himself ate, and caused all his barons to partake. And this was in accordance with the custom of the Tartars.'[10] Father Ricold, less benevolently disposed toward the Mongols, has a slightly more lurid version. 'When the Emperor Khan was giving the order for the traitor's execution the Tartar ladies and women interposed, and begged that he might be made over to them. Having got hold of the prisoner they boiled him alive, and cutting his body up into mincemeat gave it to eat to the whole army, as an example to others.'[11]

Popular belief certainly held the Tartars to be unregenerate cannibals. Vincent of Beauvais reported: 'When they capture any one who is at bitter enmity with them, they gather together and eat him in vengeance of his revolt, and like infernal leeches suck his blood.'[12] Ivo of Narbonne, when the Mongols swept over Europe in 1242, wrote that the Tartar chiefs and their dog-headed followers ate the bodies of their victims like so much bread,[13] while another chronicler embroidered on the theme. The Tartars, he said, ate *everyone* they killed, being specially fond of female flesh. The commissariat rationed out succulent young girls to officers, while the common soldiers had to make do with tough and stringy matrons. Breast meat, the greatest delicacy, was reserved for the princes' tables.[14]

Three hundred years later, during the Seven Years' War, these old beliefs were revived in regard to the Kalmuks of the Russian army. One author says that an old Kalmuk warrior confessed to him that they had done what they could to encourage the Prussians' fears by cutting up the bodies of the slain in the presence of prisoners, and roasting them.[15]

While their more boisterous neighbours indulged in such deeds as these, there were many people in India who believed that

it was a sin to eat even an insect. This was, to them, cannibalism of the soul.

The doctrine of transmigration of souls holds that, when a
living thing dies, if it has lived its life well its soul is afterwards
reincarnated at a higher level; if badly, at a lower one. By
virtuous living during successive incarnations, even the mean-
est form of life may ascend through the ranks to reach the
highest level, and then achieve the paradise of release from
the cycle of rebirth; similarly, a man of the highest rank, by
evil living, may slide down the spiritual scale until he is
incarnated as a rat or a gnat. Even an insect, therefore, is
inhabited by what may have been and may again become a
human soul. To swallow one is equivalent to committing murder—which does nothing to advance the incarnation rating
of either the swallower or the swallowed. The doctrine of
transmigration encouraged vegetarianism among Buddhists,
and compelled it for Jains, because to kill an animal for food
was as reprehensible as killing a man.

Buddhism and Jainism emerged in the sixth century B.C.,
and as the centuries passed their basic beliefs (in certain of the
more remote regions) took on some curiously logical-illogical
shapes. There was in Tibet, for example, the gorily un-
Buddhist tale of Padma's destruction of the butchers. At one
of the furthest extremities of India there was a town inhabited
entirely by butchers. To destroy these unrepentant sinners,
the guru Padma-Sambhava incarnated himself as one of their
sons, Kati. To Kati, all living things being man's kin (and
eating the flesh of animals essentially the same as eating the
flesh of man) it made no difference which he ate; and so he
began eating the butchers. But when he took to the habit of
cutting off bits of his own flesh and eating it, the people
cursed him and drove him away. Kati now made the acquaintance of a butcher named Tumpo, who was quite as regrettable
as himself, and said to him: 'Both of us live the same kind of
life and we should be good company for each other.' He
supplied Tumpo with bows and arrows and snares, and
instructed him to continue killing butchers as fast as he could,
while he, Kati, devoted himself to despatching their life-
principles back to the safe keeping of the World Soul so that
they might be redistributed to more desirable owners. Thus

all the butchers were killed off.[16] This Tibetan fable was intended to emphasise the evils of killing, and particularly of killing for food.

In India itself, not all were vegetarians, although at times the meats people were legally permitted to eat were limited. In the last two or three centuries B.C., it was prohibited to sell 'unclean meat'—a category which covered meat cut with a sword, dog meat, human meat, the village pig, carnivorous animals, locusts, camels, and hairless or excessively hairy animals.[17]

In the further reaches of the country, however, there were tribes who followed the ancient practice of endophagy. Herodotus said that 'the Padaeans' lived on raw meat. 'It is said that when a man falls sick, his closest companions kill him, because, as they put it, their meat would be spoilt if he were allowed to waste away with disease. The invalid, in these circumstances, protests that there is nothing the matter with him—but to no purpose. His friends refuse to accept his protestations, and kill and eat him just the same. Should the sufferer be a woman, it makes no odds: her women friends deal with her precisely as the men do. If anyone is lucky enough to live to an advanced age, he is offered in sacrifice and devoured.' The 'Padaeans' were later identified as the Birhors, who admitted endophagy and expressed horror at the thought of eating anyone but a near relative.[18]

Tibetan Buddhism—which was in a class by itself—made great use of blood in offerings to wrathful *dharmapalas* (a kind of demon). But just *any* blood would not do. The blood taken from a corpse or from someone suffering from a dangerous, contagious disease, especially leprosy, was believed to be specially efficacious. In writing magic formulae it was sometimes necessary to use blood wiped from a sword or taken from a healthy young man who had been killed in a fight. For other prescriptions, blood from the brain of a man who had died of insanity, or that of an eight-year-old child, or that of a child who was the fruit of an incestuous union, was required. And for others still, the blood of the Abominable Snowman![19] Human skulls were used as magical cups, and flutes and whistles were made from human thigh bones. According to one mediaeval account, the bodies of executed criminals were stored up to provide the Lamas with at least some of their ritual needs.[20] The Tibetans, like the Padaeans, were accused of endophagy. They had, said Pian del Carpine, 'a most astonishing, or rather horrible, custom, for, when anyone's father is about to give up the ghost, all the relatives meet together, and they eat him, as was told to me for certain'.[21]

Such practices, if they had ever been common around the Mediterranean shores of Europe, had largely died out by Classical times, surviving only in the Greek myths—in the tale of Cronus, for example, who married his sister Rhea. It was prophesied by Mother Earth, and by his dying father Uranus, that one of Cronus' own sons would dethrone him. When Rhea every year dutifully bore him a child, its father promptly swallowed it. First there was Hestia, then Demeter and Hera, next Hades, and then Poseidon. Rhea, not unnaturally, was annoyed, and when Zeus, her third son, was born, she made arrangements to keep him out of Cronus' way. Zeus grew in safety to manhood when, with the aid of his mother, he fed Cronus an emetic potion which caused him to regurgitate all Zeus' brothers and sisters—unhurt, and fully grown. Ultimately, Zeus struck his father down with a thunderbolt before banishing him (to the British Isles!) for ever.[22]

Many of the gods, giants, and heroes of Greek legend had cannibal tendencies. There was Polyphemus, who captured Ulysses and every evening, with the greatest relish, ate two of his crew. There was Achilles, who snarled at Hector that he wished he could eat him, and Hecuba, who in turn expressed a strong desire to make a meal of Achilles' liver. All this was legend, but it was not legend that, as late as the Christian era, children were still sacrificially eaten in some of the more backward districts of Arcadia, or that in an early version of the Dionysian revels mare-headed Maenads annually tore a boy victim in pieces and ate him raw.[23]

Although some authorities insist that, by Roman times, only slight importance was attached to blood as a sacrificial substance, this is not entirely borne out by the facts. Among the new cults which penetrated Rome during the early centuries of the Christian era were several mystery religions, into which the initiate was inducted by a symbolic rebirth ceremony. In the rites of Cybele, the initiate descended into a trench where he was deluged with the blood of a bull, slaughtered over him. 'The blood is the life. . . .' This was the *taurobolium*, and there was also the *criobolium* where ram's blood was used. (At this stage, of course, the blood had to be animal blood. There is nothing to prove or disprove that, in earlier times, human blood may have been used. Nor is there anything other than the implications of modern psychiatry to suggest that, even in Roman times, there may have been private perverts who chose to use the more potent human blood for their rituals.) After the blood-bath, the *dies sanguinis*, said Sallustius—himself an initiate of Cybele—'we were fed on milk as though being reborn'.* The rites of Isis and Attis, of Cybele and Mithras, had a precise appeal for the people of Imperial Rome. The Classical world had its own theory of transmigration of souls, propounded by Plato; it might take a man ten thousand years of rebirths before he reached the Islands of the Blest. The mystery religions, via their rebirth rites, got you there quicker.[25]

The mystery religions reached Rome, in the main, from beyond her eastern borders, and some—particularly Mithraism—were carried by the Roman army as far afield as Britain, taking on local attributes on the way. But it was not only 'pagan' beliefs that were altered to suit new lands. The Christ of the New Testament, too, was absorbed in Egypt into the persona of the resurrection god Osiris.

According to Egyptian Christians, Adam and Eve—being expelled from Paradise, where they had lived on the choicest foods—were unable to eat the coarse food they found elsewhere. They suffered greatly from hunger and want, and were soon near to starvation. At this point Jesus, who was Adam's sponsor, went to God the Father and asked him if he wished Adam to die. In reply, Yahweh told Jesus that he had better give Adam some of his own flesh to eat. Taking flesh from his

---

* 'We shall do well to avoid', said the distinguished scholar Arthur Darby Nock, the supposition that . . . the *taurobolium* was of paramount importance in determining' the development of the Christian rite of baptism.[24] For readers who were not even aware of the supposition, far less of the need to avoid it, this is an interesting area for consideration.

right side, he rubbed it down into grains and took it to Yahweh, who thereupon took some of his own (invisible) flesh, formed it into a grain of wheat, and placed it with the flesh of his Son. He then sealed the grain of wheat with the 'seal of light', and told Jesus to take it to the archangel Michael and instruct him to deliver it to Adam on earth, and to teach him how to sow it and reap it, and how to make bread from it.[26] So the flesh of Christ and God the Father was used to bring fertility to the land, much as the dissected and scattered flesh of Osiris had done in earlier times (see p. 20).

And the land needed fertility. For hundreds upon hundreds of years, the peoples of Europe and Asia—and, no doubt, of Africa and the Americas (although most records before A.D. 1200 remain undeciphered—starved when the harvest failed. The story is agonising and repetitive. In China in 206 B.C., 'people ate human flesh; and more than half of the population died'. In 178 B.C., 'tired and weak old men would exchange the dead bodies of starved children, and gnaw their bones'. In 89–87 B.C., 'human beings ate human flesh'. In 48–44 B.C., 'in the province of Lang-yeh residents ate human flesh'. In 15 B.C., in Liang and the province of P'ing-yüan, the same thing happened. And again in Ch'ing and Hsü in A.D. 21.[27]

Dramatists even made good theatre out of it. In the year A.D. 25 in the province of Honan there was a roving gang of Chinese who would settle for a while in one place, eat the inhabitants, and then move on. Not surprisingly, at news of their approach, people fled from their homes. The play *Chao-li-ch'ang-fei* ('The devotion of Chao-li') takes the subject on from there. The scene is the fields of Pien-king. Enter a high-ranking widow, Madam Chao, supported by her two sons, Chao-hiao and Chao-li, who are fleeing from the cannibal brigands. To provide their mother with some comforts, Chao-li begins cutting wood for a fire, while Chao-hiao sets out to look for herbs and roots. But scarcely has he gone a hundred yards when he comes on a most frightening-looking man, one Ma Wou. Ma Wou explains that though his talents are great, he has been rejected by an army examining tribunal because he is so excessively ugly. In revenge, he has put himself at the head of a party of other malcontents, and makes it a principle to eat a little piece of human heart or liver at every meal. Ma Wou here plants his hands on the shoulders of the politely listening Chao-hiao and drags him off to his camp. Having tried in vain to soften the heart of his murderous host, Chao-hiao—full of orthodox Chinese filial piety—implores him to allow him to pay his respects to his mother once more before he dies. Ma Wou hesitates and is fatally drawn into a philosophic discussion about the five cardinal virtues (particularly sincerity). Worsted in this, he gives Chao-hiao one hour to say farewell. In a touching scene, the young man takes leave of his parent. Her tears cannot hold him, and when his time is up, faithful to his promise he returns to the cannibal camp— hotly pursued, it need hardly be added, by his mother and brother, both of whom express a desire to take his place. Chao-li, whose *embonpoint* is greater than his brother's, bares his chest, displays his brawn, and tries to seduce the cannibal chief with the bait of greed. In the end, Ma Wou is so touched by these displays of virtue that he releases Chao-hiao and sends mother and sons on their way again.[28]

There are other casual references in Han literature to the prevalence of cannibalism in particular circumstances. In the *Chou-hou-chouen* ('Story of the river banks'), 'the hostess cheerfully served up supper and the two bowmen, spurred on by hunger, began to eat. But Wou-song, who had opened a pie and was examining it with care, interrogated her. "Are these," he demanded, "man pies or dog pies?" "Man pies!" she responded with a shout of laughter. "Where would we get human meat to make pies these days? The country is quiet; there's no war on just now!" '[29] And in the *San-kui-chi* ('History of three kingdoms'), the great Hsuan-te was being entertained by a huntsman who had had an unsuccessful day. So 'he killed his own wife to allay the hunger of Hsuan-te, and when Hsuan-te asked "What is this meat?", he replied simply "Wolf". And they supped.'[30]

Towards the end of the T'ang dynasty, in the late ninth and early tenth centuries, Arab travellers to China recorded that 'Chinese law permits the eating of human flesh, and this flesh is sold publicly in the markets'; and also that 'the Chinese eat the flesh of all men who are executed by the sword'.[31] During one of the Mongol sieges, Carpine heard, one man in ten of the army was sacrificed to feed the rest.[32] And during the anarchic conditions of the eleventh century, human meat became a commonplace in the north. Northerners, in fact, later opened human-meat restaurants in the sophisticated, bustling southern capital of the Sung dynasty, Hangchow. Dishes made from the flesh of old men, women, girls and children all had special names—and presumably special tastes. The meat was referred to, euphemistically, as 'two-legged mutton'. Cannibals of more recent times have usually described human meat as resembling pork, but pork was such a familiar item of diet in China that another name had to be found.[33]

Indian literature is rather less informative on the subject of cannibalism prior to about A.D. 1200. But there is a realistic moral tale of low life contained in the *Dasakumaracarita* ('Tales of the ten princes') which indicates that the problem was by no means unknown. There had been no rain for twelve years. 'The corn withered, plants were barren, trees bore no fruit, and the clouds were impotent; water courses dried up, ponds became mud-holes, and the springs ceased to flow. Bulbs, roots and fruit became scarce, folk-tales were forgotten, and all festive merrymaking ceased. Robber bands multiplied, and people ate one another's flesh. Human skulls, white as cranes, rolled on the ground. Flocks of thirsty crows flew hither and thither. Villages, cities, whole districts, were deserted.

'The three householders [brothers] first ate their store of grain and then one by one their goats, their sheep, their buffaloes, their cows, their maidservants, their manservants, their children, and the wives of the eldest and the middle brother. Finally, they decided that next day they would eat Dhumini, the wife of the youngest; but the youngest brother, Dhanyaka, could not bring himself to eat his darling, so that night he stole away with her. . . .'[34]

In Europe, the situation seems to have been as bad as in China. In A.D. 450 there was a famine in Italy when parents ate their children. Between 695 and 700 England and Ireland suffered from a three-year dearth during which 'men ate each other'. It was the turn of Bulgaria and Germany to starve in 845 and 851, and in 936 began a four-year famine in Scotland when 'people began to devour one another'.[35] In the latter half of the tenth century, according to one of the few authors who was born at a time when it was still possible to hear of it from eyewitnesses, 'a mighty famine swept the whole Romanised world for five years, and there was nowhere that was not reported poverty-stricken and destitute. Vast numbers of people starved to death. Then, in many areas, the terrible famine forced people to dine not only on foul animals and reptiles, but also on the flesh of living people, men, women and children. Their need was so great that they even ate their parents. In fact, so severe was the famine that young men ate their mothers and, forgetting all maternal instincts, mothers ate their little ones.'[36]

Again, in 1022, half the world seems to have starved, and in 1069 parts of William the Conqueror's English realm 'were so wasted with his wars that for want of both husbandry and habitation, a great dearth did ensue, whereby many were forced to eat horses, dogs, cats, rats, and other loathsome and vile vermin; yea, some abstained not from the flesh of men'.[37]

It is a dispiriting catalogue—and yet an unreal one. In the so-called 'dark ages', as in all ages, it was the poor who suffered most from starvation, and the poor could not write. Furthermore, there were few cities at this time, and it is in cities that the effects of famine show up most startlingly. The probability is that contemporary historians restricted themselves to bald statements on the lines of 'men ate each other' not from reasons of fastidiousness, but because that was all they knew.

Except in one case. During the great famine of A.D. 1201 in Egypt there was a doctor living in Cairo—a man in his late thirties—who saw and heard much, and wrote it down. A whole chapter of his *Useful and instructive reflections on things that I have seen and events that I have witnessed in Egypt* (written between 1201 and 1207) is devoted to the subject. Abd al-Latif's flat prose makes the story far more convincing than any professional author could have contrived, and far more harrowing. This was the reality of famine everywhere, not just in Egypt.

Since Abd al-Latif's sobering and detailed document seems never before to have been translated into English, it is given here virtually in its entirety.

'At Misr, at Cairo, and in the surrounding areas,' says Abd al-Latif, 'wherever a man directed his steps, there was nowhere that his feet or his eyes did not encounter a corpse or someone in the last stages of agony, or even a great number of people in this unhappy state. Particularly in Cairo, they picked up from a hundred to five hundred dead bodies every day, to take them to the place where they were accorded burial rites. At Misr, the number of dead was incalculable; people there did not bury them but contented themselves with throwing them outside the town. In the end, there were no longer enough people to collect them and they remained where they were, among the houses and shops, and even inside the living quarters. You would see a corpse fallen to pieces—and quite near a cook-shop, or a baker's, or other places of that kind. . . .

'As for the suburbs and the villages, all the inhabitants perished except for a small number, some of whom left home to seek refuge elsewhere. . . . Often a traveller would pass through a sizeable village without finding a single inhabitant alive. He would see the houses open, and the bodies of those who had lived there laid out facing one another, some putrefying, some still fresh. Very often he found valuable possessions in a house, for there was no one to steal them. . . .

'I heard tell of a fisherman of the port of Tennis, who had seen pass near him in a single day four hundred corpses that the river was carrying down to the sea. . . . The road from Egypt to Syria, according to the reports of a great many witnesses, was like a great field sown with human bodies, or one over which the harvester's sickle has passed. It became a banqueting hall for ravening birds and beasts, who gorged themselves; and the dogs that these people had taken with them to accompany them in their voluntary exile were the first to devour their corpses.'[38]

The full horrors of famine had begun to threaten in October 1200. Egypt's fertility depended on the natural irrigation and enrichment of the soil that resulted from the rising of the Nile. In a good year, the Nile waters rose in mid-June, reached their fullest extent in September, and then retreated, leaving behind a coating of rich black earth deposits from the Ethiopian plateau. 1200 was not a good year.

'There was no longer any hope that the Nile would rise;

and as a result the cost of provisions had already gone up. The provinces were ravaged by drought. The inhabitants foresaw a state of dearth as inevitable, and fear of famine led to disturbances. Those who lived in villages and in the countryside left for the main provincial towns. A great number emigrated to Syria, the Maghreb, Hejaz and the Yemen. . . . A vast multitude sought refuge in Misr and Cairo, where they were to meet with frightful famine and appalling mortality; for, when the sun entered the sign of Aries, the air became corrupt, and pestilence and a deadly contagion began to take their toll, and the poor, under the pressure of ever-growing want, ate carrion, corpses, dogs, excrement, and animal dung. They went further, and reached the stage of eating little children. It was not unusual to find people [selling] little children, roasted or boiled. The commandant of the city guard ordered that those who committed this crime should be burned alive, as should those who ate such meats.

'I myself saw a little roast child in a basket. It was brought to the commandant, and led in at the same time were a man and woman who were the child's father and mother. The commandant condemned them to be burned alive.

'In the month of Ramadan [June 1201] a corpse was found at Misr with all the flesh stripped off for food, and its legs tied like a sheep trussed for cooking. . . .

'When the poor first began to eat human flesh, the horror and astonishment that such extraordinary meals aroused were such that these crimes formed the topic of every conversation. No one could stop talking about them. But eventually people grew accustomed, and some conceived such a taste for these detestable meats that they made them their ordinary provender, eating them for enjoyment and even laying in supplies. They thought up a variety of preparation methods. And the custom being once introduced, it spread in the provinces so that there was no part of Egypt where one did not see examples of it. Then it no longer caused surprise. The horror people had felt at first vanished entirely; one spoke of it, and heard it spoken of, as a matter of everyday indifference.

'I saw one day a woman with a head wound being dragged, by some labourers, through the market. They had seized her while she was eating a small roast child, which they also carried with them. The people in the market paid not the slightest attention to this sight, but went on with their business. I saw in them no sign of astonishment or horror—which surprised me rather more than the crime itself. Their indifference sprang, really, only from the fact that the sight of such cruelties had already struck them a great many times, so that it fell into the category of things they had become accustomed to and no longer had the power to startle them.

'Two days before, I had seen a child nearing the age of puberty, who had been found roasted. The two young people who had been found with it confessed that it was they who had killed the child, cooked it, and eaten part of it.

'It happened one night [after dusk] that a young slave girl was playing with a newly weaned infant, the child of a rich private citizen. While the child was by her side, a beggar-woman seized the very moment when the slave's eyes were turned away, tore open the child's stomach, and began to eat the flesh, quite raw. Many women have told me of people flinging themselves at them in order to snatch their children, and that they have had to use all their strength to save them.

'Talking one day to a woman who carried a newly-weaned and very chubby child, I admired it and recommended her to take good care of it. She then told me that, when she had been walking on the canal bank, a sturdy ruffian had attacked her and tried to snatch the child from her; that she had found no other way of sheltering it than to throw herself to the ground, holding the child beneath her, until a horseman happened to pass by, which forced the man to retreat. She added that the rascal had watched avidly for the chance of getting a grip on any of the child's limbs that might stray out from their shelter, so that he might eat it. The child was ill for some time afterwards as a result of the mauling he had suffered in the tug-of-war between the robber and herself, one trying to snatch him and the other to hold on to him.

'The children of the poor, those who were young or already grown and had no one at all to care for them or look after them, were scattered through all parts of the town, even in the narrowest side streets, like locusts in the countryside. The poor, men and women alike, lay in wait for these unhappy children, carried them off and ate them. The guilty were rarely caught in the act, and only when they were careless. It was usually the women who were caught with the proof of their crime, a circumstance which in my opinion arose from the fact that women are less crafty than men and cannot so readily flee to escape pursuit. In only a few days, at Misr, thirty women were burned, among whom there was none who did not admit to having eaten several children. I saw one of them taken to the commandant with a roast child hung round her neck. She was given more than two hundred lashes to make her confess to her crime, but they elicited no response from her. You would have said that she had lost all human faculties. Then someone pulled her roughly, to lead her away, and she expired on the spot.

'When some unfortunate who had been convicted of eating human flesh was burned alive, the corpse was always found to have been devoured by the following morning. People ate it the more willingly, for the flesh, being fully roasted, did not need to be cooked.

'This mania for eating other people became so common among the poor that the majority of them perished that way. Some rich people, in decent circumstances, also shared in this detestable barbarism. Among them, some were reduced to it by need, others did it out of greed and to satisfy a taste for it. One man told me he had a friend who had been reduced to poverty by the calamities of that year, but that the friend one day invited him to come and eat with him as he had often done in former times. When he arrived at the house, he found assembled there a set of people whose appearance was wholly wretched. Before them was a fricassée containing a great deal of meat, but there was no bread at all to eat with it. This made him suspicious, and when he went to relieve himself and noticed a storeroom full of human bones and fresh flesh, he was seized with terror and took to his heels.

'Among these rascals there were some who used all kinds of tricks and pretexts to entice men, unsuspectingly, to their homes. This was what happened to three of the doctors I was associated with. One told me that his father had gone out one day and never reappeared. Another was asked by a woman, who gave him two pieces of silver, to come with her to see an invalid for whom she was responsible. This woman having led him through several narrow alleys, the doctor became uneasy and refused to follow further. When he remonstrated strongly with her, she departed hurriedly without reclaiming her two pieces of silver.

'The third doctor was approached by a man to accompany him to the home of an invalid who lived, he said, on the city's main thoroughfare. As they walked along, the man distributed some small coins as alms, saying each time: "Today is the day of retribution, and a recompense double the good that has been done; let those who act, act with a view to such a reckoning." This [extract from the Koran] was repeated so often that the doctor began to suspect the man of being up to something. However, the good opinion he had formed of him outweighed his alarms; moreover, the desire for profit urged him on. He allowed himself to be taken into the entry of a half-ruined apartment block [built over stables, warehouses and shops]. The look of the place kindled his fears again, and he stopped on the stairs while his companion went ahead to open the door. Then the man's crony came to meet him and said: "After taking so long about it, have you at least brought some good game?" These words struck terror into the doctor's heart. He hurled himself through a window which, by good fortune, he chanced to see, and landed in a stable. The master of the stable came to him and asked what was going on, but the doctor was wary of telling him, as he did not dare trust him. Then this man said: "I know what has happened to you. The people who lodge there entrap men and kill them."

'At Atfih, a grocery store was found to contain jars full of human flesh pickled in water and salt. The man was asked why he had amassed such a large quantity, and replied that he had thought that, if the dearth continued, men in future would become too skinny to eat.

'A great many of the poor had retreated to the Isle of Raudha, where they remained hidden in earthen huts and watched out for passers-by whom they could kidnap. The authorities were warned of this and decided to wipe them out, but they fled. In their huts were found an enormous number of human bones. I have it from a trustworthy source that four hundred skulls were counted.

'The following story, which was recounted by the commandant himself, received at the time great publicity. A woman came one day to see him; she had her face uncovered* and appeared to be in the grip of extreme horror. She told him that she was a midwife and had been invited in her professional capacity to the home of certain women. There, someone had given her a plate of *sicbadj*,† very well made and perfectly seasoned. She had noticed that, in it, there was a lot of meat different from the kind usually used in a *sicbadj* [viz. mutton], and this had given her a distinct distaste for it. Contriving to draw a little girl aside, she asked her what kind of meat it was, and the child said: "Miss So-and-so—the very fat one—came to pay us a visit and my father killed her; she is in here, jointed and hung." She then entered a storeroom and found stocks of meat. When the commandant heard what the woman had to say, he sent some men with her to raid the house and arrest everyone they found there. But the master of the house saved himself, and eventually did so well that he won pardon by secretly donating three hundred pieces of gold.

'Here again is another example of these barbarities. The wife of a military man who was rich and enjoyed all the comforts of life was pregnant, and her husband was away on service. Her neighbours were worthless creatures, but having sniffed the aroma of a fricassée which was coming from their house she asked to eat some of it—because of one of those cravings women are subject to during pregnancy. Finding it very agreeable she asked for more, but they told her it had all been eaten. Then she wanted to know how the dish was made, and they confessed that it was with human flesh. She then settled with them that they should try to kidnap little children for her, promising generous recognition of their efforts. A constant diet of such food made her quite ferocious and roused in her the instincts of a carnivorous beast, until her servants, who feared she might make an attempt on their lives, denounced her. As a result, the law descended on her house and found there a quantity of flesh and bones that proved the

* Only under the greatest stress would a Muslim woman appear unveiled before any man who was not of her immediate family.

† According to a contemporary recipe, this dish consisted of cubed meat, onions, and carrots or aubergines in a sweet-sour sauce, garnished with split almonds, raisins, and dried figs.[39]

truth of the accusations. She was put in irons and thrown into prison; but capital punishment was deferred, as much out of regard for her husband as to save the child she was carrying.

'If I were to record all the acts of this kind that I have heard of, or seen with my own eyes, I would risk being suspected of exaggeration or taxed with chattering too much. All the facts I have reported being an eye-witness to came under my eye without any design on my part, and without my having intentionally frequented places where such things might be expected to occur. Chance alone was responsible. Far from looking for such sights, I most often avoided them, so great was the horror they inspired in me. People who, in contrast, stayed on duty at the commandant's headquarters, saw all kinds of tragic scenes throughout the day and night. Two or three children, even more, would be found in a single cooking pot. One day, they found a pot with ten hands cooking in it, prepared like sheep's trotters. Another time, they discovered a large cauldron with an adult's head and some of his limbs simmering with wheat grains. There were parallels without number.

'Near the mosque of Ahmad ibn Touloun there were people who kidnapped men. One bookseller with whom I dealt, an elderly and corpulent man, fell into their net and escaped with great difficulty and almost at his last gasp.

'One of the officials of the Misr mosque similarly fell into the hands of another bunch of rascals at Karafa. Other people happening to come on the scene, he escaped and ran for his life. But there were many others who, having left their family to go out, never returned home again.

'One person whom I know to be scrupulously truthful has assured me that, passing a forsaken spot, she saw a woman with a bloated and decomposing corpse in front of her; that the woman was eating flesh from the thighs of the corpse; and that when she reproached the woman with the horror of such a deed, she replied that the corpse was that of her husband. Nothing was more commonplace than to hear people who were eating human flesh say that it was the body of their son, their husband, or some other close relative. An old woman eating a tiny child would excuse herself by saying that it was her daughter's son, not an infant she did not know, and that it was better that she should eat him than that someone else should do so.

'Nothing was more common than this kind of thing, and it would be difficult to find in the length and breadth of Egypt, even among people who live cloistered in monasteries, or women who spend their lives in the zenana, anyone who has not been eye-witness to such atrocities. Moreover, everybody knows that there were grave-robbers who ate or sold the bodies they dug up.

'This hideous calamity I have just described struck the whole of Egypt. There was not a single inhabited spot where eating people was not extremely common. Syene, Kush [Meroe], Fayum, Mahalleh, Alexandria, Damietta, and every other part of Egypt witnessed these scenes of horror.

'A merchant friend of mine, a man you can count on, came from Alexandria and told me of a great many events of this kind that he had seen for himself. Most remarkable of what he told me was that he had seen five children's heads in a single cauldron, cooked with the choicest spices.

'But that is enough of this subject, on which—though I have dwelt on it at length—I have still been too brief. . . .'[40]

CHAPTER THREE

The Red Elixir

IN THE year A.D. 1215, Pope Innocent III summoned not only the patriarchs of Jerusalem and Constantinople but twenty-nine archbishops, four hundred and twelve bishops, eight hundred abbots and priors, and the envoys of all the major rulers of Europe and the Levant—including the Holy Roman Emperor and the kings of England, France, Aragon and Hungary—to attend the Fourth Lateran Council. This assembly of all who were most distinguished in the Catholic world was to decree it as an article of faith that Christians must believe—when the priest at the altar pronounced the phrase '*hoc est corpus meum*' ('this is my body')—that the bread and wine were changed into the body and blood of Christ. In the words of the Definition: 'The body and blood of Jesus Christ are truly contained under the appearance of bread and wine in the sacrament of the altar, the bread being transubstantiated into the body and the wine into the blood.'[1] Those who partook of the Host had formerly eaten it as a symbol of the body of Christ. Now it was to be no longer a symbol but an actuality, and anyone who doubted it was guilty of heresy.

This was the culmination of more than a thousand years of disagreement within the Church as to what Jesus had meant when he spoke to his disciples on the occasion of the Last Supper. In the words of Mark: 'As they were eating, he took bread, and blessed, and broke it, and gave it to them, and said, "Take; this is my body." And he took a cup, and when he had given thanks he gave it to them, and they all drank of it. And he said to them, "This is my blood of the covenant, which is poured out for many." '[2] Matthew's version was much the same, and so was Luke's, although Luke added that Jesus had also said: 'Do this in remembrance of me.'[3]

There seems to have been little doubt about the words actually used. After the crucifixion and the resurrection, the disciples began to recall every detail of the Last Supper and to emphasise the mystic communion of the bread and wine. Mark, the first gospel to be written down (*c.* A.D. 65–70, more than thirty years after the event) was based on the reminiscences of Peter, who had been present. The authorship of Matthew is a matter of debate, though some churchmen attribute an early date to it and claim that it was written by the apostle himself. Luke, a Greek-speaking convert, gathered other men's memoirs, written and oral, fragmentary and complete, into a gospel designed to meet the needs of the mission to the gentiles. The fourth gospel, John, was compiled at the beginning of the second century A.D. by an unknown second-generation Christian who drew on a tradition that at some points conflicted with the first three gospels. Nevertheless, the historical Jesus, according to all contemporary opinion, did equate the bread with his body and the wine with his blood. And as one modern scholar remarks, the paradox, for a Jew, of any suggestion of drinking blood virtually guarantees the authenticity of the record. It is much harder to imagine someone else inventing these words than Jesus uttering them.[4]

To begin with, however, no one seems to have been greatly concerned over whether Jesus intended what he said about transubstantiation to be taken literally or not. It was the general tenor of the message that was more immediately important. Were his words meant to imply that he was the intermediary in a renewed covenant between Yahweh and the Jews? Or that his forthcoming death was to be seen as a sacrifice, a sin-offering to God on behalf of all mankind?

It was to be St Paul, a Hellenistic Jew who was not one of the original disciples—who was, indeed, in bitter ideological conflict with them in their role as leaders of the church at Jerusalem—who was to be responsible for resolving the question in such a way as to shape the whole future of Christianity. If the Jerusalem leaders had had their way, it might well have remained welded to Judaism. But Paul, in attempting to make Jesus intelligible to gentiles and particularly to the Greeks, was to lay the foundations of Christianity as a religion of universal salvation.[5]

Astutely, he brought a number of different interpretations together and dovetailed them into a whole. The virtual simultaneity of Passover and crucifixion allowed the redemption element in the first to be transferred to the second, so that Jesus could be presented to potential Jewish converts as the new Redeemer. At the same time he became a sacrificial figure, the Paschal lamb offered up at Passover. In an age saturated with sacrificial ideas, this interpretation satisfied gentiles as readily as Jews. For gentile and Jew alike, the natural form of homage to the gods was sacrifice; the crucifixion, viewed in this way, brought Christianity within the familiar orbit of Greek religious ritual. The blood covenant, too, was as familiar to gentiles as to Jews; it needed only to be expanded into a covenant with *all* mankind.

Whether or not Jesus had intended his symbolic acts and words to become a rite, continuously repeated, is uncertain, but ritual re-enactment was a long-established religious custom, and Paul emphasised it strongly in his correspondence with the Greeks. In Paul's description of the Last Supper, he has Jesus say, after breaking bread: 'Do this in remembrance of me.' After passing the cup, he again says: 'Do this, as often as you drink it, in remembrance of me.' And Paul himself adds at the end: 'For as often as you eat this bread and drink the cup, you proclaim the Lord's death until he comes.'[6] It is perhaps worth noting that the only gospel to quote Jesus as saying: 'Do this in remembrance of me'—that of Luke—was written after Paul's correspondence with the Corinthians, and that Luke was a close associate of Paul.

What developed out of such adjustments was the Mass, that ceremonial recreation of the events surrounding the death and rebirth of Christ. Even the word 'Mass' itself was an indication of how far Christianity had strayed from Jerusalem by the fourth century. It came from the Latin, as did the name given to the consecrated bread of the Eucharist —the Host—which is derived, significantly enough, from *hostia*, 'sacrificial victim'.

In some parts of the newly Christian world, the view of Christ as a human sacrifice and of the bread Host as representing his body were interpreted in the most literal fashion. In the liturgy of St Chrysostom, the priest is required to divide the Host into four parts 'with care and reverence', saying: 'The Lamb is broken and distributed; he that is broken and not divided in sunder; ever eaten and never consumed. . . .'[7] St John Chrysostom, archbishop of Constantinople, was of course a preacher noted for what modern Catholic biographers, with commendable restraint, describe as 'directness of attack'. He did not hesitate to tell his hearers that Christ 'gave us his body pierced with nails, that we might hold it in our hands and eat it, as a proof of his love; for those whom we love dearly we are often wont to bite'; or that there was no need to shrink from eating human flesh and drinking human blood, 'for in order that the disciples should not be horrified, Christ first drank his own blood and so led them without fear or dread into the communion of his mysteries'.[8] The human sacrifice message was visually but no less bluntly expressed in Europe when the particles of the Host were arranged in such a way as to represent the human form. This practice, however, was denounced by the Council of Tours in 567.[9]

There were others like St John Chrysostom who believed that the bread and wine *were* the blood and flesh of Christ. When forced to defend their view, their arguments were ingenious if not always valid. St Gregory of Nyssa, for example, satisfactorily explained Christ's claim that he was 'the bread of life'[10] by saying: 'When we see bread, we may, as it were, see the human body in it, because bread, when it enters the body, becomes itself the body; similarly the bread that was eaten by Christ later became one with him.'[11] This disposed of the problem of the bread eaten *by* Christ, but not of that eaten *as* Christ by disciples or worshippers.

For centuries, some men believed in transubstantiation, but the majority held that the words at the Last Supper had been intended symbolically. The former had a literal turn of mind and total faith. The latter, more inquiring, perhaps, more sensitive to the ancient Hebrew tradition, echoed the early Christian *Didache*, whose eucharistic ritual said: 'O Almighty Lord . . . to all men thou hast given meat and drink to enjoy, that they may give thanks to thee, but to us thou hast graciously given spiritual meat and drink together with life eternal, through thy Servant.'[12]

In A.D. 1215, however, the inconsistency had to be resolved. This, the beginning of the great century of papal supremacy, was not a time for either tolerance or dissent. The Church intended to wield temporal as well as spiritual power, and it could do so only if its followers submitted absolutely to the 'will of God'. Pope Innocent III was a mystic but a worldly one, and perhaps the doctrine of transubstantiation was something of a test case. Whatever the reason, Christianity adopted into its most sacred ritual an act of pure cannibalism, of unequivocal god-eating on the most primitive level. To the faithful, the bread became not a symbol of the flesh of Christ, but as real as if the flesh itself had been sliced and baked.

Some of the repercussions were unexpected. Within a few decades, Christians had become so convinced that the Host was the real and sentient body of Christ that they were prepared to massacre Jews accused of torturing it.

In the early centuries of the Christian era, the bread for the Eucharist had been large and wreath-shaped, but in the eleventh century the custom had grown up of baking rolls not much larger than a walnut. It had been realised, too, that Jesus, as a Jew, would scarcely have eaten leavened bread in the week of Passover. By the thirteenth century, therefore, the Host was customarily made from unleavened dough and baked in a waffle iron which imprinted it with Christian symbols. The little wafers were kept in a vessel known as the pyx. Every so often, a few disappeared into the pouches of farmworkers who believed they might persuade a cow to give richer milk or bees sweeter honey.

After the doctrine of transubstantiation had been promulgated the wafers of the Host assumed a far more awesome power. They were synonymous with the body of Christ, and it was easy to endow them with fleshly attributes. Easy, too, to believe that they had as much magical potency for associates of the devil as for Christians. Theft of the wafers became sacrilegious, even demonic. When some of them were seen to bleed—as a result, it was discovered centuries later, of a red bacillus that sometimes grows on stale food kept in a warm place—the conclusion that they had been tortured was almost inevitable. Irreproachable witnesses had seen the Host bleeding, had even seen the spots of blood spread from day to day (as the bacilli multiplied). In the conditions of the time, Christians leapt to the conclusion that the Jews, who had hated Christ and crucified him, were responsible. By less than forty years after the Council of 1215, there had begun an epidemic hysteria that was to last for well over two centuries.

In 1253, the entire Jewish community of the town of Belitz, near Berlin, was put to death. There was a massacre in Paris in 1290, and another in a suburb of Vienna in 1298. In the years that followed, Jews were burned in Ratisbon, Cracow, Güstrow, Deggendorf, Poznan, Prague, Breslau and Segovia. In 1370, in Enghien, some thieves murdered a Jewish banker but his wife and son escaped to Brussels. Fearing retribution, the thieves spread a rumour that the eucharistic bread in the Brussels church of Saint-Gudule had been seen to bleed—with the outcome that the whole Brussels Jewish community (which fortunately numbered only four families) was burned. Even as late as 1510, thirty-eight Jews were burned in Berlin for tormenting consecrated wafers, though by that time they were not held quite so automatically to blame. Witches were now believed to eat 'red bread' at the Black Mass.[13]

The blood of Christ played a less lethal role in the mediaeval legend of the Holy Grail, a composite of ancient Celtic belief and later Christian didacticism, whose best-known version is to be found in Malory's *Morte d'Arthur*. In some of the literary romances built on this theme, the Grail is simply an updated version of the classical horn of plenty, but in others it is the very cup from which Christ drank at the Last Supper and which was afterwards used by Joseph of Arimathea to collect the blood that flowed from his wounds when he was crucified. The dating of the early Grail texts—mostly between 1190 and 1250—and the strong eucharistic associations of the story have led some authorities to suggest that the romances were a weapon in the debate over transubstantiation, committed to the spiritual rather than the literal interpretation.[14] The coincidences are certainly striking.

It is also striking that this relatively sudden and acute preoccupation with the blood of Christ should have manifested

itself just at a time when man, all over Europe, was being
lectured about the importance of his own blood. Though this
was a subject that had been integral to his thinking in much
earlier times, it had to some extent been submerged by more
sophisticated beliefs in the classical period. But the theory
of medicine newly formulated at Salerno in the eleventh and
twelfth centuries brought it back into sharp relief.

The great medical school at Salerno had developed a 'regimen of health' based on the works of the Greek physician
Galen and amplified by the results of Arab and Italian
research. This regimen, disseminated throughout Europe by
Crusaders who had paused at Salerno to recruit their strength
before (or after) their exertions in the Holy Land, was founded
on the proposition that man and his food contained within
them the same four elements as made up the cosmos. Air was,
in man, transmuted into blood (sanguine), fire into yellow or
green bile (choler), water into phlegm, and earth into black
bile (melancholy).

> Foure humors raigne within our bodies wholly,
> And these comparèd to foure Elements,
> The Sanguine, Choler, Flegme, and Melancholy . . .
> Like ayre both warme and moist, is Sanguine cleare,
> Like fire doth Choler hot and drie appeare.
> Like water cold and moist is Flegmatique,
> The Melancholy cold, drie earth' is like.[15]

Some people and some foods were believed to suffer from an
excess of one or other of these four 'humours', as they were
called, and Salerno's solution was a judicious balancing act—
hot, dry foods for people of 'flegmatique' temperament, cold,
moist foods for people of 'choleric' temperament, and so on.
The permutations were, in fact, endless, and beyond the
grasp of most laymen, but the Salerno regimen was riddled
with references to food that bred 'ill blood' or 'good blood',
and to the states of 'hot-bloodedness' and 'cold-bloodedness'.
These appear to have helped revive in the popular mind all
the old beliefs about the properties of blood, as well as intro-
ducing a few new ones concerning the relative value of different kinds.

One of the most notable figures whose name was associated with the Salerno regimen—by way of the occasionally acid 'commentaries' he wrote on it in the thirteenth century—was Arnald of Villanova, physician, astrologer, alchemist, social reformer, and diplomat. Arnald is sometimes credited with one of the greatest discoveries of all time, the distilling of wine into spirits. Fundamentally, the process of distilling consists of heating a substance so that part of its liquid content turns into vapour; this vapour, if condensed, is the pure, concentrated essence of the parent liquid. Distilling had been for many centuries an essential process in alchemical experiments, but Arnald (or some other thirteenth-century genius) tried distilling wine and succeeded in producing almost pure spirits. These were at first known as *aqua vitae* or 'water of life', later translated into *eau de vie, akvavit,* and *uisge beatha* which became, via the abbreviated *uisge,* 'whisky'.

Whether or not Arnald was responsible for distilling wine to make *eau de vie,* he did distil blood to make what he claimed was a medicinal liquid of great occult virtue against all diseases, capable even of prolonging life. The secret, he said, was discovered 'under divine favour', and when he passed it on to his very dear friend, James of Toledo, he instructed that it should never be revealed either to fools or to men possessed of great worldly power. It was essential to use for this medicine the blood of healthy men of sanguine or choleric temperaments, aged between twenty-five and thirty. The blood was to be collected in April and May, and was to be pure and without spot, as red as a rose. After hanging for a time in a fine linen bag so that all the surplus wateriness might drain out, it was to be placed in a well-sealed glass alembic over a slow fire. The first element would distil out as a clear liquid; the second as a yellow water; the third as a red. Each element had to be distilled again, three times, with the juices of fruits and flowers. Arnald said that when the red distillation had been given to a certain count who lay as if dead, he revived for a whole hour—enough to enable him to make his last confession. This, in the thirteenth century, was a considerable recommendation.[16]

Blood in its more everyday form did not, o course, go out of fashion as an ingredient in medicine and magic. In 1483, for example, Louis XI of France was dying. 'Every day he grew worse, and the medicines profited him nothing, though of a strange character; for he vehemently hoped to recover by the human blood which he took and swallowed from certain children.'[17]

For almost two thousand years, blood was regarded as the sovereign remedy for leprosy. According to Pliny, when this disease, in Egypt, 'fell upon princes, woe to the people; for, in the bathing chambers, tubs were prepared, with human blood, for the cure of it'. In the early English romance of Amys and Amylion, one of the knights—with the full approval of his lady—yields the lives of two of his infant children to cure his brother's comrade; since this is fiction, the leper is cured and the children are miraculously restored to life. But in sober fact, such authoritative scientists as Michael Scot stated that bathing in the blood of a dog or of two-year-old infants mixed with hot water 'undoubtedly' cured leprosy. The belief persisted throughout the Middle Ages in Europe and until as late as the 1870s in China, and no doubt elsewhere. 'Just two years ago,' said one of those Europeans who were such avid collectors of information about the seamier side of life in nineteenth-century China, 'a number of lepers were reported to have made their appearance at Whampoa and its vicinity, attacking and killing healthy men, that they might drink the blood and eat the intestines of those killed, which, lepers are under the firm belief, will cure them of their loathsome disease. . . . A Chinaman, who was employed on board one of the river steamers, caught the disease, and, as was currently stated at the time, resorted to the *modus operandi* stated above.'[18]

It was not always necessary for people who were sick to commit murder in order to acquire blood medicine. In Germany and Hungary, until the eighteenth century, it was one of the official executioner's perquisites to sell the blood from a criminal executed on the block as it streamed from the headless trunk. In West Africa and among the Shans of Burma, the executioner himself drank—or at least tasted—the blood, though in this case the motive was to prevent him from being possessed by the ghost of the man he had slain. But in nineteenth-century China again, 'after an execution . . . certain large pith balls are steeped in the blood of the defunct criminal, and under the name of "blood-bread" are sold as a medicine for consumption. It is only to the blood of decapitated criminals that any such healing power is attributed.'[19]

Some of history's more manic criminals were men—and women—who killed ostensibly because they needed blood for alchemical purposes.

Alchemy was not a matter of sizzling cauldrons and magic incantations but a perfectly serious, and usually highly moral, attempt 'to make the noble metals, and colours, and many other things better or more abundantly by art than they are made in nature. And the science of this kind is greater than all those preceding because it produces greater utilities. For not only can it yield wealth and very many other things for the public good, but it also teaches how to discover such things as are capable of prolonging human life for much longer periods than can be accomplished by nature.'[20]

The primary aims of alchemy were to discover how to turn base metals into gold, and how to produce an elixir of life. The basic reasoning was that the four elements which made up the cosmos (discussed on p. 62 in relation to the Salerno regimen) were contained in all things; the proportionate relationship of the elements determined the physical structure of each and every substance. By adjusting the proportions of a structure, therefore, it should be possible to change the substance—to turn lead into gold, for example. The agent of change was known as the 'philosopher's stone' or the 'grand elixir'. Quite how the alchemists' reasoning was expanded to prove that the elixir could also give man eternal life is by no means clear, but the Chinese, at least, seem to have settled the matter to their own satisfaction by as early as the second century B.C.

Although mediaeval credulity permitted some fairly bizarre ingredients to find their way into alchemical recipes, alchemy on the whole was a respectable science, rarely guilty of black magic, necromancy, or the invocation of demons. Indeed, its practitioners tended to claim divine inspiration at the drop of an alembic. It was the charlatans who were the problem, for the prospect of easy money was no less attractive then than now.

Some of them were disarmingly ingenious. In the eleventh
century in Damascus, for example, there was one who blended
some gold filings with charcoal, glue, and other substances,
made the mixture into pills, then, dressed as a dervish, sold
them to a druggist as '*tabarmaq*', swearing the druggist would
find them a useful item in his pharmacopoeia. Next day,
disguised this time as a man of substance and claiming to be
an expert alchemist, he contrived to be summoned before the
Sultan who expressed the desire to witness a transmutation.
Certainly, agreed the villain, provided the appropriate chemicals could be supplied. The Sultan's men had to scour the
city to find one essential ingredient—and the druggist was no
doubt delighted to sell it again so quickly, and at a handsome
profit. The Sultan was deeply impressed when the alchemist
placed all the ingredients, including the *tabarmaq*, in a crucible,
heated them, cooled them, and produced a small bead of pure
gold. Having rewarded the man, the Sultan consulted with
him about acquiring further supplies of the vital drug and the
latter said he knew of only one source, a cavern in Khorassan.
The Sultan would not hear of sending a full-scale expedition.
This was something that had to be kept secret. So he equipped
the alchemist with every possible traveller's aid, including a
large sum of money, and sent him on his way. It was the last
he ever saw of him. [21]

To play this kind of confidence trick on a reasonably sane
and balanced prince was one thing. But the sharks only too
often found their victims among the unstable or neurotic. It
was difficult enough for an honest man to understand the
vocabulary of alchemy, which used hundreds, even thousands
of 'cover' names. True practitioners knew that 'the black
crow' meant lead, 'the white eagle' sal ammoniac, 'celestial
dew' mercury, but there was nothing to prevent a shyster
from assuring his victim that 'the black crow' meant the
blood of a black-haired man, if he thought this would appeal
to him. For hundreds of thousands of years blood had been
credited with both real and magical potency, and for some
types of psychotic it held a morbid fascination. In any case,
almost everyone knew something about the colour of the
famous elixir that turned lead into gold or gave eternal life.
For many centuries there had been an insistence on the

importance of colour changes during the process of transmutation, and there had gradually grown up an accepted
sequence in which the colours had to appear if the process
were to be successful. The layman might be vague about the
first stages—black, then white, then iridescent, then yellow,
then purple—but he knew that when it turned blood-red the
elixir was a success.

One of the gorier cases that studded the archives of late
mediaeval Europe was that of Gilles de Rais, baron and
marshal of France, comrade in arms to Joan, Maid of Orleans.
Gilles was to pass into legend as Bluebeard. He was said to
have murdered anything from one hundred and forty to eight
hundred children, and in fact even before he wasted away his
fortune and looked to alchemy to repair it, he seems to have
been wholly committed to what church and state for so long
unctuously described as 'unnatural appetites'. In his case, this
meant masturbating against the bodies of dying or newly dead
children. When the Italian alchemist and initiate of the forbidden arts, Francisco Prelati, came to him at Tiffauges in
1439, Gilles' crises of conscience were soothed by the presence
of this tonsured clerk—who was in holy orders, however
minor—and by the knowledge that the blood of the children
he murdered for his pleasure could be used for the divinely
approved purpose of converting base metals into the gold he
so badly needed. There are strange areas of suppression in the
trial records of Gilles de Rais. Prelati denied using the children's blood or flesh for alchemy, or for summoning up the
devil. Gilles swore that he had killed only for carnal delight.
Here and there in the printed French and Latin records there
is a blank. But in view of Gilles' personality and practices and
of what is known of the alchemical and occult experiments
that took place at the castle of Tiffauges, it is virtually impossible that blood should not have been used. Whatever the
truth, nine years and five months after Joan of Arc had gone
to the stake, Gilles de Rais —a model of penitence and piety—
followed her.[22]

In the early 1600s, Hungary had its female equivalent of
Gilles de Rais in the Countess Elisabeth de Báthory. The
Countess Elisabeth did not need money and did not employ
an alchemist. But she did number among her retainers one of

those sinister peasant women who throw such a dark and inhuman shadow over many of history's most chilling scenes. Dorotta Szentes (Dorka) was always there to aid the Countess in being uninhibitedly mad, bad, and dangerous to know— especially for any girl who happened to be a blonde and buxom virgin. To the Countess, a virgin's blood was the elixir of life and youth.

The lady's early career was not particularly notable in terms of her time. Married at the age of fifteen to an up-and-coming soldier who belonged to one of Hungary's most powerful families, she was perhaps a little more vain, a little more lesbian, and a little more sadistic than most. From her husband she learned some of the tortures used in the brutal Turkish wars. From her aunt she discovered the sexual stimulus of whipping naked, busty servant wenches. On her own account, she discovered the pleasure to be derived from disfiguring any sewing girl or serving maid who transgressed. So far, even when she tore the girls' flesh with her special silver pincers or lit torches between their thighs, she still remained within the bounds of what was acceptable in a bored aristocrat in a lawless and corrupt society. No one in authority would have dreamed of listening to peasant whisperings about what went on in the remote castle of Csejthe in the Carpathians; no one in authority ever saw the Countess in her blood-soaked gown working herself into a frenzy of sexual ecstasy over the sights in her torture chamber.

When her husband died in 1604, the last shreds of restraint seem to have gone. She was a considerable beauty, and her vanity had always been narcissistic, but now—perhaps with a second husband in mind—she became possessed by it. She was forty-three, almost elderly in seventeenth-century terms, and the wrinkles were beginning to show despite creams, lotions and herbs, magic spells and incantations, attempts to propitiate the powers of evil. One day, she found occasion to slap a chambermaid so viciously that blood gushed from her nose and splashed on to the Countess's face. When it was washed off, it seemed to the Countess that her skin was whiter and finer than before. It was an observation that exactly fitted with her instincts, and could be made to fit with what she knew of the properties of blood in medicine, alchemy, and sorcery. If blood were the red elixir of life, virgins' blood must be the red elixir of youth.

She began to bathe, at four each morning—the magical hour before the dawn—in virgins' blood. And really bathe in it. Her later victims were killed by being shut in an Iron Maiden, an enormous box moulded into the shape of a naked woman; it was hinged to open sideways, and lined with spikes. This box was gradually closed around the victim who was slowly pierced by the spikes, and the blood ran down into a catchment area to be gently warmed over a fire and used for the bath at daybreak. She drank blood, too, from the wounds and burn blisters of girls who were tortured and dying. According to some of those who, astonishingly, survived, 'some of their fellow victims were forced to eat their own flesh roasted on the fire. The flesh of other girls was chopped up fine like mushrooms, cooked and flavoured, and given to young lads who did not know what they were eating'.

With the Countess using up serving maids at the rate of at least five a week, there was soon something of a shortage in the vicinity of the Báthory castles. If the records of this case are to be taken seriously, they provide an instructive commentary on the licence enjoyed by the aristocracy. The Countess easily found women who were prepared to range the countryside in search of good-looking blonde 'serving girls' for her, though they knew why she wanted them. Parents were easily persuaded to give up their daughters to her, though some suspected why she wanted them. And the local Lutheran pastor was easily bullied into burying the mutilated, blood-drained bodies secretly in the village churchyard, sometimes as many as nine in a single night. Other ministers whose living depended on the Countess were less amenable, even daring to denounce her from the pulpit, but their words at first had little effect. When burial with the proper obsequies—on which the Countess at first insisted, being a good Christian—became too troublesome, she simply instructed her retainers to throw the bodies out in the fields. For a time, the villagers believed them to have been killed by some bloodsucking ghoul.

Yet despite all this activity, the Countess's beauty baths were failing to have the desired effect and she began to despair until a forest sorceress told her that the blood she had been using was of inferior quality. Peasant blood was not good enough; blue blood was what was required.

This was not quite so easy, but in the winter of 1609, with macabre humour, the Countess arranged to accept twenty-five daughters of the minor nobility whom she was prepared to instruct in the 'social graces'. It was the beginning of the end. Explaining away the deaths or disappearances of numerous well-born girls was very different from merely shrugging off the fate of peasants. And the Countess made another disastrous mistake. She had the bodies of four naked girls tossed over the ramparts one winter night when wolves were on the prowl, and the villagers found them before the wolves did.

The Countess was at last denounced, but as the widow of one of the most distinguished Protestant peers of the realm she could not be arrested without an Act of Parliament. To her considerable indignation, the Act was passed. Nevertheless, she did not go on trial. Three of her retainers—including Dorka Szentes—were tried and sentenced to death, two being publicly tortured and then burned alive, the third decapitated and then burned. As for the Countess herself, the Lord Palatine of Hungary (her cousin) said: 'The families which have won in the eyes of the nation such high honours on the battlefield shall not be disgraced by the murky shadow of this bestial female. . . . Everything is to be done in secret. For if a court were to try her the whole of Hungary would learn of her murders, and it would seem to contravene our laws to spare her life. But having seen her crimes with my own eyes, I have to abandon my plan to put her in a convent for the rest of her life.' (Fortunately for the convent, in view of the Countess's predilection for virgins.) The Lord Palatine therefore ordered that this 'bloodthirsty and bloodsucking Godless woman' should be sentenced to lifelong imprisonment in her own castle at Csejthe. She was immured in a small room with only a food hatch to link her with the outside world, and died three and a half years later. It was believed that she had been responsible for the deaths of six hundred and fifty girls.[23]

The ferocious pair just described murdered perhaps a thousand harmless people between them, to satisfy their demented belief in the efficacy of blood. Ironically, only

7. "How the savages roast their enemies." From *La Cosmographie Universelle* by André Thévet, 1575.

8. Another view of Brazilian cannibalism from *Americae tertia pars* by Theodor de Bry, 1592.

9. A family supper in Brazil from *Americae tertia pars* by Theodor de Bry, 1592.

10. Aztec sacrifice—the priest rips out the living heart of the victim. From the Codex *Magliabecchiano* in Florence.

11. A prisoner of war being dressed to simulate the god to whom he will be sacrificed. From the *Codex Florentino: Illustrations for Sahagun's Historia General de las Cosas de Nueva España.*

12. Vlad the Impaler at breakfast, surrounded by spiked burghers.
A Strasbourg woodcut of 1500.

twenty years after the death of the Countess Elisabeth de
Báthory, their record was cast wholly into the shade by a
kind, amiable, tolerant Burmese monarch who sacrificed six
thousand human beings because their hearts were needed to
help him fulfil his dream of bringing the whole world under
the gentle rule of Buddhism.

Thiri-thu-dhamma* ascended to the throne of Arakan in
1622, having inherited from his father not only the kingdom,
but a belief that its ruler was destined one day to become
Lord of the World, the instrument by which the teachings of
the Buddha would be disseminated to all mankind. He already
possessed the Seven Gems, the magical symbols essential for
any claimant to the Universal Throne. No one knows what
the first five of these actually were; they were called 'the
golden wheel, the divine guardian of the treasury, the jewel
maiden, the horse, and the jewel that wrought miracles'. The
sixth was 'the general who could never be defeated'—which
could be applied to any general who had never *been* defeated
(so far). The seventh was 'the white elephant', which was in
fact a much-pampered albino with pinkish-yellow eyes, a
pale brick-coloured hide, white-edged ears and a white-tipped
trunk. But Thiri-thu-dhamma's father and grandfather had
both possessed the Seven Gems, and neither had become
Lord of the World. Clearly, something more was needed.

Another problem preyed on Thiri-thu-dhamma's mind. It
had been prophesied that he would die soon after his coronation so he postponed it, and postponed it, until twelve
years had passed and he could scarcely postpone it much
longer. He could not embark on his attempt to rule the world
without first being ritually invested as king of Arakan.

In 1634, there arrived at court a Muslim sage who claimed
that he had made the pilgrimage to Mecca and was possessed
of occult secrets. Soon enough, the sage revealed to Thiri-thu-
dhamma that he could 'make your Majesty invisible and
invincible so that not only will you be safe from the death
prophesied to follow your coronation, but you will obtain
possession of the vast empire of the Mughal [of India] and
of the kingdoms of Burma and Siam'.[24] Thiri-thu-dhamma
was neither more nor less credulous than most people before

* Pronounced Tirri-too-dahmah.

the advent of the Age of Reason, and the particular nature of his dream of sovereignty made him as susceptible to the sage's promises as Gilles de Rais' golden bloodlust had made *him* to Prelati's.

The king was excited and enormously relieved. When the sage mentioned an elixir, it came as no surprise. When the sage said that the ingredients were rare and difficult to come by, it was only what the king expected. As Lord of the White Elephant, possessor of the Seven Gems, he would have found an elixir compounded from commonplace materials not only inapposite but impossible to have faith in. It was when the sage descended to details that Thiri-thu-dhamma came face to face with the hideous reality of what was being suggested. 'Two thousand hearts of white doves,' said the doctor. 'Four thousand hearts of white cows.' And, in conclusion, 'six thousand human hearts'. A Buddhist king, dedicated to the Eightfold Path of Compassion, was faced with the choice between mass murder and failing to conquer the world for his faith. It was the age-old dilemma of ends and means, and like so many before and after him Thiri-thu-dhamma finally decided that the ends justified the means.

Bypassing the normal channels of administration, the king commanded his personal police to seize six thousand of his subjects, kill them, and deliver their hearts to the 'alchemist'. The utmost secrecy was to be observed. The victims were to be seized when no witnesses were present, unless a whole group could be taken at once. Houses were to be entered at night, victims arrested in back streets and alleys. People thus apprehended were to be taken to the thickly-wooded hills around the city and there disposed of. If any policeman was caught at his murderous task, he could expect no royal protection but would be impaled according to judicial precedent.

Carefully, the police singled out widows and orphans, vagrants and slaves, people whose absence would cause little comment. But soon, these resources were exhausted and they had to winnow out the poorer quarters of the city. Rumour began as a whisper and became a roar. There was a place in the mountains where the kidnapped were slaughtered and thrown into burial trenches. There was a magician who screamed incantations while he stirred a sullen, simmering cauldron. Some citizens barricaded themselves inside their homes. Others turned savage and urged mass revolt. A few policemen were caught, tried, and died on the spike. But the others went doggedly on, gathering the hearts that were needed for the Grand Elixir.

One night, a few weeks after the start of the terror, there was a volley of cannon from the palace walls. Lights sparkled around the state buildings. Rockets and fireworks sizzled into the sky. The royal orchestras played on the ramparts.

Next morning it was proclaimed that the coronation would take place after the monsoon rains.

Thiri-thu-dhamma had drunk the elixir of immortality and invincibility, and went light-heartedly to be crowned in his sky-blue velvet cloak laden with pearls and precious stones, wearing the famous ruby ear-drops that were as large as a bantam's eggs.

Did the elixir work? The prophet proved wiser than the sage—Thiri-thu-dhamma *did* die soon after his coronation. Though there is only madness, no blood, involved, it is worth carrying the story to its conclusion.

The gathering of the hearts had alienated many of the nobility of Arakan when the story leaked out, as it was bound to do, and Thiri-thu-dhamma's principal queen took advantage of the fact. A formidable woman with a passion for power, she offered herself and the throne to the captain of the Household Troops, a young man of the blood royal named Kuthala. With the situation as it was, it seemed unlikely that the murder of the king would provoke any great opposition, but Nat Shin Mé—'Mistress of Paradise'—believed just as deeply in the elixir as did Thiri-thu-dhamma. Magic would have to be countered with magic.

The source of Nat Shin Mé's murderous magic was the great Yattara bell, thickly engraved with diagrams based on mathematical calculations. When the bell was struck in a certain way it was believed to disrupt the astrological field of the man or men against whom its power had been directed. First it was necessary to calculate the astrological relationship between Kuthala's horoscope and that of the king, and to make an adjustment to improve Kuthala's astrological rating, so that it would be superior to the king's. Once this had been done—by burying inscribed stone squares at a certain place at a certain time—Kuthala would have control over the king's astrological field. The influence of the squares was reinforced by the chanting of poems written to a special rhythm and constructed from a special sequence of symbolic letters.

The news that sorcerer's songs were being intoned in the city was brought to Lat Rone, the king's chief minister, who instigated an investigation. The result was that he went to the king with the suspicion—no proof—that Nat Shin Mé and Kuthala had mounted a magical conspiracy against him. The king refused to believe him. Lat Rone therefore suggested that *taran* omens should be taken, and the king reluctantly agreed. According to the theory of *taran*, forthcoming events sent a shock-wave before them which was subconsciously felt by people who were ruled by instinct rather than reason. These people were quite likely, in the course of casual conversation, to betray their significant foreknowledge to anyone who, wiser than they, was listening for it. Confidential agents were sent out, and the results of their eavesdropping profoundly shocked Lat Rone, but not the king, armoured in his elixir of immortality.

Thiri-thu-dhamma summoned Nat Shin Mé and taxed her with conspiring against him, but her personality, as so often before, overrode his. Lat Rone observed the queen's unassailable dominance with the eye of self-preservation and wisely took himself off to a monastery.

Some months later, according to the bald statement of the palm-leaf manuscripts from which the tale of the king's downfall is drawn, Thiri-thu-dhamma died 'by the action of the Yattara squares'. He had survived his coronation by just over three years.[25]

CHAPTER FOUR

Blood for the Gods

B Y RENAISSANCE times the use of blood for magical purposes was found more often in the realm of private enterprise
than public endeavour. But only in the Old World. When the
Spaniards began to colonise the New, they ran head on into
something they had never before encountered or even dreamed
of—a whole civilisation founded on, and in the most literal
sense sustained by, the heart's blood of its people. When
Cortés and his little band of conquistadors set off from the
coast in 1519 on the march that ended in the beautiful, bloodstained capital city of the Aztecs, the cultural shock was
profound. Nothing in the twenty-seven years of Spain's presence in the Indies had prepared them for Tenochtitlan.

The Aztecs turned out to be a very different proposition
from the uncivilised Caribs who had done violence to the
principles, and occasionally to the persons, of Columbus and
the early settlers, but who were now well on the way to being
wiped out. Columbus had made his landfall in the Americas
in 1492 and had soon discovered that the islands round the
Caribbean were populated not only by the 'gentle, peaceful and
very simple people' he had met on first landing,[1] but by the
far from gentle and peaceful Caribs, the red-painted Vikings
of those sunny waters. It is virtually impossible to discover
the unvarnished truth about the early Caribs because layers of
legend were so quickly built up around them, but they were
undoubtedly superb seamen and warriors to be reckoned with.
They had already driven the Tainos (or Arawak) out of the
Lesser Antilles and were raiding into Jamaica and Puerto
Rico by the time Columbus arrived. They were to hold out
strongly against the Spaniards, too. But what startled and
horrified the newcomers was not the Caribs' lobster-coloured
warpaint or their swift belligerence or even their poisoned

arrows, but the fact that they were said to make a habit of eating people.

The Spaniards first came across them when Columbus put some men ashore for a night on Guadeloupe. Returning next day to pick them up, he found the party had been enlarged by half a dozen women, who indicated (by means of sign language) 'that the people of that island ate men and were holding them captives and that they did not wish to stay with them'. The women further conveyed that, although there were many people still on Guadeloupe, the king himself had gone off 'with ten large canoes and three hundred men to raid the neighbouring islands and steal their people in order to eat them'.[2] Despite the notorious unreliability of sign language, Columbus seems to have had no doubts about his interpretation of what the women were trying to say, and resolved to remove his ship immediately from this dangerous vicinity. Unfortunately, nine other men had gone ashore in the meantime and disappeared. In a rage, Columbus sent out a search party and for four days the Europeans blithely wandered about the island, marvelling at the number of rivers, the richness of the vegetation, and the variety of the bird life. The admiral himself ventured no further than into one of the Carib houses, where he saw a number of skulls hung from the ceiling and some baskets full of what he took to be men's bones. Finally, the entire crew drifted back on board again, uneaten, and Columbus set sail. As they passed the island of Montserrat, the refugees encouragingly remarked that it had been totally depopulated by the Caribs, who had eaten all the inhabitants.[3]

The legend of the fearful cannibal Caribs soon began to grow, a legend that, like most such, was constantly being improved on. When the Spaniards captured four anonymous Indians and discovered that they 'had had their virile members cut off', they promptly deduced that the Caribs castrated their captives 'as we do to fatten capons, to improve their taste'. It was also said that: 'The men captured they split in two . . . guts and limbs eaten, and the rest salted and dried like our hams.' In fact, the peoples of the Caribbean knew nothing about the process of salting until they learned of it from the Europeans. The indigenous method of preserving was by smoke drying on a greenwood lattice over a slow fire.* There was, too, a popular belief that the Caribs were true connoisseurs of human flesh, though their preferences seem to have depended largely on the fancy of the chronicler. According to de Rochefort, the Caribs thought the French were delicious, the English so-so, the Dutch tasteless, and the Spaniards so tough as to be virtually inedible. An earlier writer however—also French—said 'the Caribs avowed that the flesh of the English was the most delicate and desirable of any they had tasted, being far superior to that of the Spaniards or French'.†[4]

On the whole, the truth seems to be that the Caribs' cannibal habits were a product, not of greed, but of the need to express triumph or vengeance in the most ostentatious manner—an idea which has been by no means uncommon among other peoples during the course of history. One indication of this is that they only ate men, never women or children. Another, that they kept the skulls of those they had killed in a kind of trophy rack. From the purely dietary point of view, they had certainly no need to eat human flesh, for the islands they inhabited and the waters surrounding them supplied a rich and endless variety of food. In any case, for at least three hundred years after the arrival of the Spaniards, the Caribs continued to regard the bodies of their enemies as emblems of victory. In 1694, for example, the reverend Father Labat recorded that a number of Caribs arrived at Martinique with, displayed in the poop of their pirogue, 'the arm of a man barbecued in the buccaneer fashion, that is to say, dried with a slow fire in the smoke. They offered it to me very civilly, and informed me it was the arm of an Englishman, whom they had lately killed in a descent on Barbuda, when they massacred six persons'.[6]

* The Carib name for this was *boucan*, adopted by the French as *boucanier*—from which the buccaneers, who appropriated the process, took their name. The Spaniards came to call the lattice *barbacoa*, from which 'barbecue' was later derived.

† Natives of the southern half of the British Isles may perhaps find it useful to know that sharks in the Caribbean also prefer the English. 'If they find an Englishman, a Frenchman and a Spaniard in a boat or in the water, they will always attack the Englishman first. This has often been verified, both in regard to the common shark and the paracota.'[5]

The personality of the early Caribs remains elusive. By the time Europeans came to know them on less inimical terms, the bitter confrontation with the Spaniards had reduced their numbers to only a few hundred and their temperament to a state usually described as mild and melancholy, alleviated by valiant attempts to appear cheerful. Only when they were angered or offended did they become quite implacable. In the eighteenth century, one sure way to offend them was to call them cannibals.[7] They were in the unhappy position of having had their name and reputation immortalised in several European languages by the Spanish transliteration of Carib into *Calib* into *Canib*—whence the word 'cannibal' itself.

To the Spaniards, the Caribs had been not much more than troublesome savages with peculiarly nasty habits. When the conquest of Mexico began, however, they discovered a whole nation where the 'sacrilegious desecration of the human body' was a vital instrument of state. It was not to be tolerated. The soldiers of Christ arose, put their armour on[8]—and destroyed not only the Aztec state but, in a mere matter of thirty years, twenty million of its inhabitants as well.[9]

In the Caribbean, the Spaniards had found it profitable to exact gold-mine and plantation labour from the Indians in return for instruction in the Spanish language and acceptance into the Christian religion. They hoped to extend this system into Mexico if they found natural resources worth exploiting. But when they established a base at Vera Cruz on the gulf of Mexico and began making forays into the surrounding countryside they quickly realised that things might not be so simple.

Soon, their nostrils were twitching at the smell of idolatry and human sacrifice. In hastily abandoned villages, they found temples with 'the bodies of men and boys who had been sacrificed, the walls and altars all splashed with blood, and the victims' hearts laid out before the idols. [They] also found the stones on which the sacrifices had been made, and the flint with which their breasts had been opened to tear out their hearts. Alvarado told us,' said Bernal Diaz, one of the conquistadors, 'that most of the bodies were without arms and legs, and that some Indians had told him that these had been carried off to be eaten.' Further north, at Cempoala, it was the same. The feet, arms and legs of the victims 'were cut off and eaten, just as we eat beef from the butcher's in our country. I even believe that they sold it in the markets.'[10]

Hernando Cortés read the Cempoalans a bracing sermon in which he adjured them to 'give up human sacrifice and robbery and the foul practice of sodomy'—one thing apparently led to another—'and to cease worshipping their accursed idols', but both priests and dignitaries pointed out that this would be wrong, as their gods 'brought them health and good harvests and all they needed'. Their 'insolent reply' so much enraged Cortés that he ordered all the idols to be overturned and smashed. Setting up an altar and a cross, he made it clear to the Cempoalans that they were to consider themselves Christians from then on.[11]

As the conquistadors marched inland towards Moctezuma's capital city, they left a trail of crucifixes behind them. It was only at Xocotlan that their resolution began to waver. Cortés gave his customary sermon on the evils of sacrifice, but the town's dignitaries remained grimly silent. Slightly daunted, Cortés remarked: 'I think there is nothing else we can do except put up a cross,' and to his relief, no doubt, Fra Bartolome de Olmedo intervened with: 'In my opinion, sir, it is too early to leave a cross in these people's possession. They have neither shame nor fear and, being vassals of Moctezuma, may either burn it or damage it in some other way. What you have told them is enough until they are better acquainted with our holy religion.' Fra Bartolome's caution may have been tinged with an instinct for self-preservation. Like Bernal Diaz, he had probably observed that 'in the square where some of their temples stood were many piles of human skulls, so neatly arranged that we could count them, and I reckoned them at more than a hundred thousand. I repeat that there were more than a hundred thousand. And in another part of the square there were more piles made up of innumerable thighbones. There was also a large number of skulls and bones strung between wooden posts, and three priests, whom we understood to have charge of them, were guarding these skulls and bones.'[12]

Reaching Tlascala, however, a city that was friendly with anyone who might be expected to pose a threat to Moctezuma, the Spaniards' militancy revived. Finding cages 'in which men and women were imprisoned and fed until they were fat enough to be sacrificed and eaten', they broke them open and released the prisoners. Cortés 'showed the elders of Tlascala how indignant he was and scolded them so furiously that they promised not to kill and eat any more Indians in that way'. 'But I wondered,' added Bernal Diaz a little disconsolately, 'what use all these promises were, for as soon as we turned our heads they would resume their old cruelties.'[13]

The conquistadors, horrified by cannibalism, were never to appreciate that the eating of sacrificial victims was as much a religious rite as sacrifice itself—or even that by no means all victims were destined for the pot. When the people of Cholula, sixty miles from Tenochtitlan, laid an ambush for the invaders, the Spaniards' thoughts did not fly first to sacrifice but to a vision of some hideous cannibal banquet. 'How anxious these traitors are,' said Cortés, 'to see us among the ravines so that they can gorge themselves on our flesh. . . . In return for our coming to treat them like brothers, and tell them the commands of our lord God and the king, they were planning to kill us and eat our flesh, and had already prepared the pots with salt and peppers and tomatoes.'[14]

But Cortés and his men survived to reach Tenochtitlan at last, and were met by Moctezuma with the utmost graciousness. It must have been strange to watch Cortés and his four hundred scruffy soldiers make their entry into this dazzling, magnificent city, with its green gardens and gleaming white buildings set in the midst of blue lakes and ringed by lofty mountains. Stranger still to observe the captain, his doublet and hose pungent from constant wear, confronting the emperor Moctezuma—who was 'neat and clean and took a bath every afternoon', and 'did not wear again till three or four days later' the rich and jewelled garments he laid off at night[15]—and lecturing him on the evils besetting Aztec society.

'He very carefully expounded the creation of the world, how we are all brothers, the children of one mother and father called Adam and Eve; and how such a brother as our great emperor, grieving for the perdition of so many souls as their idols were leading to hell, where they burned in living flame, had sent us to tell him this, so that he might put a stop to it, and so that they might give up the worship of idols and

make no more human sacrifices—for all men are brothers—
and commit no more robbery or sodomy. He also promised
that in the course of time the king would send some men who
lead holy lives among us, much better than our own, to
explain this more fully, for we had only come to give them
warning.' Moctezuma listened to this discourse with slightly
surprised courtesy, but replied: 'We have worshipped our own
gods here from the beginning and know them to be good. No
doubt yours are good also, but do not trouble to tell us any
more about them at present.'[16]

The Aztecs, in fact, had so many gods that even neighbouring peoples were never able to put a number to them. In the
two hundred eventful years that had transformed a rough
tribe of nomads into the rich and sophisticated rulers of much
of the valley of Mexico, the original tribal pantheon had been
considerably enlarged by borrowing or adapting other deities
from the traditions of the valley and beyond.

The people of Tenochtitlan (the site of modern Mexico
City) believed that they lived under constant threat. They
were now in the period of the 'fifth world' or 'fifth sun'. The
four worlds that had gone before—and the men who inhabited
them—had been annihilated in four great spasms of destruction. The same destiny awaited the fifth world. When the
appointed time came, earth and sky would be torn apart and
the monsters of the twilight would throng out to engulf the
whole human race. Although Mexicans believed in a primordial god and goddess (Ometecuhtli and Omeciuatl), they
regarded them rather in the light of senior citizens, and
attributed most of the purposeful action that influenced the
world's affairs to the younger members of the pantheon. It
was they who had been responsible for the creation, of which
the most important part in Mexican eyes was the birth of the
sun. This came about when the gods gathered in the twilight,
and one, small and leprous, threw himself into a huge brazier
as a sacrifice. He rose from the flickering red-gold furnace
transformed into a sun—but a sun that could not move until
it had been imbued with life and strength in the form of
blood and heart's blood. So the other gods sacrificed themselves, too, and the sun began its passage across the heavens.

As long as the sun continued in its course, the fifth great

cataclysm would be postponed and the monsters of the twilight contained behind the western sky. But the sun, born in
sacrifice and blood, had to be sustained by sacrifice and
blood. It was their preoccupation with the recurring miracle
of sunrise that made the religion of the Aztecs so much more
blood-soaked than other early faiths. Theirs was no seasonal
fertility offering, no annual re-enactment of the creation
myth, but a daily magical struggle—engaged in by priests,
dignitaries, and common people alike—to ensure that the
world would go on.* Day after relentless day, ritual and
sacrifice were invoked so that there need be no fear-racked
hour before the following dawn. But the Mexicans continued
to fear.

They feared, especially, when it came to the last day of
their fifty-two-year cycle. In city and countryside, the fires
were put out after nightfall and the people crowded to the
slopes of the mountain Uixachtecatl, from whose top the
priests observed the Pleiades. If the seven stars stopped at
their zenith, the heavens would rip and the world would end.
At the crucial moment, the priests stretched out a prisoner on
the sacrificial stone at the summit of the Hill of the Stars.
They struck the sacred knife into his chest and then twirled
the sacred firestick in the wound. When the stars passed the
meridian, a new flame sprang up from the firestick and the
watchers knew that a new cycle of life had begun. Almost
hysterical with relief, they scattered to their homes while
runners lit torches from the flame and sped off to carry fire
again to all the temples in the valley of Mexico.[17]

The Mexican year consisted of eighteen months, each of
twenty days, and every month in addition to daily sacrifices
there was a major festival that also involved sacrifice, usually
human. In the first month, children were drowned as an
offering to the rain god. The second month saw the feast of
Xipe Totec, 'our lord the flayed one', god of spring and the

---

* Aztec sacrifice was an extreme version of a phenomenon familiar
to anthropologists as 'substitute theophagy'. In early societies kings
were often seen as earthly incarnations of the gods, responsible for the
country's well-being. They were expected to sacrifice themselves before
their powers began to fail. Sometimes, however, they were reluctant, and
in that case the only substitute for the one, all-embracing divine sacrifice was the continual outpouring of the blood of lesser men.

renewal of nature. But there was no bucolic charm here; indeed, the Xipe Totec ceremonies (which appear not to have been native to the valley of Mexico but imported from the south) were horrific even by Aztec standards. The victims were first peppered with arrows so that their blood fell to the earth like rain. Afterwards, they were flayed and the skins were dyed yellow. Then, in culmination, Xipe's priests dressed themselves in the skins as a symbol of the way in which the earth donned its new mantle of vegetation when the rainy season ended.

The fifth month brought the feast of Texcatlipoca, which might have been devised as the scenario for some 'twenties Hollywood melodrama. A year before the festival, the hand-somest and bravest prisoner of war was chosen and taught by the priests how to behave as a great ruler. As he walked about the city—playing divine melodies on his flute—he was awarded all the homage due to the god himself. A month before the fatal day, four beautiful maidens, dressed as goddesses, were brought to him to care for him and supply his every want. At last, he took leave of his weeping consorts and placed him-self at the head of a procession, glittering, joyful, and mag-nificent, which bore him to the temple that was to see the climax of his year of honour. The eight priests who had attended him throughout that year preceded him up the ceremonial stairway, and as he followed he broke, at each step, one of the flutes he had played during the happy days of his incarnation. When he reached the platform at the top, the priests stretched him, face up, on the sacrificial stone. The sacred knife was plunged into his chest below the breast-bone and brought down in a sweeping arc to the base of the stomach. Then, with a skilful twist, his heart was torn out and offered to the god. His destiny had been fulfilled.

In the sixth month, victims personifying the gods of rain and water were sacrificed; in the seventh, a woman represent-ing the goddess of the salt waters; in the eighth, one who personified Xilonen, the goddess of young maize. Her face was painted red and gold, and she wore a plumed headdress made from the shimmering emerald feathers of the sacred *quetzal* bird, with a gold and turquoise necklace, embroidered clothes, and red sandals upon her feet. For a few hours she *was* the goddess. No one slept the night before the sacrifice. Women intoned the hymns of Xilonen, and at dawn the dances began. Through the early light there was a procession of dancing, singing worshippers, everyone carrying a stalk of maize, propelling the goddess on toward the temple. They arrived, she entered, and on the instant the officiating priest struck off her head with the ceremonial gold-hilted flint knife. The maize cob had been cut. Afterwards, for the first time in the new season, the people ate maize cakes and offered them to the gods.

And so it went on. In the tenth month, prisoners of war were dedicated to the god of fire; in the eleventh month, a woman who represented the mother of the gods was sacrificed; in the twelfth, there were hideous ceremonies for the fire god; in the thirteenth, it was the turn of the agricultural gods; in the fourteenth, of the god of hunting; in the fifteenth, there were mock battles and sacrifices to the war god; in the seventeenth a woman died for the old-time goddess of corn and earth; and in the eighteenth, children were immolated in honour of—yet again—the god of fire. Observant readers will have noticed that only four months out of the eighteen were free of sacrificial festivals that involved violent death for one or many. In the third, fourth and ninth months, flowers were offered instead; in the sixteenth month, the people fasted and offered their food and drink to the rain gods.

Human sacrifice on the Aztec scale demanded a considerable number of victims.* As a result, the Aztecs lived in a state of almost perpetual war with their neighbours. It was not the kind of war familiar in Europe, for the main purpose

---

* It should perhaps be explained here why human sacrifice had not been superseded by animal sacrifice, as in most other great civilisations. Partly it was because Aztec civilisation was scarcely a hundred years old, but more important was the fact that there were no suitable animals. The native American horse had been wiped out in prehistoric times; the cow and sheep were unknown in America till after the Spanish conquest; the caribou and bison were not to be found so far south. Game was scarce, and the wild deer and great seasonal migrations of ducks, geese and other wildfowl that brought welcome relief to the Mexican diet were not reliable enough to meet daily sacrificial needs. The only domesticated livestock were the dog and the turkey, and these were too contemptible to be worthy of the gods.

of all concerned was to take prisoners, not to kill. When a battle began, archers and javelin-throwers first loosed their missiles and then the ranks broke and the warriors rushed in with sword and shield. The battlefield disintegrated into innumerable separate duels as each man did his best to defeat another and hale him off to the sidelines, where non-combatants waited with ropes to tie the captives up. So deeply ingrained was the habit of capturing rather than killing that the Aztecs clung to it even when they found themselves face to face with the Spaniards, who had no such inhibitions; it was at least partly responsible for their defeat.

When serious war was impracticable, either because the economy could not stand it or because the nearest suitable enemy was too far off, the old custom of the War of the Flowers was revived. This, which had been known since at least the mid-fourteenth century, was a friendly war between friendly states, a combat designed for the specific purpose of producing losers who could be sacrificed.

The best sacrifices for everyday wear, so to speak, were war captives, especially those who were brave men of high rank. Slaves, however, might also be used. There were two types of slave who almost invariably ended their lives on the sacrificial stone—prisoners of war who had not been sacrificed immediately after capture, and barbarians paid as imperial taxes by cities in tributary relationship to Moctezuma. Of civilian slaves, only one category could be offered in sacrifice, men who had been so unsatisfactory that three successive masters had been forced to get rid of them. These delinquents could be bought by tradesmen or artisans who had no opportunity of capturing prisoners of war.

Most victims appear to have gone to their deaths quite philosophically, especially the military captives. They had been indoctrinated since birth with the idea that, some day, they might well have to die so that the world could go on living. Nothing was born or could endure without the sacrifice of man's blood and heart's blood, and the man whose blood and heart were sacrificed knew that his death was a divine necessity—however much he may have wished that someone else had been chosen. He went to his death, in most cases, dressed, painted and ornamented to simulate the god for whom he was intended; it was the god himself who was sacrificed, in re-enactment of that first occasion when all the gods had given themselves so that the sun might begin its passage across the heavens. So soldiers went steadfastly to their deaths, while the civilian slaves, ritually bathed, luxuriously dressed and adorned for the occasion, were mercifully stupefied by the 'divine' *pulque** they had drunk.

The ceremonial cannibalism that sometimes followed was an extension of the sacrifice itself. The head of the victim was removed and hung on a skull rack, one thigh was presented to the supreme council and other choice cuts to various nobles and to the victim's captor. By eating this flesh, the great men and good soldiers of Aztec society not only identified themselves directly with the sacrifice and, through him, with the god, but also absorbed strength and life-force that would enable them to maintain the successes that were necessary if the god's requirements were to continue to be met. The victim might, perhaps, have objected to his bonier remains being tossed to the animals in Moctezuma's private zoo, but even they had a religious role as guardians of the temples.

The scale on which sacrifices were carried out is generally agreed to have been considerable, although it never again reached the high peak claimed for 1486, when 20,000 victims were said to have been slaughtered in four days at the dedication of the great temple to the war god at Tenochtitlan. The city's new monarch, aided by the ruler of neighbouring Texcoco, began the work of sacrifice with his own hand and teams of lesser dignitaries then took over, working systematically in relays through the two endless lines of victims. Recently it has been pointed out that if, as the records say, the victims were dealt with two at a time and if the entire ceremony took up all the daylight hours for four days, then the figure of 20,000 must be a gross exaggeration. At a conservative estimate of one victim per team per minute, and assuming a

* Made from the fermented sap of the agave, or American aloe, and not unlike a heady cider. There were fearsome laws against drunkenness; a plebeian first offender had his head shaved, and repetition of the offence was punishable by death. (Priests, and nobles found drunk in public, were not even given a second chance.) Because of this, few people were inured to the effects of alcohol and *pulque* could be used almost as an anaesthetic.

twelve-hour working day, not more than 5,760 victims could possibly have been disposed of in the time.[18] Today, the question is academic; though it was not so to the 14,240 debatable victims in the year 1486.

Thirty-three years had passed by the time Cortés and his men visited the temple, but it still stank of blood and death. Moctezuma welcomed the conquistadors at the top of the great flight of one hundred and fourteen steps that ended on an open platform. It was here, said Bernal Diaz, 'that the great stones stood on which they placed the poor Indians for sacrifice. Here also was a massive image like a dragon, and other hideous figures, and a great deal of blood that had been spilled that day.' The temple dominated the city and gave the Spaniards a bird's eye view of temples and shrines 'that looked like gleaming white towers and castles: a marvellous sight'. Then they were shown the images of the gods— Uitzilopochtli, the war god, who had 'huge terrible eyes' and 'so many precious stones, so much gold, so many pearls and seed-pearls stuck to him . . . that his whole body and head were covered with them', and Tlaloc, the ancient god of rain and green growth. 'There were some smoking braziers of their incense, which they call copal, in which they were burning the hearts of three Indians whom they had sacrificed that day; and all the walls of that shrine were so splashed and caked with blood that they and the floor too were black.' In the shrine of Tlaloc, similarly, 'all was covered with blood, both walls and altar, and the stench was such that we could hardly wait to get out. . . . In that small platform were many more diabolical objects, trumpets great and small, and large knives, and many hearts that had been burnt with incense before their idols; and everything was caked with blood. The stench here too was like a slaughterhouse, and we could scarcely stay in the place.'

Emerging into relatively clean air again, Cortés was tactless enough to laugh and make another attempt to convert the emperor. 'Lord Moctezuma,' he said, 'I cannot imagine how a prince as great and wise as your Majesty can have failed to realise that these idols of yours are not gods but evil things. . . . Allow us to erect a cross here on the top of this tower, and let us divide off a part of this sanctuary . . . as a place where we can put an image of Our Lady, and then you will see, by the fear that your idols have of her, how grievously they have deceived you.'

This extraordinary suggestion gave deep offence to Moctezuma and his priests, and it says much for the emperor's willpower that he did not order the Spaniards to be sacrificed on the spot. Instead, he banished them from the temple and they went off to see what other specimens of blood and barbarity they could find to disgust them. They found idols, blood, smoke, skulls, bones, as well as great pots and jars and pitchers in the house where 'they cooked the flesh of the wretched Indians who were sacrificed and eaten by the priests. Near this place of sacrifice there were many large knives and chopping blocks like those on which men cut up meat in slaughterhouses . . . I always called that building Hell,' concluded Bernal Diaz.[19]

The day finally came when it was not 'wretched Indians' but Spaniards who had their hearts torn out in honour of the Aztec gods during the last bitter battles that ended in the destruction of the whole of Aztec civilisation. Wounded and exhausted, a little group of conquistadors heard from their temporary refuge the terrifying sound of the sacred drum, conches and horns. 'When we looked at the tall temple from which it came we saw our comrades who had been captured in Cortés' defeat being dragged up the steps to be sacrificed. When they had hauled them up to a small platform in front of the shrine where they kept their accursed idols we saw them put plumes on the heads of many of them; and then they made them dance with a sort of fan in front of [Uitzilopochtli]. Then after they had danced the priests laid them down on their backs on some narrow stones of sacrifice and, cutting open their chests, drew out their palpitating hearts which they offered to the idols before them. Then they kicked the bodies down the steps, and the Indian butchers who were waiting below cut off their arms and legs and flayed their faces. . . . Then they ate their flesh with a sauce of peppers and tomatoes.* They sacrificed all our men in this way, eating their legs and arms, offering their hearts and blood to their

* This was a guess; the Mexicans ate sweet peppers and tomatoes with almost everything.

idols as I have said, and throwing their trunks and entrails to the lions and tigers [i.e. pumas and jaguars] and serpents and snakes that they kept in the wild-beast houses.'[20]

But in the end, after the appalling siege in which the people of Tenochtitlan died like flies not only from hunger and thirst but from the new diseases brought in by the invaders—even the common cold was a killer for people who had no immunity to it—the conquistadors experienced the faintest twinge of doubt about whether the Mexicans were quite such unregenerate cannibals as they had thought. In the houses, streets and courts of the city, even in the lake stockades, there were so many corpses that Bernal Diaz said, 'I do not know how to describe it. . . . We could not walk without treading on the bodies and heads of dead Indians. . . . The stench was so bad that no one could endure it.' The survivors were allowed to leave, and 'for three whole days and nights they never ceased streaming out, and all three causeways were crowded with men, women and children so thin, sallow, dirty and stinking that it was pitiful to see them'. The city itself 'looked as if it had been ploughed up. The roots of any edible greenery had been dug out, boiled, and eaten, and they had even cooked the bark of some of the trees. There was no fresh water to be found; all of it was brackish.' Bernal Diaz had the grace to note, although only in passing, that despite the famine in the besieged city 'the Mexicans did not eat the flesh of their own people, only that of our men and our Tlascalan allies whom they had captured'.[21] Only, in fact, that of people who had been sacrificed to the gods in a last despairing attempt to stave off the end of the Aztec world.

Considered dispassionately and from the victim's point of view, there was a great deal to be said for the Aztec sacrificial system. Life was uncertain everywhere in the sixteenth century, and death under the expert knife of the priest was quicker and possibly less agonising than many other deaths. It was certainly better than a slow spilling of guts on the battlefield. Better than being burned alive, broken on the wheel, impaled, disembowelled, or torn apart in a tug-of-war between horses—all common methods of execution in 'civilised' Europe. Nor was it preceded by the tortures of the Inquisition (though these were soon to be introduced into

Mexico), the rack, the boot, thumbscrews, the Iron Maiden, or the original hot seat that *half*-roasted the victim sitting on it. It was a sharp and purposeful death, and where the priests had doubts, as in the case of civilian slaves, or where the ceremony required a protracted end, as in some sacrifices to the fire god, the victims were usually anaesthetised either with *pulque* or *yauhtli*, Indian hemp.

What aroused such fear and disgust in the breasts of the invading Spaniards was not only the combination of human sacrifice and cannibalism—both regarded with the deepest loathing by the Catholic church—but above all the scale of it. The remorseless character of the confrontation between Spaniards and Aztecs was perhaps less a product of religious belief than of the conquistadors' gut-reaction to the all-pervading reek of blood.

In the decades after the conquest, the reek of blood gave way to the smell of burning flesh as the process of converting the heathen began. Spanish justice was imported, with all its casual cruelties. Mexicans were forced into the mines and ruthlessly exploited. Millions died from the new diseases that came with the conquistadors from Europe—colds, measles, smallpox. Some of those who refused baptism no doubt did so for the same reason as the 'gentle and peaceful' Taino who went to the stake in Cuba because he feared that, if he were converted and went to heaven instead, he would find more Christians there.[22]

Before the time of Cortés, it has been estimated that central Mexico had 25,000,000 inhabitants. By 1605, only 1,075,000 remained.[23]

Towards the end of the sixteenth century, an Italian merchant found himself in what had once been Tenochtitlan. It was still 'an earthly paradise', with floating gardens and many 'very beautiful' buildings. The buildings now were churches and convents, some of them—the 'very sumptuous' Jesuit College, and the new cathedral—still under construction. Carletti remarked that one could still see 'a tablet formed from a huge, thick stone worked in a round shape on which are carved various figures in half-relief, and with a small gutter in the middle through which ran the blood of the men who here were sacrificed in the times of the Mexican nobles'.

And the Aztec gods, too, remained on display, vanquished and powerless, 'walled up in the exterior walls of the buildings erected by the Spaniards, placed there to express the triumph of their foundation'.[24]

CHAPTER FIVE

The Nonconformists

GERMANY IS almost entirely occupied with building fires for them. Switzerland has been compelled to wipe out many of her villages on their account. Travellers in Lorraine may see thousands and thousands of the stakes to which they are bound . . . I say nothing of other more remote lands. No, no; there are witches by the thousand everywhere, multiplying upon the earth even as worms in a garden . . . I would that they should all be united in one single body, so that they might all be burned at once in a single fire.'[1] The year was 1590, the author of these intemperate words the chief judge of St Claude in Burgundy, a distinguished lawyer named Henri Boguet, who had written a procedural manual for the guidance of other judges engaged on witchcraft trials.

Not that Boguet and his fellows were entirely convinced of the existence of witchcraft. Indeed, they quibbled endlessly about the executive capabilities of Satan and his familiars. But they had no doubt that *witches* existed, or that they injured people, cattle and crops, sold their souls to the devil, took part in obscene and blasphemous rites that parodied the sacred rituals of the church, and murdered newborn babes, whose flesh they ate at sabbat feasts and whose fat they used for compounding a magical salve that was as valuable for getting a broomstick airborne as for poisoning an enemy.

The unfortunate witches who perished in the holocausts of the sixteenth and seventeenth centuries attracted accusations of cannibalism as readily as modern politicians attract charges of corruption. They were the inheritors of a long tradition of attributing to any minority that the establishment thought dangerous the most unattractive characteristics that could be devised.*

* This was true not only of the Western world. In India, tribal

In the Western world, among the first to suffer from this kind of polemic had been the Jews. In the second century B.C., Antiochus IV (Epiphanes) of Syria had sacrificed swine's flesh in the Temple at Jerusalem. This deliberate pollution of a place of worship had outraged not only the Jews but much of the Hellenistic world. To retrieve the royal reputation, the public relations experts of Antioch disseminated a carefully calculated fable about how the king, entering the Temple, had found there a plump Greek captive who assured him that it was the Jewish custom to 'kidnap a Greek foreigner, fatten him up for a year, and then convey him to a wood, where they slew him, sacrificed his body with their customary ritual, partook of his flesh, and, while immolating him, swore an oath of hostility to the Greeks'.[2] Since the Greeks knew very little about Jewish religious custom, this tale had its effect and the myth of ritual murder was well on the way to being established. It did not, however, gather momentum for several centuries, because in the meantime Christianity appeared on the scene.

Roman concern over the dynamism of this new minority led to charges that the Christians sacrificed and ate humans, usually children, and that they dipped the Host in their victims' blood. But this was one case in which Christians resolutely refused to turn the other cheek. They retaliated with enthusiasm, and by the third century had mounted a full-scale propaganda campaign not only against their Roman detractors but, prompted by Clement of Alexandria, against almost every 'heretical' sect in the book. The Carpocratians ate their own progeny; so did the Manichaeans; the Montanists baked bread from flour and children's blood; the gnostics cooked and ate human embryos; and the Euchites always met nine months after an orgy to dine on the babies that had been conceived at it.[3] It was all good uninhibited fun—and reasonably harmless for as long as religious belief was not backed by the force of law.

As the centuries passed, however, the Church gained

peoples were (and are) almost automatically accused of cannibalism, while in the middle mediaeval period there were several obsessively nonconformist cults such as the Shakta and the Kalamukhas who were charged with blood sacrifice, sex orgies, eating food out of skulls, and smearing their bodies with the ashes of the dead.

ground and heretics found themselves brought to trial and condemned to death for just such practices. In Orléans in 1022, for example, a group of Reformists were accused of having gone to a secret place at night, bearing torches and chanting the names of demons. When one of these obligingly materialised, the lights were put out and a sex orgy took place. The devil himself appeared and was duly worshipped. The cross was desecrated. Children conceived at the orgy were burned eight days after birth and the ashes made into a parody of the Host. The accused claimed that they had visions and could be transported instantly from one place to another—the first known record of the broomstick phenomenon.[4]

During the next four hundred years, the Catharists, Bogomils, Albigensians and Waldensians—not to mention the Henricians, the Apostolici, the Luciferans and Adamites—were among the numerous heretical sects charged with crimes that were already a cliché in the history of religion and were to become a cliché in the history of witchcraft.

But before the massacre of the witches, it was the Jews' turn to suffer. Strictly speaking, the Christian church could hardly count the Jews as heretic. If anything, it was the other way round. But hundreds of years of indoctrination had led the ordinary people of Europe to canalise many of their fears and animosities in the direction of the hook-nosed, black-avised, subservient Semites, the people who were legally bound to wear distinguishing badges or clothes and, in many areas, to live in separate ghettoes—an easy target for a lynch mob. The fact that popes and emperors consistently supported the Jews against their enemies may well have added to the virulence of the mobs.[5]

Since the first century A.D. it had been indelibly imprinted on the minds of ordinary Christians that the Jews had a deep-rooted hatred for Christianity—a charge not without foundation at that time. When the concept of the Antichrist arose a hundred years later, the Jews came to be seen as his allies, and since the Antichrist, according to some theologians, was not a living tyrant but Satan himself the inescapable conclusion was that the Jews had made a pact with the devil. What they gained from this pact was expertise in the mysterious arts of fortune-telling, medicine, and high finance. What they gave in return was blood sacrifice.

The idea of ritual murder that had first appeared in the days of Antiochus IV had been reiterated time and time again in the centuries that followed. There had been sporadic outbursts of violence, houses had been burned, synagogues destroyed or converted into churches, and in A.D. 414 there took place the first recorded expulsion of the entire Jewish population of a city—Alexandria. When the Crusades began, there was a renewed upsurge of hysteria that could never have been sustained without the precedent of a thousand years of denigration. In 1095 Pope Urban II preached a crusade to rescue the tomb of Christ from the heathen. The response of the European poor was no less intense than that of the rich. But in Normandy a band of fanatics raised the cry that it was madness to risk their lives in crossing half the world to save the tomb of Christ while his murderers remained at home in luxury. The massacres began in Rouen and continued wherever the People's Crusade passed on its way to the Holy Land.

In an era saturated with ideas of self-sacrifice, ever more lurid tales began to circulate about the sufferings of early Christian martyrs at the hands of the Jews. It was only a short step to belief in the sufferings of contemporary Christian martyrs at those same hands. The first serious accusation was made in 1144 at Norwich in England, where a Christian child— a twelve-year-old named William—was found dead. It was claimed that he had been ritually murdered on behalf of the Jewish community, for 'it was written that the Jews, without the shedding of human blood, could neither obtain their freedom, nor could they ever return to their fatherland'.[6] Fifty years later, at Bray in France, the Jews were accused not only of crucifying a boy in the weeks before Passover but of using his blood to mix their Passover bread.[7] Such accusations soon became commonplace, and it was enough for a Christian child to die under unusual circumstances, or even simply to disappear, for the cry of ritual murder to go up.

In 1329 two Savoy Jews were accused of having committed ritual murder 'with the knowledge and consent of all the Jews of the County of Savoy'; they were fortunate, for the authorities investigated and discovered that their accuser had been bribed. In 1401, however, a man living in Diessenhofen, Switzerland, murdered a four-year-old boy and confessed (under torture) that he had promised to sell the boy's blood to a Jewish visitor from Schaffhausen. The visitor and all the Jews of Diessenhofen were burned; so, soon after, were many of the Jews of Schaffhausen.[8]

And so it went on. The Jews' own special talents as well as their religion set them apart from others. The moneylenders among them attracted not gratitude but envy and dislike. Few men love their creditors, and it is clear that the main aim of at least some of the rabble-rousers who helped to stimulate the pogroms of the Middle Ages was simultaneously to wipe out a loan and its lender. Some Jews, too, had powers of healing that were regarded as supernatural, stemming from the devil and as likely to be used for harm as for good. It was easy enough to believe that they used human blood for their physics and spells. Easy enough, too, to blame the appalling ravages of the Black Death on Jewish poisons, and to torture, burn, drown or hang the supposed criminals in a futile attempt to force them to remove the pestilence they had brought. And—always—easy to believe that the Jews still hated Christ so much that they would torture the sacred Host until it bled (see pp. 60–61).

Because Judaism had a considerably longer history than Christianity, there was plenty of material for the fabulists to work on. They were able to produce a gratifyingly large number of typically 'Jewish' crimes without even having to refer to the files. But when the eye of the judiciary fell on witchcraft, it became necessary to dust off some of the charges that had been used so successfully against heretics in the past.

There had been witches since time immemorial, often evilly-disposed. When they committed a crime, they were punished according to the law; otherwise, administrators were inclined to turn a blind eye to their procuring, their brewing of aphrodisiacs, and their distressing habit of turning themselves into owls and taking off for the nearest graveyard. As paganism gave way to Christianity, the witch tended to become caretaker of the old customs, sorceress by repute, and dispenser of drugs, simples, and other folklore remedies.

The Salic Law of the Franks, in about A.D. 500, decreed no

more than a fine (admittedly a heavy one) of two hundred
solidi, or shillings, for any witch found guilty of eating someone. During the next one hundred and fifty years, however,
there are indications that the populace had begun to exercise
its own rough justice, for an edict of A.D. 643 made it illegal to
burn women for the crime of cannibalism—on the engaging
principle that the crime itself was impossible. At the end of the
eighth century, in regulations dealing with the administration
of newly-conquered pagan Saxony, Charlemagne's attitude
at first appeared to be ambivalent. 'If anyone, deceived by the
devil, believes after the manner of pagans that any man or
woman is a witch and eats men, and if on this account he
burns or gives her flesh to be eaten, or eats it, he will be
punished by capital sentence.' The involved syntax of this
statement has led some authorities to interpret it as meaning
that it was forbidden to believe in cannibalism, and also forbidden to *be* a cannibal—a clear case of each-way betting. On
the whole, however, it seems more likely that the death
penalty was being decreed for anyone who was misled by the
devil into making a false accusation and burning or eating
someone who was in fact innocent. In any case, Charlemagne's
twelfth capitulary made it clear that there was no longer any
ban on believing in cannibalism; the punishment for sorcerers
of either sex who ate human flesh themselves or fed it (spit-
roasted) to others was death.[9]

What may be deduced from all this (although it cannot be
proved) is not that witches were particularly prone to cannibalism, but that the name of witch was casually applied—for
want of a better word—to anyone found guilty of it. The word
'cannibal' itself was not invented until Columbus discovered
America. The Greek *anthropophagos* would have done, but the
Greek language, like Greek learning, had been lost to the
West after the split in the Roman empire and was not to be
rediscovered until the twelfth century.[10] Latin had no single
word for people who ate people, and it is possible that some of
the vernacular languages that were gathered within the
frontiers of Charlemagne's empire suffered from the same
lacuna. Many of the Franks were or had been cattle herders,
and cannibalism is usually rarer in a pastoral than in a
crop-based economy. Nevertheless, the implication remains

that whether or not witches indulged in cannibalism they were certainly regarded as being fairly disreputable.

Witchcraft, as such, was not yet a crime, although *maleficium* (harmful magic) was. But the concept of witchcraft was gradually changing. It was now being held distinct from sorcery. Sorcerers, those mediaeval scientists who dabbled in the unknown, were often respectable men of high degree with whom it was unwise to tangle. Witches generally inhabited a lower level of the social scale. The magic of sorcerers was high magic, an intellectual aid to speculations about the structure of the universe. The low magic of the witches was sanctified by no such grandiose vision. Witches read hands, not the heavens, brewed their potions in cauldrons, not crucibles.

The witch's spells began to take on a heretical tinge, partly because she dealt not in vague concepts but in the realities of ordinary life. It was axiomatic that only God and the saints could work miracles—yet the witch's tiny miracles (like those of the itinerant Jewish doctor) were an everyday denial of this holy truth. There could be but one explanation, and it was reinforced by the fact that witches usually came under the notice of authority only when they were accused of being *malefici*. It was that their powers (like those of the Jews) were the product of a pact with the devil. By the end of the eleventh century, to the now traditional accusations of cannibalism and child murder were added the crimes of blasphemy and satanism. This was what brought witchcraft within the jurisdiction of the Inquisition and led to the mass trials of the sixteenth and seventeenth centuries.

Curiously enough, it was only at the end of the fifteenth century that witches were saddled with the group image and activities that still added so much colour to trials involving the heretical sects. Now, for the first time, references to the coven and the Black Mass appeared in the indictments.[11] Implying organisation, collusion, a conspiracy against both the Church and the social order, they made witchcraft appear much more dangerous, and also made the multiple trial possible. An inquisitor convinced of the existence of the coven and the Black Mass felt justified in continuing to torture a suspect until she admitted who else had been present. Driven beyond endurance, perhaps even by what the witch-hunters regarded as 'the very gentlest questions'—'being suspended hardly clear of the ground by her thumbs'[12]—she would blurt out the names of a few people she knew of by reputation in a despairing attempt to avoid implicating family and friends. Statistics relating to one area of Germany show that the people most often denounced in such a case were individuals of notoriously bad reputation (especially midwives) and the better-known public figures—the magistrates, teachers, innkeepers, merchants and their wives.[13]

The first great handbook of the witch inquisitors, the *Malleus Maleficarum* of 1486, advised judges to be wary about torture, for some people were 'so soft-hearted and weak-minded that at the least torture they will confess anything, whether it be true or not. Others are so stubborn that, however much they are tortured, the truth is not to be had from them. There are others who, having been tortured before, are the better able to endure it a second time, since their arms have been accommodated to the stretchings and twistings involved. . . .'[14]

The judges who were intent on stamping out the heretical evil of witchcraft scarcely seem to have questioned whether it was an organised—and, therefore, arguably dangerous—cult, or merely an individual habit of mind. They used torture and carefully phrased questions to elicit the answers they expected. And as the witch mania grew, they were rewarded by having 'witches' come forward voluntarily to confess, just as dozens of people today confess to some crime they have read of in the newspapers.

Cannibalism, necrophagy and the obscenities of the Black Mass were of particular interest to the inquisitors. Usually, the cannibal charges related to unbaptised babies, not for gastronomic reasons, but because it was believed such children could not enter the kingdom of heaven—which delayed the day when the number of the elect would be complete and postponed the Last Judgement and the downfall of Satan.[15] Midwives, who had access to a great many newborn children, were commonly believed to be among the devil's main procurers, and were no doubt unjustly blamed for most cot or crib deaths at the height of the witch craze.

Although in Germany witches might dine on turnips, in

Alsace on fricassée of bats, and in England on roast beef and beer, it was not unusual for babies to appear on the menu at demonic feasts. In fifteenth-century Berne, one witch confessed that she and her cronies secretly took just-buried babies from their graves and cooked them in a cauldron, 'until the whole flesh comes away from the bones to make a soup which may easily be drunk'.[16] In sixteenth-century Spain, it seems to have been more customary to bake them in a pie.[17] But, either way, the general opinion was that the food at demonic feasts was terrible; some complained that it was tasteless (salt was banned at all witchly tables, which did not help), others that it was actively revolting.

But the infant's more important role in the mythology of witchcraft was to supply materials for magical powders and salves. At Todi in 1428, baby's blood was regarded as so effective that the only other ingredient needed was a vulture's fat. Other recipes were much more complex. In Artois, for example, one witch was accused of feeding toads on consecrated bread and wine, of killing and burning them, and then of mixing the ashes with the powdered bones of dead Christians, children's blood, herbs, and a number of other ingredients, unspecified. In 1450 in Savoy, the recommended recipe was as follows. Tie a naked, red-haired, male Catholic to a bench and subject him to the unrestrained attentions of a number of venomous animals. When he has expired from the bites and stings, hang him upside down, with a bowl underneath to catch the drips. Mix these with the fat of a man who has been hanged, the entrails of children, and the corpses of the venomous animals who caused his death. Use as required.[18]

One of the main uses of this unguent was for anointing a chair or broomstick, 'whereupon [witches] are immediately carried up into the air, either by day or by night, and either visibly or, if they wish, invisibly'.[19] Though some commentators sourly remarked that all the ointment did was 'send these old hags to sleep, and afterwards make them dream marvellous dreams',[20] there were enough reported sightings to confirm belief in the practice. The ointment could also be used to harm men and animals. One witch rubbed some on the butt end of a cow and the cow died next day. Another smeared some on the doors of houses in Geneva, which 'caused so great a plague in the city that the greater part of the inhabitants died of it'.[21] And if the witch wanted to transform herself into an animal—especially a werewolf (see pp. 108–20)—she rubbed herself all over with the magic salve.

For a powder with the special virtue of enabling a witch to remain silent under torture, it was best for her to roast her own firstborn male child, not yet baptised, in an oven, with other ingredients 'which it is not expedient to mention', and then to grind the results down into a powder; 'and if any witch or criminal carried about with him some of this substance he would in no way be able to confess his crime'.[22] This belief was already established in Germany in the 1480s and was still current in Scotland as late as 1661, when Helen Guthrie and four other women dug up the body of an unbaptised infant from a churchyard in Forfar 'and took several pieces thereof, as the feet, hands, a part of the head, and a part of the buttock, and . . . made a pie thereof, that they might eat of it, that by this means they might never make a confession (as they thought) of their witchcrafts'.[23] Witches could not be condemned and burned without first having confessed.

When they did confess, it was as if they had dredged all the murkier cesspools of the human subconscious. How much the witches' crimes owed to the repressed imaginations of their judges, how much to the suggestibility of weak minds under stress, and how much to the truth, no historian has ever been able to decide. But there is a grubby repetitiveness in the pages of the witch-hunters' manuals that makes them suspect as well as pitiably sordid.

What does emerge with startling clarity from these bizarre documents is the atmosphere of town and village life in times of panic—the credulity, the corrosive jealousies, the random suspicions of a world that knew only two states of being, monotony and disaster. The old woman who had not been invited to a wedding called down a thunderstorm upon it. The neighbour who had been refused a jug of milk made the cow barren. The beggar chased off for stealing an apple would blight the whole crop. These were the kind of allegations that landed unpopular villagers first in the torture chamber and then in the flames.

It was an atmosphere that infected great cities as much as remote villages, the aristocracy as much as the peasants. The average provincial beldame accused of witchcraft probably never attended a Black Mass in the whole course of her life, but some of the most beautiful women at the Sun King's court frequently did. Their tongues were as vicious, their minds as susceptible to the supernatural as any peasant's; their rank, however, nearly always protected them.

The volumes of the Bastille archives that deal with the great poison scandal that rocked Paris in the 1670s suggest that half the great ladies of Versailles went to have a Black Mass said on their behalf, a Mass designed to reinforce the power of the aphrodisiacs or poisons that the notorious Catherine de Montvoisin specialised in supplying. La Voisin's original trade was that of beautician, creator of creams and lotions, but when it became clear that few things were more destructive of a court lady's beauty than an unwanted pregnancy, she expanded into the manufacture of abortifacients. Business acumen suggested that some use might be made of the by-products—and the next step was blood sacrifice and Black Masses.

One of La Voisin's customers was Athénaïs de Montespan, mistress of Louis XIV and concerned about the royal fidelity. La Voisin promised to supply a love philtre. A special Black Mass was arranged. Madame de Montespan lay down on a bench, her legs hanging down in front, her head resting on a cushion, and hitched her skirts up to her chin so that the Abbé Guibourg—a seventy-year-old priest, with a high complexion, an atrocious squint, and an even worse reputation—might say Mass on her bare stomach.* La Voisin's daughter brought in 'a child that looked as if it had been born prematurely, put it in a basin, Guibourg cut its throat, poured [the blood] in the chalice, and consecrated the blood and a sacred wafer, celebrated the Mass [the chalice, Host and cross meanwhile being balanced on Madame de Montespan's stomach], then removed the child's entrails; Mother Voisin took blood and wafer next day to Dumesnil, to be distilled into a glass vial that Madame de Montespan took away.'[24]

* Ladies of lower rank were expected to strip completely on such occasions.

The police finally succeeding in arresting La Voisin—for poisoning, not witchcraft—and began to interrogate more than two hundred witnesses. La Voisin had been in business for fifteen years, the Abbé Guibourg for at least twenty, and trying to piece together the events of those years took more than another three. The pages of the depositions are littered with abortions, with cupboards and ovens full of infant corpses, with distillations of blood and entrails. La Voisin's potions, compounded equally of chemicals, magic, and satanism, had been very profitable indeed, especially as they were sold entirely on a cash-with-order basis, but she went to the stake in the end, perhaps one of the closest approximations to a real witch of any of the thousands of women who were burned in the sixteenth and seventeenth centuries.

The great witch-hunting mania had by now begun to subside, partly because social conditions were changing, partly because the disruption caused by the hunt had become intolerable. But this did not mean that people had ceased to believe in magic, or forgotten the old accusations that had for so long been hurled at nonconformist minorities. In 1782 it was the turn of the gypsies in Hungary. Forty-one men and women were hanged, beheaded, broken on the wheel or quartered, for having smoke-cured, cooked and eaten forty-four people who were subsequently discovered to be alive and well. Similar accusations cropped up again as late as 1920 and 1929.[25] Nor had the Jews seen the end of the ancient myth of ritual murder, which remained current in the nineteenth century within the domains of the Orthodox Church, and was resurrected yet again, with hideous effectiveness, by the Nazis. It was even to surface once more in 1960, in a local newspaper in one of the Muslim republics of the USSR.[26]

'Cannibal' in Europe in the 1450s was a term of invective much on a par with 'Reds under the bed' in America five hundred years later. But the genuine article did exist, men who, from hunger or sheer perversity, were prepared to eat their fellow men.

Scotland, as wild and lawless as the remoter regions of continental Europe until well into the sixteenth century, still has a proprietorial affection for some of her more stylish reprobates. As far back as A.D. 367, the Roman province of Britain was invaded by Picts, Scots, Saxons and Franks, reinforced by the Attacotti, a cannibal tribe from Argyllshire, who later turned respectable and enrolled in the Roman army. But a thousand years after, there were still some who clung to the old ways. There was one family that inhabited a cave near St Vigeans in Forfarshire and lived, literally, off passing travellers. The picturesquely named Christie o' the Cleek was similarly addicted to human flesh, though he was almost as famous for the fearsome hooked axe with which he hauled his victims from their ponies as he was for his gastronomic tastes.[27] The moss troopers (or freebooters) of the Borders are said to have eaten the flesh and drunk the blood of their enemies, and are reputed to have boiled a certain Lord Soulis alive and then quaffed the broth.[28]

But best known of all—no doubt because he was immortalised by a best-selling eighteenth-century anthologist—is Sawney (Sandy) Beane. Born not far from Edinburgh towards the end of the fourteenth century, he wandered away with a local girl and finally settled in a cave on the beautiful, lonely coast of Galloway, on the other side of the country. Cattle raising was not an occupation for an impoverished (and possibly lazy) peasant, and cattle rustling was perhaps the most dangerous occupation imaginable at that time. Sawney and his wife made do with people.

Sallying forth from their vast and well-hidden cavern, they waylaid travellers, slaughtered them, and took them home for dinner. As the family increased—Sawney and his wife raised eight sons and six daughters, and they in turn produced eighteen grandsons and fourteen granddaughters—the whole mob would go hunting together. People began to shun the coast road on which so many travellers mysteriously disappeared and where severed limbs were often cast up by the tide, 'to the Astonishment and Terror of all the Beholders'. The Beanes, first and last, were estimated to have disposed of more than a thousand victims.

One day, however, some twenty-five years after Sawney and his wife first took up residence in their cave, a party of horsemen rode into sight while the Beanes were still busy dismembering a woman they had killed. The villains fled, but were traced at last with the aid of bloodhounds. When the pursuers found their way into the secret recesses of the cave, they were met with the sight of arms, legs, and haunches hanging from the roof as neatly as in a butcher's shop. That Mrs Beane was a thrifty housewife was proved by the other choice cuts that had been put up in pickle. But the law wasted no time on compliments and the whole Beane clan was dragged back to Leith, there to be summarily and painfully exterminated in the year 1435.[29]

At the other end of Europe, and the other end of the social scale, there flourished in the second half of the fifteenth century Vlad V of Walachia, the original of Bram Stoker's Dracula. But though Vlad had many failings, being a vampire was not one of them.

Vlad the Impaler, as he was affectionately known to his contemporaries, ruled the principalities of Walachia from 1456 until 1462 and again for a short period in 1475–76. He did his best to strengthen the central power, and to curb the *boyars*, the feudal barons, while promising improvement to the peasantry and damnation to the Turks. His methods were primitive but effective. When he heard of a plot to depose him, 'he robbed the St Jacob church and set fire to the outskirts of the town [Kronstadt, in Transylvania]. And early next day he had women and men, young and old . . . impaled and had a table put in their midst and partook of breakfast with great appetite.' Some *boyars* who offended him were beheaded; the heads were fed to crabs, and the crabs were then served up at a feast attended by the victims' friends and relatives. Mothers were forced to eat their children, husbands their wives. When three hundred Tartars wandered into his territory, Vlad took the three best of them 'and had them fried. The others had to eat them, and he said unto them: "You will have to eat each other in the same manner unless you go to fight the Turks." ' The Tartars went and fought the Turks.

The exploits of Vlad the Impaler, thanks to the recent invention of movable type and the activities of the news media, became almost as popular with horror fans in the late fifteenth century as those of his heir, Count Dracula, did with *frisson*-seekers of the nineteenth and twentieth.[30]

There were, of course, other cannibals driven by a less

calculated form of insanity. There was the fourteen-year-old French girl who had a compulsive thirst for blood; the Italian brigand, Gaetano Mammone, who triumphantly drank the blood of his captives; and the cave dweller on the Côte d'Azur who strangled and violated a twelve-year-old girl and then drank her blood and devoured her flesh.[31] There was the hungry colonist in the newly settled state of Virginia in 1610, who murdered his wife, then salted (powdered) and ate part of her before he was discovered; 'now whether she was better roasted, boyled, or carbonado'd, I know not,' remarked one Jamestown chronicler, 'but of such a dish as powdered wife, I never heard of.'[32] And in Clovelly in Devon, in 1740, there was John Gregg who was said to have emulated Sawney Beane with a precision that from today's viewpoint looks highly suspicious.[33]

True ritual cannibalism also continued to flourish in some parts of the world, even if not in Europe. In sixteenth-century Brazil, said Montaigne, who had his information from a merchant who had lived there for some years, 'everyone for a trophy brings home the head of an enemy he has killed, which he fixes over the door of his house. After having treated their prisoners well for a long time and given them all the regales they can think of, he to whom the prisoner belongs invites a great assembly of his friends.' On this happy occasion, the prisoner having been tidily despatched, 'they roast him, eat him amongst them, and send some chops to their absent friends'.[34] A hundred years later, a Dutch clergyman reported that the Mohawks of the area round present-day Albany held religious cannibal feasts. 'The common people,' he said, 'eat the arms, buttocks, and trunk; but the chiefs eat the head and the heart.' There were similar reports of the Hurons and the Miamis.[36]

But famine was still one of the commonest reasons for cannibalism. In Ireland in 1588–89, 'one did eate another for hunger'. In 1594, when Henri IV besieged Paris, bread was made from the bones of the charnel house of the Holy Innocents. In 1601–3 cannibalism was again reported in Ireland.[37]

In those parts of the world that depended for their productivity on the whims of the monsoon wind, famine was endemic. Especially in India. In 1631, early in the reign of

Shah Jahan—who was to build that most coolly exquisite of all the world's monuments, the Taj Mahal—people were reduced to 'scraping on the dunghills for food. . . . All the highway was strowed with dead people, our noses never free from the stink of them, especially about towns. . . . Women were seen to roast their children; men travelling in the way were laid hold of to be eaten and having cut away much of his flesh, he was glad if he could get away and save his life, others killed outright and devoured. A man or woman no sooner dead but they were cut in pieces to be eaten.' This European traveller's account was endorsed by that of the official historian of the time, Abdul Hamid. 'The inhabitants of these two countries [Gujarat and the Deccan],' he said, 'were reduced to the direst extremity. Life was offered for a loaf, but none would buy; rank was to be sold for a cake, but none cared for it. . . . Destitution at last reached such a pitch that men began to devour each other, and the flesh of a son was preferred to his love.'[38]

CHAPTER SIX

Werewolves and Vampires

'WHAT BIG eyes you have, grandma!' exclaimed Little Red Riding Hood.

'All the better to see you with, my dear.'

'What big ears you have, grandma!'

'All the better to hear you with, my dear.'

'What big teeth you have, grandma!'

'All the better to eat you up with!' snarled grandma, as she tossed back the coverlet and leapt out of bed. *Sic transit* Little Red Riding Hood.

Grandma, in fact, was a werewolf, one of the more fearsome monsters among the many who have terrified mankind since the dawn of history. The werewolf was a human being who could, at will, change his or her shape into that of a wolf— larger and stronger than the ordinary wolf, and endowed not only with that animal's bestial ferocity but with human intelligence and cunning. The wolf incarnation was most common in central Europe, where the snows of winter drove the wolf packs down to prowl by night round the very walls of isolated villages, chilling the peasants' blood with their unearthly howls. But the concept itself was worldwide. There were tales of were-hyenas and were-lions in Africa, were-tigers in Sumatra and were-leopards in Assam, were-jaguars in Central America and were-bears in Scandinavia.[1]

In Europe, belief in the predatory man-wolf was so long-established and widespread that in the horror-haunted sixteenth and seventeenth centuries there was even what amounted to a werewolf epidemic in the Slav territories and in some of the more mountainous regions of France, notably the Auvergne. Many of the cases then tried followed the basic pattern laid down fifteen hundred years before in classical Rome and described with colloquial vigour in *The Satyricon* of Petronius.

The storyteller in Petronius's narrative—a slave called Niceros—described first how he had persuaded a soldier acquaintance to go with him 'as far as the fifth milestone' on the way to visit his mistress. 'We stumbled off,' continued Niceros, 'with the moon shining down as though it were high noon. But where the road leads down between the graves, my man went off among the tombstones to do his business, while I sat by the road mumbling a song to keep my courage up and counting the graves. After a while I started looking around for him and suddenly I caught sight of him standing stark naked with all his clothes piled up on the side of the road. Well, you can imagine: I stood frozen, stiff as a corpse, my heart in my mouth. The next thing I knew he was pissing around his clothes and then, presto! he changed into a wolf . . . then started to howl and loped off for the woods. . . .

'I pulled out my sword and slashed away at the shadows all the way to my girlfriend's house. I arrived white as a ghost, almost at the last gasp, with the sweat pouring down my crotch and my eyes bugging out like a corpse. I don't know how I ever recovered. Melissa, of course, was surprised to see me at such an hour and said: "If you'd only come a little earlier, you could have lent us a hand. A wolf got into the grounds and attacked the sheep. The place looked like a butcher-shop, blood all over. He got away in the end, but we had the last laugh. One of the slaves nicked him in the throat with a spear."

'That finished me. I couldn't sleep a wink the rest of the night and as soon as it was light, I went tearing back home like a landlord chasing the tenants. . . . When I got home,' concluded Niceros, 'I found the soldier stretched out in bed like a pole-axed bull and the doctor inspecting his neck.'[2]

That a wounded werewolf had to return to human form, and that the wounds stayed with him, were still essential aspects of the werewolf belief in sixteenth-century France, and when legend became entangled with reality, the result could be disastrous for the suspect. There was a sensational case reported from a village in the Auvergne in 1588 in which a huntsman was attacked by a wolf of enormous size. He fired at it, but to no effect. (Against werewolves, *silver* bullets were mandatory, although in parsimonious Normandy it was sufficient for the ammunition to have been blessed by a priest.) Fortunately, the man also had a knife, and during the course of the struggle succeeded in lopping off one of the beast's fore- paws. The animal fled and the huntsman, much shaken, set off for home with the paw in his pouch. On the way he met a gentleman to whom he had promised some game, and told him what had happened. He took the paw out to prove his story—only to find that it had turned into a woman's hand, complete with wedding ring. Worse still, the gentleman recog- nised the ring. It was his wife's. Going in search of her, he found her seated in the kitchen with her arm tucked inside her apron, trying to conceal a bleeding stump. The unfortunate woman was arrested and publicly burned alive, a sacrifice to the powers of legend.[3] What the truth behind this strange sequence of events really was has never emerged, although to the modern eye it looks very much like a successful plot to dispose of an unwanted wife.

There were more ways than one of forcing a werewolf to return to human form. If something made of iron or steel were thrown over it, its skin would split horizontally across the forehead and the man or woman would emerge. If it were hit between the eyes with a fork or blood-rusted key—how many of *those* were there lying around?—or wounded three times between the eyes so as to draw three drops of blood, it would also have to revert. The least dangerous—and, it may be suspected, least efficacious—method was to recognise the man implicit in the beast and address him by his baptismal name.[4]

Werewolf lore was not confined to detection and disposal. Centuries of observing deviations from the normal human pattern had helped to compile a kind of guidebook to ways of becoming a werewolf. Among some of the Slav peoples, any child born with a caul (second skin) or with teeth already appearing was undoubtedly either a werewolf or a vampire.[5] In Denmark, if a woman experienced painless childbirth (possible, it was believed, only if she repeated a secret charm) all her sons were fated to be werewolves and all her daughters *incubi*, or 'nightmares'. In Germany, if a woman bore seven daughters in succession, one of them was bound to be a were- wolf. And in Greece, any child who was so irreverent as to be born on Christmas day—or, in some districts, at any time between Christmas and Twelfth Night—was known as 'feast-blasted' or *callicantzaros*, and condemned to be a werewolf for the twelve days of Christmas every year.[6] The *callicantzaros*, in fact, was not quite a werewolf but more an anonymous monster on the lines of Grendel in *Beowulf* (though somewhat miniaturised) or of those man-eating multiform Indian demons, the *raksasas*. It behaved with manic fury; its nails grew like talons, and its hands curled into claws; the Aegean islanders believed that it was particularly prone to devour its own brothers and sisters.

All these were what might be described as constitutional werewolves. But it was also possible for a man or woman to become a werewolf by malice aforethought or even by sheer bad luck. Witches often changed shape to make the journey to the sabbat, and for as long as real wolves roamed the forests and plains of Europe that was the form they preferred; the fashion for black cats came later. In 1610, two witches were condemned at Liége for having changed themselves into werewolves and killed a great number of children, whom they tore in pieces and then guzzled.[7] Sometimes, however, a sorcerer was believed to direct his spells and potions at some innocent victim, which explains why the pages of legend occasionally tell of a beneficent or kindly werewolf who is usually fortunate enough—like the prince who was turned into a frog—to be released from his bondage through the love of a beautiful maiden.

The simplest way of becoming a werewolf, however, providing the facilities were available, was by donning a wolf's pelt. The standard version of this tale is to be found in the northern *Völsunga Saga*, in which Sigmund and his son Sinfjotli sally forth into the forest in search of loot. Coming upon a house in which two men are sleeping the deep sleep of exhaustion, they see wolf shirts hanging on the wall. The *Saga* explains that the men are werewolves, bewitched princes who are only permitted to remove their wolf skins once every ten days until someone else comes along to release them from the spell. Sigmund and Sinfjotli cannot resist trying on the shirts, but once they have them on they cannot get them off again—and when they speak to each other it is in the language of wolves. For nine days the two heroes range the forest, urged on by a wolfish instinct to destroy and kill. At last they return to their own lair to wait for the dawn of the tenth day. Being heroes, they have no doubts about what to do next, though lesser mortals were generally believed to be reluctant to give up the wolf persona. When dawn comes, Sigmund and his son tear off their wolf shirts and throw them in the flames, praying (rather late in the day) 'that they might bring harm to no one'.[8]

In this part of the Sigmund legend, scholars see the reflection of an ancient initiation rite, and something of the sort may indeed help to explain the whole peculiar history of were-animal beliefs. If such beliefs are to persist, and even to gain in strength over the centuries, they have to be reinforced in contemporary terms. Learned churchmen in mediaeval times argued that this reinforcement was supplied by the activities of the devil. Not, said St Augustine, that the devil was actually capable of transforming a man into a wolf or vice versa. He was, however, capable of 'transporting man's fantasy in a bodily shape unto other senses'[9]—in other words, he could make a man feel like a wolf and look like a wolf. Which, for all practical purposes, was just as good.

But if Satan is left out of the reckoning, and if the occasional coincidence of a wolf and a human having similar wounds is taken to be inadequate, what was it that maintained the strength of the werewolf belief?

It seems clear that at some time in the mists of prehistory a multiplicity of attitudes, instincts and convictions had converged to create the basic idea of were-animals. As has been explained earlier in this book (see pages 10–11), primitive man lived on level terms with the animals who shared his world; he found nothing strange in the thought that the soul of man or animal might, by mistake, come to inhabit the wrong body.*

Further, many tribes had totem animals with whom they closely identified themselves, often because a particular

---

* Small children today—in that brief moment when they will believe anything, preparatory to disbelieving everything—are equally ready to accept this proposition. How often does a child question the matter of Beauty and the Beast, or Puss-in-Boots conversing with Dick Whittington, or butterflies having a ball?

species (providing meat, skins, and the bone or horn from which tools were made) was essential to the whole tribal economy. Shamans, or medicine-men, in prehistoric times as today, customarily dressed themselves in an animal skin, taking on the animal's power to fortify their magic, and there were special totem ceremonials in which the whole tribe took part, mimicking the animals with grunts, howls or roars. In some parts of Africa and Australia today such rituals can still be observed. Finally, when early man went hunting, one of his favourite techniques was to disguise himself as an animal which his quarry would not instantly either attack or run from, but, for preference, be hypnotised by. In the 1830s, the Sioux Indians were still dressing themselves in the pelts of white wolves when they went hunting buffalo.

As the world began to change, a number of the animals that had once been hunted were brought into the barnyard. The rampaging wild bull of early times was transformed into the stolid and lacklustre ox. The vicious red-eyed wild boar became a cantankerous domestic pig. Subtly, man's emotional allegiance was transferred to the independent, untameable predators that still roamed free—the wolf in Europe, the leopard in Assam, the tiger in Sumatra, and so on. For the largest and fiercest animal in his immediate vicinity, man developed a curious fascination compounded of love, hate, awe and revulsion.

By Roman times doctors had begun to recognise a form of disturbance now known as lycanthropy, in which fascination developed into identification. According to a medical treatise of the second century A.D., the sufferer was attacked by a kind of delusion which led him to believe he was a wolf and endowed him with a wolf's savagery and lust for raw flesh. Men were chiefly overcome by this madness in January and February.[10] Interestingly enough, the eleventh-century Arab physician Avicenna also mentioned February as the worst month, and so, by implication, did Robert Burton in his *Anatomy of Melancholy* (1621).[11] February was the hungriest time of year for man and beast alike, the time when wolves actively hunted human prey and men were at their lowest physical and mental ebb.

In some cases, the lycanthrope may have been certifiably

insane, but more often he seems to have been possessed by a temporary hysteria. Trailed along in the backwash of the early animal-worshipping religions were groups of believers who never quite gave up the old ideas, and these ideas, in time, contributed to the evolution of animal-cult societies marked by the practice of group lycanthropy. Herodotus, in the fifth century B.C., recorded that the Scythians believed their neighbours, the Neuri, turned into wolves every year for a day or two. 'Of course, I do not believe this tale,' Herodotus hastened to add. 'All the same, they tell it and even swear to the truth of it.'[12]

In the eighth century A.D., the archbishop of Canterbury, echoing the sentiments of earlier prelates in Ravenna, Turin, and Scythopolis (Palestine), prescribed: 'If anyone at the Kalends of January goes about as a stag or a bull; that is, making himself into a wild animal and dressing in the skin of a herd animal, and putting on the heads of beasts; those who in such wise transform themselves into the appearance of a wild animal, penance for three years because this is devilish.'[13] By this time what had once been hunting-magic rites were, in all probability, more an excuse for feasting and merry-making, but the participants remained bound by a special kind of fellowship. This, or the memory of initiation rites into an animal-oriented warrior society, was (as has already been mentioned) enshrined in the tale of Sigmund, Sinfjotli and the wolfskins. And the berserkers of Norse history and legend, who fought in a state of wild frenzy and were free from the laws that governed ordinary members of society, traditionally wore animal skins; accordingly, they were called either 'wolf-coats' or 'bearshirts' (i.e. *berserkr*). One celebrated berserker, the champion of King Hrolf of Denmark, was said to fight in the form of a great bear while his human form lay at home asleep, and this idea of one soul with alternative bodies—as distinct from one soul with one, transformable body—was a recurring feature of the werewolf tales.

There is no specific association with man-eating in any of these cases. Arguably, there may have been with Sigmund and the berserkers, but this is the kind of material that tends to be pruned when historical truth is elevated into heroic legend. Villains can be cannibals, heroes must not.

Some authorities believe that in parts of Europe in the sixteenth and seventeenth centuries, organised animal cults—quite distinct from witch cults—still existed.[14] Certainly, there are indications that this may have been so. In France, in Nivernais, Poitou, and—inevitably—the Auvergne, there was a firm belief in what were known as 'wolf leaders'. These were sorcerers who donned a bewitched wolfskin and then marshalled together a pack of about thirty wolves to roam by night along the highways and byways and in the neighbourhood of tumbledown buildings. The wolf-leaders forced stray wayfarers or belated roisterers to pay up and then gave them an escort of a couple of wolves to see them home. Anyone who fell was instantly devoured by his escorts. Wolf leaders were believed to receive a monthly allowance from the devil for the upkeep of their pack. This particular version of the protection racket had such a bad reputation in the Auvergne that, according to an author writing in 1857, 'very recently an inhabitant of St Gervais, having been called a wolf leader during an argument in the market at Riom in the presence of several witnesses, took legal action for slander'. At a number of sixteenth-century French trials accused 'witches' admitted to consorting with others in wolf form, while the Swedish cartographer Olaus Magnus recorded that werewolves were accustomed to meet in a ruined castle at Courland on the borders of Latvia to perform their ceremonies and set special tests of agility to members of the pack.[15]

All this is suggestive. The modern world is by no means unfamiliar with the kind of secret society that gives its officers special titles and establishes a corporate identity by means of ritual, ceremonial, and exotic clothing; that permits the individual to behave as he would not in daily life, releasing him from the bonds of self-reliance into a world of temporary irresponsibility. Today, it is all harmless enough, an excuse for conviviality, sugared with a little philanthropy and spiced with a dash of mystery. But the Ku Klux Klan of a hundred years ago, though it substituted sheets for wolfskins, approaches much more closely to the kind of association that may have existed in the dark valleys of Europe in the sixteenth and seventeenth centuries—an instrument first, perhaps, for revenge or self-protection, later for simple terrorism. And an instrument unrecorded except in rumour and folk memory, because in those dark valleys even the *curé* was not necessarily less credulous or more literate than his flock.

The world of rural France was one in which, according to a modern historian, 'everything is the object of fear; and, more important, everything is possible. . . . It is a world in which there is no distinction between natural and supernatural, reason and unreason—a world, in fact, in which such a distinction has no meaning. . . . The worship of saints readily commingles with superstitious practices, so termed after the beginning of the seventeenth century. Moreover, belief in the unmitigated power of sorcerers, sorceresses, neighbours endowed with the evil eye who are in the habit of riding broomsticks and rambling through clearings at night—all occupy an enormous place. The devil is at least as often present as the benevolent God. . . . The maleficent supernatural is always present to the mind.'[16]

Occult terrors, chronic malnutrition, age-old animal superstitions, the ever-present threat of plague, of harvest failure, the depredations of soldier mercenaries, or of the brigands who swooped down from their mountain lairs with feral savagery, the inturned, almost incestuous nature of French village life where mild dislike could so quickly burgeon into unreasoning hate—it was a world pulsating with suspicion. And when a pack of wolves or a lone killer began to pad the forest margins, there was often someone who could be matched to the werewolf tradition—an emaciated consumptive who coughed blood, one of those stray children who turned up occasionally, having been reared by animal foster-parents, someone afflicted by a dermoid cyst,* or even a man or woman who, oversensitive to atmosphere, had lapsed into the nightmare of lycanthropy.

In some parts of sixteenth-century France and in Bohemia and Hungary there were a number of outbreaks of murder and cannibalism that were firmly associated in the public mind with werewolfism. In 1522, for example, two men named

* A subcutaneous lump that, when opened, turns out to contain growing hair. One such cyst, as large as a boy's head and containing hair five feet long, is said to have been removed in a London hospital in the early twentieth century.[17]

Pierre Burgot and Michel Verdun were burned alive at Besançon 'for having danced and sacrificed to the devil, having changed themselves into wolves and having devoured children'. In the Pyrenees district alone, one official was responsible for burning two hundred alleged werewolves or *loups-garous*. In 1573, at Dôle, near Dijon, Gilles Garnier was accused of having terrorised the countryside. He admitted killing a child of twelve, tearing her in pieces with his teeth and wolf claws, eating some of her, and considerately taking the rest home to his wife. Aided by the rack, he also recalled killing another girl and tearing a thirteen-year-old boy limb from limb. There were fifty witnesses to testify against him, and he was condemned to the stake (after being forced to pay the costs of his own prosecution.) Occasionally, doubts would creep in. In 1598 and 1603 there were two cases in which men were tried and convicted, but judged insane. In one of them, some witnesses swore they had seen the accused in the guise of a wolf when he attacked his victim. Others, simultaneous witnesses of the same act, flatly contradicted them.[18]

Even as late as 1764 in the Cévennes, there was a wolf so strong, so cunning, and so destructive, that everyone believed he must be a werewolf. Children were attacked and two devoured, then the wolf moved on to larger prey, killing and eating a pair of adolescents (see illustration 14). Five hundred dragoons and twelve hundred peasants, led by one of the king's best wolf hunters, set out to beat the forests for the animal, but he gave them the slip. A price was put on his head, and with this encouragement it is said that twenty thousand men were raised to hunt the Beast of Gévaudan. Still he escaped them. Next, the king's Chief Gun-Bearer and Lieutenant-General of the Royal Hunt came in on the act, backed up by all the gamekeepers and bloodhound-handlers of Versailles and St-Germain-en-Laye, as well as a mob of beaters who were familiar with the local mountains and valleys. But the wolf had moved on to the Aveyron. Finally, three years after its crimes had begun, it was wounded by some villagers and then tracked down and shot by the king's Chief Gun-Bearer. Or, at least, *a* wolf was wounded and then shot. It was just an ordinary wolf, not even particularly large. People wondered for a long time afterwards whether it really was the Beast of Gévaudan or whether some man or woman still walked among them who had once been a *loup-garou*.[19]

Against the combined attack of the church and civic authorities, the European 'werewolf' had few defences and gradually faded out of history and into folklore. But when, in the nineteenth century, missionaries and anthropologists erupted into the private world of the heathen in what had formerly been the more secret corners of the globe, they were horrified to find cannibalistic animal cults not only flourishing, but flourishing openly.

They discovered that among the Kwakiutl tribes who inhabited the Pacific coast of Canada just north of the forty-ninth parallel, young men were accustomed to put themselves under the protection of one or other of a miscellany of tribal spirits. Those who were accepted as disciples of Baxbakuala-nuxsiwae—a bear-like monster whose entire body was covered with gaping, bloodstained mouths—became Hamatsas, a tribal élite of licensed cannibals. The initiation rites consisted of the re-enactment of a legend so gory, so laden with detail, that it is almost impossible to distinguish what is fundamental to it from what was added later.[20]

The youth who hoped to become a Hamatsa was first dispatched alone into the forest where he was expected to remain for three months absorbing the habits and temperament of his alarming patron. During this period he would return at least once to the outskirts of his village, gaunt, hysterical, making a piercing whistling sound and crying 'Hap! Hap! Hap! Hap!'—'Eat! Eat! Eat! Eat!' Charging into the village, he would bite mouthfuls of flesh out of the arms or chest of anyone he happened to encounter, and would then rush back into the forest again.

In the forest he would build a hut, to which, some days before the end of his exile, members of the tribe brought a mummified corpse that had been soaked in salt water, cleaned, and split open.

On the appointed day, senior members of the Hamatsa cult went to the hut, solemnly greeted the initiate, and were invited to inspect the corpse—which had been smoke-cured, in the meantime—and choose which of the cuts they preferred. A woman impersonating the slave of the original legend then carried the corpse through to the rear of the hut and, carefully watched by the Hamatsas, ate four ritual mouthfuls of it. In order of seniority the Hamatsas now tucked in to their share, swallowing each mouthful whole, as ritual demanded, and washing it down with an emetic gulp of salt water. After this epicurean repast, they all adjourned for a swim. The initiate had now been accepted as a Hamatsa, and the ceremonies concluded with a prolonged dance that vibrated with cannibal symbolism.

From this time on, the new Hamatsa was at liberty to bite a piece out of anyone he chose, to kill, if he liked, a slave for his dinner, or to take down and eat one of the mummified corpses hung from a Burial Tree (which was apparently more palatable then fresh flesh). To offset this freedom there were innumerable tabus. After swallowing a human meal, he had to take an instant salt water emetic, in order to get rid of it again. On the credit side, however, he was not allowed to do any work for sixteen days.

By the end of the nineteenth century, this Kwakiutl ritual had been considerably modified. Dogs were substituted for corpses, and instead of biting bits out of people the Hamatsa merely shaved off a sliver of skin and sucked it. Nowadays, the ceremonial dance has even become something of a tourist attraction.

In Africa, the missionaries found, not bear-monster cults but leopard cults that were considerably more manic and gruesome and much more difficult to emasculate. Membership of a Leopard Society was a distinction that conferred special privileges, and the initiation rites were correspondingly severe —though less for the member than for his family. Each initiate had to produce, for sacrifice, a teenage girl of his own or his wife's blood.

On the night before the night of sacrifice, after eating a meal of human flesh and conducting the necessary negotiations for supply of the victim, the initiate and four companions ranged the forest all through the hours of darkness, roaring like leopards. Then on the night itself members gathered from near and far, wearing leopard masks and armed with leopard knives—pronged, clawlike, with double-edged blades. One man, the executioner, would be fully clad in a leopard skin.

The victim was set on her way along an agreed track by a parent or guardian, stumbling, terrified, oppressed by the humid menace of the jungle at night and the sense of hidden presences. A low leopard growl broke the throbbing silence, the executioner leapt from his hiding place, and the girl's throat was torn open with one swift slash from the leopard knife.

The body was carried to a secret clearing and there dissected so that the internal organs could be studied with as much care and concentration as any Babylonian or Greek diviner ever bestowed on his hieromantic sheep's liver. Afterwards, the flesh was cut up and distributed to members of the society, the choicest cuts, as always, for the chief. The victim's father or mother was traditionally presented with a small portion—a not unusual feature of cannibal ceremonies, though more often found when a tribe was executing criminal justice on some wrongdoer. Parents, by accepting a morsel of their child, signified that they accepted the verdict and waived the right to start a blood feud.

Leopard Society members argued that their bloody ritual was designed to create powerful medicine to strengthen themselves and their tribes.* This belief, in fact, made the society more than a simple animal cult on werewolf lines. It carried right into today's world—for some authorities believe that the Leopard Society has not yet been entirely relegated to the pages of history—the paleolithic belief that flesh was strength and blood was life. [21]

Closely associated with the idea of the werewolf in Europe was that of the vampire, one of the most lurid horror comics ever dreamed up by man and yet, oddly enough, one of the least harmful. Though the forces of church and state burned vampires, decapitated them, tore them limb from limb, or transfixed them with stakes through the heart, the vampire was in most cases dead already and knew nothing about it. There were none of those appalling holocausts that purged the countryside of living 'witches' and 'werewolves', schismatics

---

* It might be thought that the flesh and blood of a lusty young warrior would have supplied more potent magic than that of an adolescent girl, but the girl was clearly intended as a direct substitute for the man of her family who was being initiated.

and other sinners in the sight of the Lord. Nevertheless, the psychological effects of the vampire myth were unpleasant enough at a time when the human mind was under constant assault.

In the late seventeenth century, Hungary, Moravia, Silesia and Poland suffered from epidemics of plague, smallpox—and, soon after, vampirism.

'Vampires,' said Zopfius, one of the earliest authorities to write on the subject, 'issue forth from their graves in the night, attack people sleeping quietly in their beds, suck out all their blood from their bodies and destroy them. They beset men, women and children alike, sparing neither age nor sex. Those who are under the fatal malignity of their influence complain of suffocation and a total deficiency of spirits, after which they soon expire. Some who, when at the point of death, have been asked if they can tell what is causing their decease, reply that such and such persons, lately dead, have arisen from the tomb to torment and torture them.'[22] Nor could men deliver themselves from these visitations, added Dom Augustin Calmet, 'unless they dig the corpses up from the graves, drive a sharp stake through the bodies, cut off the heads, tear out the hearts; or else they burn the bodies to ashes. The name given to these ghosts is Oupires, or Vampires, that is to say, bloodsuckers, and the particulars that are related of them are so singular, so detailed, accompanied by circumstances so probable and so likely, as well as with the most weighty and well-attested legal deposition that it seems impossible not to subscribe to the belief . . . that these apparitions do actually come forth from their graves and that they are able to produce the terrible effects so widely and so positively attributed to them.'[23]

The particulars related of them were certainly, as Dom Calmet remarked, detailed. Almost anyone who had been unpopular in life could be suspected of maliciously turning into a vampire at death—the ingrate, the libertine, the lecher, and especially the werewolf. The same was true of those who had incurred the displeasure of the Church—the suicides, the unbaptised, and the excommunicate. Even mismanagement during the obsequies of the righteous could result in vampir-dom—if a cat leaped over the corpse, or something went wrong at the burial service. Those unfortunates who had been attacked by a vampire were frequently suspected of having caught the habit—in an attempt to make up for lost blood, no doubt.

The vampire's personal appearance was guaranteed to fill the observer with revulsion. It was deathly pale, and its eyes glinted with the fires of hell. Full red lips framed teeth that were white and gleaming, the long canines curving like fangs. The palms of the hands were hairy, the nails curved, crooked, and clotted with dried and blackened blood. The spectre's breath stank of the charnel house. At sight of this vision, the victim was said to subside into a trance-like sleep (a dead faint, more probably) whereupon the vampire first greedily kissed his or her throat and then sank its fangs deep into the jugular vein and drank the blood. The victim was usually left lethargic and weak, but still alive—for the time being, anyway—except if he was unfortunate enough to be embraced by one of the red-headed Children of Judas, who drained all his blood at a single gulp. In that case, the corpse would be left with three scars forming the Roman numeral XXX, signifying thirty pieces of silver or the price of a life.[24] When the vampire returned, sated, to its grave, it was no longer pale and lean but ruddy-cheeked, puffy and bloated. And what set the final seal on this marrow-freezing image was the state in which the vampire was found when its grave was opened.

In view of the number of possible candidates for vampirdom, it was of course necessary to decide which grave to open first. A young officer in the army of the Holy Roman Empire, stationed in south-east Hungary in the early 1730s, described how such a decision was made. 'They choose a young lad who is a virgin, that is to say, who they believe has never performed the sexual act. He is set upon a young stallion who has not yet mounted his first mare, who has never stumbled, and who must be coalblack without a speck of white. The steed is ridden into the cemetery, in and out among the graves, and the grave over which the steed refuses to pass despite the blows rained down on him is the one in which the vampire lies.'

When the grave was opened, no decaying body, no bundle of bones, was found. Instead, 'they find a sleek, fat corpse, as healthily-coloured as though the man were quietly and happily sleeping in calm repose. With one single blow of a sharp spade they cut off the head, whereupon there gush forth warm streams of blood rich red in colour and filling the whole grave. It would undoubtedly be supposed that they had just executed a fine sturdy fellow of the most sanguine habit and complexion.'[25] Some of these reputed vampires, however, had been underground for as much as thirty years.

Another imperial officer told a professor at Freiburg of his own investigations into the vampire phenomenon. A soldier, he said, stationed on the frontiers of Hungary, was sitting with his landlord at table one day when a stranger came in and joined them. Everyone appeared to be terrified, and next day the apparently healthy landlord died. The soldier asked what it was all about and was told that the stranger had been the landlord's father, dead and buried for more than ten years, who had come to tell his son of his impending end. The soldier repeated this story to his friends, and the officers of the regiment, hearing of it, appointed the Count of Cabreras to investigate. The count, attended by several other officers and with a surgeon and notary in tow, went to the house and took depositions. Everyone swore that the apparition had been the landlord's father, and that he had indeed been dead for years; other villagers confirmed it.

As a result, 'the body of the spectre was dug up and found to be in the same state as if it had just died, the blood like that of a living person. The Count of Cabreras ordered the head to be cut off and the corpse buried again.

'He then proceeded to take depositions about other apparitions of the same kind, and particularly about a man who had been dead for over thirty years and had visited his own house occasionally at mealtimes. On his first visit he had fastened upon the neck of his own brother and sucked his blood; on his second, he had treated one of his children in the same manner, and the third time, he fastened on a servant of the family. And all three had died instantly.' The Count had this vampire dug up, too, and he was found like the first, 'with his blood as fluid as if he had been alive'. A great nail was driven through his temple, and he was buried again.[26]

Although beheading the corpse or driving a nail through its

temple were perfectly canonical ways of dealing with a vampire, the most generally approved was to transfix it through the heart with a stake cut from an aspen, maple, or hawthorn tree. This had to be done at a single stroke; more than one blow would have the opposite of the desired effect. It was advisable to cut off the head as well, using a gravedigger's shovel, because it was said that in 1672, near Laibach, one vampire transfixed with a sharp thorn stake had pulled it out again and flung it scornfully back at his would-be exorcists.[27] Sometimes the body was burned, and sometimes the heart was boiled in oil or vinegar. Sometimes the vampire was bottled; in Bulgaria there were people who made a fulltime profession of vampire-bottling. The bottler's technique was to arm himself with an icon for protection, and then to pursue the vampire during its forays into the land of the living, manoeuvring it until it was cornered and had no place to go except into a bottle baited with a small quantity of blood. Once the vampire was in the bottle its persecutor popped the cork in, and that was that. Bottle and vampire together were consigned to the flames.[28]

A less energetic way of neutralising a vampire was to splash holy water on it, or to inter with it a fragment of the Host. But this, besides being less flamboyant (and perhaps less fun) than the other methods, also smacked of blasphemy and was frowned on by the Church. The vampire did, however, loathe garlic—strangely enough, since the general consensus was that his breath was so bad already that a little garlic would have been a positive improvement. If the mouth of a vampire were stuffed with garlic and further handfuls strewn around the coffin, its depredations were guaranteed to cease.*

The vampire belief that haunted the wide stretch of Europe between the Adriatic and the Black Sea in the last years of the seventeenth century and the first half of the eighteenth had a completeness, a unity about it that set it apart from similar beliefs in earlier periods of history. It had the well-

---

* In the mundane surroundings of the English town of Stoke-on-Trent in 1973, there was a pathetic reminder of this occult practice. A Polish immigrant of twenty-five years' standing still believed in vampires and the efficacy of garlic against them. He even went to sleep at night with a clove of garlic in his own mouth—and choked to death on it.[29]

rounded narrative logic of a work of fiction—which indeed it was. But it was a fiction that had written itself out of a composite of old fallacies and new facts.

The Balkan vampire, by definition, was a spirit that left its grave to gorge itself on the blood of the living, then returned to the grave to inhabit a body that did not decay. Among the vampire's ancestors were the demons of many lands. There were the *vetālas* of Vedic India, evil spirits who took up their abode in corpses, and the *ghuls* or ghouls of Arabic folklore, spectres who feasted on the living. There were the *lamiae* of ancient Greece and Rome, nebulous witches who sucked blood,* and the *strigae*, ghostly but lascivious, who raped people or drank their blood with cheerful impartiality. (In post-classical times, the names of *lamia* and *strix* or *striga* were transferred to living witches, to the detriment of the latter's reputation.) But the majority of vampire-like stories featured either straightforward ghosts with a liking for blood, or 'living ghouls', who were merely human beings with depraved tastes. Although writers on vampirism—reluctant to give a sucker an even break—are inclined to latch on to any blood-drinker they happen to encounter, the Scythians and Mongols, the alchemists and lepers, the Burgundian warriors and Hungarian noblewomen who drank blood for their own clear-cut purposes were no more vampires than the modern hospital patient who has a blood transfusion. Belief in the regenerative qualities of blood, a belief that was age-old and worldwide, may have been the most striking element in the vampire legend, but it was the form rather than the content of the legend that was characteristic.

There are, however, a handful of tales that anticipate the vampire legend almost in its entirety. They come from regions as far apart as England, China, and Baghdad, and all are highly suspect. The probability is that they represented no general belief but were individual and conscious works of fiction. The basic elements in the vampire legend—the evil spirit, the blood-sucking, and the unnatural condition of the dead—were all firmly entrenched in people's minds, and any

---

* Their name was derived from Lamia, the legendary queen of Libya, whose children were slain by Hera and who, in demented revenge, thereafter roamed the world sucking infants' blood.

good thriller-writer could have strung them together to make
a vampire. The fact that such tales are so few tends to confirm
that they were the product of single minds rather than of
popular nightmares.

One such story was told by the twelfth-century romancer,
Walter Map, who compiled a witty, discursive set of reminiscences entitled *Courtiers' Trifles*. According to Map there was
a Welsh wizard who was reported to return from the dead to
dine on his neighbours' blood. The clergy, at this time, were
constantly on the look-out for improving tales that could be
used to impress on their parishioners the dreadful consequences of an insufficiency of virtue. Map's work began to
circulate in 1180. In 1196, William of Newburgh, gathering
material from priests and deacons for a 'modern history' of
England, recorded what may well have been an adapted and
purposefully expanded version of Map's original tale.

The squire of Alnwick, said William, 'a stranger to God's
grace', after death began to issue forth from his tomb and
wander about the streets and into people's houses during the
night. 'The air became foul and tainted as this fetid and
corrupting body wandered abroad, so that a terrible plague
broke out . . . and presently the town, which a little while
before had been thickly populated, seemed to be well-nigh
deserted, for those who had survived the pestilence and these
hideous attacks hastily removed themselves to other districts
lest they also should perish.' William, in fact, seems to hold
the mere presence of the malignant spirit responsible for the
plague, and although he uses the epithet *sanguisuga* ('blood-
sucker') it may simply be meant metaphorically. However,
the young men of the town decided that action was necessary
and went off to the cemetery, armed with sharp spades. They
had scarcely begun to dig, when 'suddenly they came upon
the body covered with but a thin layer of earth. It was gorged
and swollen with frightful corpulence, and its face was florid
and full, with great red puffed-out cheeks. . . . They at once
dealt the corpse a sharp blow with the keen edge of the spade,
and immediately there gushed out such a river of warm red
blood that they realised this *sanguisuga* had battened on the
blood of many unfortunate souls. Accordingly, they dragged
it out of town and built a large pyre.'[30]

The Chinese were devotees of the detective story and thriller long before this form of literature became current in the West, and in Ming works in particular (sixteenth century) it is sometimes difficult to discover where fact shades into pure horror-film fiction. That the Chinese enjoyed having their blood curdled is evidenced by the following story, probably a furbished-up version of a real case. One morning, the wife of a man named Liu went to wake her husband and found in his bed only a headless corpse. There was—a real touch of imaginative genius—not a trace of blood. The local magistrate, whose manifold duties included detecting crime as well as punishing it, suspected the woman of murder and took her into custody, but two or three days later a neighbour gathering faggots on the hillside saw a huge coffin, its lid partly open, standing near an old, neglected grave. Summoning a number of villagers to provide moral support, he investigated the coffin and found inside a corpse with glaring red eyes, long white teeth, and bloodstained lips. Clutched in its bony hands was the head of the wretched Liu, sucked completely dry of blood. It proved impossible to remove the head from the corpse's grasp without severing the arms, and when this was done a great tide of blood welled out of the corpse until the coffin was awash. The magistrate ordered that the coffin and its tenant should be burned. Liu's widow was immediately released.[31]

In the *Arabian Nights* there are a number of almost-vampire tales, some of them stemming from India (from which the originals had reached Baghdad by the tenth century, or before). By the fifteenth century, when the following yarn is said first to have seen the light, the Arabs expected their 'entertainments' to be exuberantly sensational. The hero, in the present case, was a young man named Abdul Hassan who fell in love with and married a maiden of surpassing beauty *and* intellect. After several happy weeks, marred only by concern over his wife's birdlike appetite, Abdul Hassan discovered that she was in the habit of slipping from his bed at night and not returning until just before dawn. One night he followed her secretly, and was led to a remote cemetery. Gliding in pursuit, he peered into a tomb and saw his beautiful Nadilla seated round a table with a party of loathsome ghouls.

With every evidence of enjoyment, the entire company was munching away at a newly buried corpse. Abdul Hassan fled.

The following evening, when Nadilla declined to join him at supper, he flared out: 'So you prefer to keep your appetite for supper with the ghouls!' It was a mistake. When he had retired to bed and fallen asleep, his wife seized him by the throat, tore open a vein with her sharp nails, and began to drink his blood. Abdul Hassan awoke, seized a dagger, and plunged it in her heart. Next day she was buried, but three nights later reappeared in her husband's room at midnight and again went for his throat. This time, Abdul Hassan ran for it.

Nadilla's grave, when opened, revealed her body apparently asleep and floating in a sea of blood. The incensed widower confronted his father-in-law with this information, and was then told that Nadilla had been a vampire for quite some time, having been murdered several years earlier by a previous, equally angry husband! Abdul Hassan dug the lady up again and disposed of her once and for all by reducing her body to ashes.[32]

But stray stories from widely separated parts of the world provide no pedigree for the vampire epidemic that reached a peak in Hungary and the Balkans in the 1720s and '30s. People did try to account for it at the time—after all, the eighteenth century was doing its best to earn the title of the Age of Reason. Thoughtful men, however, were still inhibited by a belief in miracles. They did not so much wonder *whether* a vampire really left its grave to prey on the living; they wondered *how* it did so.

'How,' meditated Dom Calmet, 'can a corpse which is covered with four or five feet of earth, which has no room even to move or to stretch a limb, which is wrapped in linen cerements, enclosed in a coffin of wood, how can it, I say, seek the upper air and return to the world. . . . ? And after all that how can it go back again into the grave, when it will be found fresh, incorrupt, full of blood exactly like a living body? Can it be maintained that these corpses pass through the earth without disturbing it . . . ? Let us suppose that these corpses do not actually stir from their tombs, that only the ghosts or spirits appear to the living, wherefore do these phantoms

present themselves and what is it that energises them?* . . .
And if these bodies are spectral, how do they suck the blood
of the living?' The abbé ended up in a sad tangle, unable to
attribute everything to the machinations of the devil because,
according to dogma, the devil's powers were limited by what
God would permit.[34]

It is easy enough to dismiss the whole vampire phenomenon
as a product of fevered imaginations, peasant gullibility, and
morbid coincidence. But this puts too low a premium on the
quality of the human mind. There was undoubtedly some
concatenation of circumstances, even if only in a handful of
villages, that gave the legend a logical, believable start in life.
After that, it could indeed be sustained by coincidence and a
kind of infective hysteria, even by the activities of practical
jokers who switched crosses between old graves and new when
the imperial investigators hove portentously into sight.

There were, in essence, four basic components of the vampire belief—the lifelike state of the exhumed corpse; the presence of a malevolent spirit; the bloodsucking aspect; and the
death of the vampire's 'victims' from something resembling
acute anaemia. All, separately, are susceptible to reasonable,
non-magical explanations, though not, two and a half centuries
after the event, to anything resembling solid proof.

The imperial tribunals who dug up the lifelike vampire
corpses were on the alert for anything that might explain their
state of preservation. It was common knowledge that perfectly
ordinary corpses decomposed at different rates, and the
investigators did their best to make allowances for differences
in the preservative qualities of the soil. Their powers of
observation, however, were hampered by the difference of
opinion between the Roman and Orthodox Churches on the
spiritual meaning of lack of decomposition. Too many saints
had survived years of interment in perfect condition for the
Roman Church to be happy about the idea of vampires doing
the same. This may partly account for the investigators'

* Nineteenth-century spiritualists had an answer for that one. If a
body were buried too quickly, the astral soul might be caught only half-
way out. Terrified, it would retreat right back in again. Afterwards, the
theory was that it could go where it liked as long as it did not break the
phantasmal link connecting it with the body.[33]

highly libellous descriptions of the appearance of the corpses they dug up; it would have been disastrous if anyone had accused them of decapitating or transfixing a saint by mistake.

The most frequently canvassed possibility is that some of the disinterred corpses were lifelike because they were, quite simply, alive. The pages of medical history are studded with cases of premature burial. Patients in a state of catalepsy—a kind of suspended animation sometimes induced by self-hypnosis—have been buried alive, or come very near to it, on many occasions, and so have sufferers from epilepsy. The late-Victorian author William Tebb compiled from contemporary medical sources alone a list of 219 narrow escapes from being buried alive, 149 premature burials that actually took place, 10 cases where the body was dissected before life was extinct, 3 others where this very nearly happened, and 2 cases where the corpse revived when embalming had already begun. Nowadays, despite electrical tests to establish brain-death— a much surer indication than the apparent cessation of the heart—there are still frequent reports of people (usually victims of barbiturate poisoning) waking up in the morgue. In 1974, in Britain, a surgeon engaged in removing the kidneys from a 'dead' body was horrified to find the body coming back to life, while in the United States an awkward legal problem arose when a man was put on trial for murdering someone whose heart was still, in fact, beating when doctors removed it for transplant.[35] It is not difficult to conceive of similar accidents occurring in eighteenth-century Hungary.

How long a prematurely buried man can survive, only the dead can tell. There are ghastly tales of patients returning to consciousness and scrabbling bloodily at their coffins in a vain attempt to fight free. But on the whole, it seems likely that unless consciousness returned almost instantly after burial, those who were prematurely interred quickly suffocated as the small supply of oxygen in the coffin was used up. The cataleptic, however, because of the nature of his trance, might survive for some days. If his body were dug up and transfixed with a stake or decapitated, the blood would still flow as if he were alive—because he was.

One of the mysteries of the vampire epidemic is how the panic-stricken villagers (as they seem to have done) almost unerringly identified the graves of the undead, whose numbers must have been proportionately very small indeed. Possibly, in the plague-stricken atmosphere of the time, burials were indecently hasty, which would be quite enough to worry mourners who placed great dependence, as peasant societies almost invariably do, on the correct formalities. Possibly, too, in the earliest vampire cases—those that crystallised the legend—epileptics may have been involved. The epileptic, socially speaking, has had a hard time all the way through history, always being looked on with suspicion, and frequently regarded as a witch. It is conceivable that digging up a hurriedly buried 'witch' in the search for a vampire could have turned up an epileptic in an unusually protracted state of unconsciousness.

Once the vampire belief was established and the psychological pressures piled on, the people most susceptible to the belief would also be the type of people most susceptible to catalepsy. So when a vampire's 'victim' was dug up, on the principle that he or she, too, was a vampire, the diggers were quite likely to exhume someone who had retreated into a cataleptic trance.

That the undead were literally not dead was not, however, the only possibility. Normally, when someone dies, 'some hours after death the blood begins to coagulate or clot . . . and this is fairly complete some thirty hours after death. . . . Where, however, death is from suffocation or burns or certain poisons, the blood remains fluid longer and in some cases hardly changes at all, and if the body is moved or handled may flow. . . . [Or] when putrefaction has advanced to a certain stage, gas forms in the cavities of the body exerting great pressure, and the laying on of hands or putting fingers in wounds may loosen tiny clots and let the blood out.'*[36] Since suffocation or asphyxia can result not only from smothering or choking, but from the effects of carbon monoxide or benzene

---

* In some parts of Greece it was believed that the corpses of the evil did not disintegrate, 'but having, so it seems, a skin of extreme toughness become swollen and distended all over, so that the joints can scarcely be bent; the skin becomes stretched like the parchment of a drum, and when struck gives out the same sound, from which circumstance the *vrykolakas* [vampire] has received the name *tympaniaios* ("drum-like")'.[37]

poisoning, and even from a number of common diseases of the lungs or circulatory system, it is possible that the blood of quite a few of the genuinely dead in vampire country may still have remained fluid for some time after burial.

Too much attention need not be paid to the imperial investigators' reports of lifelike bodies dug up thirty years after death. In the more isolated parts of the eighteenth-century world, the resting place of the peasant dead (especially of the evil among them) was rarely marked by granite headstones. In a countryside constantly ridden over by advancing and retreating armies, where villages were sometimes abandoned for a time and then reoccupied, grave-markers may easily have been displaced. And the fact that the investigators who descended on such areas as southern Hungary had no knowledge of the local languages merely added to the confusion.

The second component of the vampire equation was the malignant spirit, and the question of why malignant spirits should have been abroad—in vampire or any other form—was one that could have been answered in so many different ways that, had the Church not chosen to make capital out of it, no one would have troubled to ask. Ever since man had first discovered the existence of the soul (see pages 10–11), he had been convinced of the existence of uneasy, often baleful, ghosts, souls that for any one of dozens of reasons had been prevented from making the transition from this world to the next. Generally, the ghost's physical form was relevant only in the sense that it mirrored its owner's shape at the moment of death—hence the decapitated aristocrat wandering the ramparts with its head tucked underneath its arm, and the aboriginal habit of cutting off a dead enemy's thumb so that his ghost will be unable to throw a spear.[38]

To the traditional catalogue of reasons why certain souls were unable to throw off their earthly bonds, the Christian Church had added excommunication and burial in unhallowed ground. Further, according to the doctrines of the Greek Orthodox Church, the body of someone who had been excommunicated did not decompose after death unless the corpse was granted absolution.* The Roman Church, on the other

---

* It raised something of a theological problem when it was discovered that the majority of excommunicated corpses decayed just

hand, held that God preserved only saintly corpses from decay. In practice the conflict was resolved by the conviction of the Roman Church that the devil rejoiced in parodying the works of the Lord—so if the bodies of the evil were preserved, it was a sure indication that Satan had been at work.

Under normal conditions, this kind of debate would simply have passed by the great mass of peasant worshippers, but conditions were far from normal on the southern borders of Hungary in the last years of the seventeenth century. For one hundred and fifty years the Turks had occupied large areas of Hungary; the Balkan states to the south for considerably longer. After 1459, when Serbia fell to the Islamic invaders, many Serbian peasants had moved north to the Danube, only to be overtaken by the Turkish irruption into Hungary. After 1686, when the Turks were driven out of Hungary again, the Serbs once more moved north into the territory of their Christian neighbours. But Hungarian Christians belonged to the Roman Church, while the Serbs were Orthodox; indeed, the latter found Rome less tolerant of their faith than the Muslims had been.

At the beginning of the eighteenth century, therefore, the devastated southern regions of Hungary were sparsely inhabited by native Magyar-speaking peoples, by Serbian and other immigrants from the Balkans, and by Germans imported by the Holy Roman Empire to colonise the empty spaces. There was a clash of languages, of nationalities, and of religions, the whole exacerbated by the determination of the Hapsburgs to favour the Germans and Serbs at the expense of the unruly Magyars, and of the Catholic Church to assert its dominance over the Orthodox Serbs.

In Hungary's southern border areas the 'vampires' who were investigated all had Slav names—were, in other words, Serbs or other aliens of the Orthodox persuasion.[40] What appears to have happened was that something convinced the local population that there was a plague of evil spirits around; that the theological argument over the state of excommunicated bodies translated itself, in the peasant mind, into a simple conviction

as effectively as those of the righteous. The problem was solved by deciding that if an excommunicant crumbled it meant he was already in hell and beyond hope of redemption.[39]

that Orthodox sinners (evil before and after death) had bodies that did not decay; and that these two beliefs, shored up by jealousy and the age-old habit of blaming the minority, led to the fusion of evil spirits, undecomposed bodies, and Orthodoxy. This was presumably the stimulus that first led to the digging up of graves—an activity essential to the history of vampirism, but one not usually indulged in without good reason in the ordinary course of events.

In the bloodsucking habits of the vampire, many commentators reared on a diet of Havelock Ellis and the Marquis de Sade have seen little more than sexual fantasising. Undoubtedly there was a strong sexual element in hallucinations about vampires, but so there was in many dreams about the dead; psychiatrists' files today remain littered with reports of women whose dead husbands have returned in the night to make love to them. Unless the peasant bedrooms of the Danube were swept by a sudden craze for the love-bite—which seems, on the whole, unlikely—a more substantial explanation has to be found.

The entire history of the world's belief in the blood as the life lay behind the vampire's kiss. But, almost certainly, this particular expression of it had a source in more recent experience. Contemporary commentators often mentioned that vampires attacked not only people but cattle and sheep, and though this is usually regarded as of secondary importance, it may in fact provide a useful clue.

For much of recorded history, cattle-herding peoples—and nomads in particular—had used the blood of living animals for food. In the ninth century, for example, a Chinese traveller recorded that people who lived south of the Gulf of Aden 'often stick a needle into the veins of cattle and draw blood, which they drink raw, mixed with milk'. The eleventh-century Byzantine scholar Michael Psellus said of the Patzinak tribes—who were Slavs, related to the Serbs—that when they were thirsty 'each man dismounts from his horse, opens its veins with a knife and drinks the blood'. Marco Polo and other travellers reported that the Mongols (or Tartars) did not burden themselves with provisions when they went on a journey, being accustomed to live on the blood of their horses —'every rider pierces a vein of his horse and drinks the blood'.

13. A Cranach woodcut, early sixteenth century, of a wild man making off with a baby.

14. A 1764 engraving showing the Beast of Gévaudan attacking a young girl.

15. A witches' sabbat, from *L'Histoire des Imaginations Extravagantes de Monsieur Oufle* by Abbé Laurent Bordelon, 1710.

16. "Hunger, Madness, and Crime." The artistic motivation of the nineteenth-century painter, Antoine Wiertz, was impeccable—his execution perhaps less so.

Even today, the Masai of Tanzania tap the jugular veins of their cattle or sheep by shooting a special arrow (which has a stop below the point to prevent it from penetrating too far) into the neck, draining off as much blood as they need, and then closing the wound with a plug.[41]

The eastern margins of Europe had been on the receiving end of nomad incursions from Central Asia for fifteen hundred years, off and on, and even when no major invasion was in progress stray bands of nomads were still liable to appear on the settled agricultural scene—like the unfortunate Tartars whose encounter with Vlad the Impaler was described on page 105. The people of Hungary and the Balkans must occasionally have watched the nomads sucking blood from the necks of their animals, and probably reacted in the same way as most 'civilised' peoples—with disgust and a kind of horrified fascination. It is the kind of detail that sticks in the mind, and it is easy to see how it might have been transplanted into the vampire legend. The Serbs themselves, when food was short, may even have resurrected the habits of their Patzinak ancestors; but whether they did or not, eastern Europe was familiar enough with the custom to prove receptive to the idea of the vampire's kiss.

But the question still remains—what was the catalyst that activated the vampire epidemic, what was the factual foundation on which these other facts, prejudices and superstitions built themselves up into a whole, beautifully mortared edifice of fear and legend? It had to be something unfamiliar and undiagnosed, something slightly uncanny, and producing a perceptible increase in the mortality rate in rural areas. The condition of the vampire's early victims must be the key—the apparently healthy people (in terms of the times) who for no recognisable reason turned pale and languid, suffered from abstraction and delusions, and then quietly lay down and, in the space of a few days or weeks, died.

The medical detectives who have diagnosed syphilis in King Henry VIII and porphyria in King George III might care to focus their microscopes on the problem of what killed the vampire's victims. Some form of anaemia, perhaps, sparked off by lead poisoning or exacerbated by a vitamin deficiency? By the beginning of the eighteenth century, lead was being used in eastern Europe not only for pots and pans but in local silver smelting and for decorative glassware. Lack of certain B vitamins can also be a crucial factor in anaemia, and maize—a comparatively new staple food in the Balkans at this time—is notorious for failing to provide other vitamins of the B complex. Or might it have been a type of leukemia? This can be caused by prolonged inhalation of benzene, which was a constituent of the wood tar that formed such a valuable byproduct of the pre-industrial charcoal heap. Or may there have been a few cases of fulminating tuberculosis in an area where the disease had previously been unknown? Or even a handful of people who, like the weak and fearful of modern New Guinea and Papua, pined away and died from the power of auto-suggestion?

Such illnesses as these could produce not only the appropriate symptoms; with some, the blood would also remain fluid for an unusually long time after death. But unless a specialist in medical jurisprudence bends his or her mind to the subject, the mystery of the vampire's death-dealing kiss will remain what it has been for so long, one of the hardest-worked and, for the entertainment industry, most profitable mysteries of all time.

CHAPTER SEVEN

Who's for Dinner?

'I HAVE been assured', said Jonathan Swift in 1728, 'by a very knowing American of my acquaintance in London, that a young healthy child well nurs'd, is, at a year old, a most delicious, nourishing, and wholesome food, whether stewed, roasted, baked, or boiled; and I make no doubt that it will equally serve in a fricassée, or a ragoût.'[1]

Swift, as much a giant among satirists as his Gulliver had been among Lilliputians, was intent on scourging the politicians and landlords who kept Ireland in a state of poverty and servitude and then complained that it was a nation of beggars and thieves. Swift's *Modest Proposal* was designed to reduce the beggary and thieving—and the population—by encouraging mothers to raise their children for a year and then sell them, at a small profit, to the landlords. 'I grant this food will be somewhat dear,' he admitted, estimating a selling price of 50p. ($1.25) per child, but it would still be perfectly suitable for landlords, 'who, as they have already devoured most of the parents, seem to have the best title to the children'. In fact, 'I believe no gentleman would repine to give ten shillings for the, carcase of a good fat child, which . . . will make four dishes of excellent nutritive meat'. The fore or hind quarter, he suggested, would 'make a reasonable dish, and seasoned with a little pepper or salt will be very good boiled on the fourth day, especially in winter'.[2]

Infants' flesh would be in season throughout the year, 'but more plentiful in March, and a little before and after, for we are told by a grave author, an eminent French physician, that fish being a prolific diet, there are more children born in Roman Catholic countries about nine months after Lent than at any other season'. Swift suggested that Dublin should have special shambles, or slaughterhouses, to deal with this new

137

baby food, which he felt certain would be extremely popular in taverns, 'where the vintners will certainly be so prudent as to procure the best receipts for dressing it to perfection, and consequently have their houses frequented by all the fine gentlemen who justly value themselves upon their knowledge in good eating; and a skilful cook, who understands how to oblige his guests, will contrive to make it as expensive as they please'.

In short, Swift concluded, there could be no serious objection to his 'modest proposal' which, at a stroke, solved most of the economic, social and gastronomic problems of Ireland. He looked forward to the day when 'a well-grown fat yearling child', roasted whole, would be the *pièce de résistance* at village revels and mayoral banquets alike.[3]

But cannibalism had by no means passed wholly into the realms of satire. Rather the contrary, especially when the eighteenth century gave way to the nineteenth and great numbers of ordinary people—many of them empire-builders (secular or religious)—found themselves far from home, trapped in situations they were not equipped for and could not control. Often, they came face to horrified face with genuine, practising cannibal tribes; sometimes they were lost or shipwrecked, and confronted with the alternative of eating the dead or of dying themselves. But the prim, well-padded nineteenth-century exterior concealed a mind that was remarkably tough, and an endurance that was sometimes little short of miraculous. The Victorians, in particular, did what they had to do, and (if possible) made money out of it afterwards.

There was, however, no profit for anyone in the first tragic saga of the century, the retreat of Napoleon's Grande Armée from Moscow, an army that at one stage numbered almost 600,000 men but was reduced in the end to no more than 30,000.[4] As the endless columns of hungry, exhausted, undisciplined French, Germans, Italians and Poles straggled back across the wintry plains of northern Russia, followed on a parallel route by the army of the Tsar and attacked at every opportunity by bands of peasant guerrillas, the men first cut steaks from the haunches of their cold-numbed horses as they plodded through the snow. When the horses at last died, they ate them. And when there were no more horses they ate their fellow soldiers. Even before Smolensk, when the weather by Russian standards was still comparatively mild, the Russian General Kreitz discovered some Frenchmen in a wood, eating the flesh of a dead comrade. 'Hunger has compelled them to eat horses' carcasses, and many of us have seen them roasting the flesh of their compatriots. . . . The Smolensk road is covered, at every step, with dead men and horses,' wrote another Russian from Elna in November. By December, 'witnesses such as Stein, the Muravievs, Fenschau and others . . . related that they had often met Frenchmen in some barn, sitting round a fire on the bodies of their dead comrades, from which they had cut the best parts to satisfy their hunger. Later, they grew weaker and weaker, and fell dead only to be eaten in turn by other comrades'. Before Vilna, twelve thousand men of a corps numbering fifteen thousand perished of cold and hunger in just three days. No one who lived through the last weeks of the retreat, who dragged himself over that final two hundred miles from the Berezina river to Kovno on the Polish frontier, ever succeeded in describing the experience. Always, the account broke off with the statement that no words were adequate to express the horrors of those days.[5]

Inability to find the right words was not one of the problems that beset the survivors of the wrecked French frigate, *La Méduse*, four years later. In their attempt to exact compensation from the government, they told all—and they told it in what is aptly known as *le style catastrophe-horreur!* For once, it was not a tale of noble suffering and sacrifice, but one of murderous out-and-out panic.

On July 2, 1816, the criminally incompetent captain of the *Méduse*—a government frigate carrying French soldiers and settlers to the colony of Senegal—ran his ship aground off the West African coast. When it became clear, two days later, that the ship would have to be abandoned, it proved impossible to load four hundred passengers and crew into the six lifeboats, which were of varying sizes and in varying stages of dilapidation. A sizeable raft was constructed to take one hundred and fifty persons. On July 5, the captain and senior officers piled into the more seaworthy boats and left the others to take their chance. Junior officers, soldiers, the ship's surgeon, a naval engineer, and a solitary woman were herded on to the raft, which was submerged to a depth of three feet by the time all one hundred and fifty were aboard. The boats began to tow the raft in the direction of the shore, but before they had gone very far the men in the boats cut the cables linking them to the raft's dead weight and left it wallowing at the mercy of wind and current, with no means of navigation, no food, and only a few casks of wine.

'All the soldiers and sailors,' recorded Savigny, the ship's surgeon, 'gave themselves up to despair, and it was with great difficulty that we succeeded in calming them.' Night fell, and the passengers huddled together, waist deep in water, terrified to move. The wind freshened, the waves rose, and next morning twenty were dead. Some had been swept away from the edges of the raft, but a dozen had caught their feet in the interstices between the planks in such a way that they could not rise again and were drowned.

The second day passed in foreboding and resentment. The waves rose higher and the raft lurched sluggishly in and out of the troughs. As darkness came, the men who had been clinging grimly to the slippery circumference began to press toward the safety of the centre. Bodies were crushed against bodies, hands scrabbled for a hold, feet scuffled for a space to rest on. And all in the unstable, menacing dark. The soldiers and sailors contrived to broach the wine casks and drank themselves, not into a stupor but into suicidal madness. One man with a hatchet began to cut the ties that bound the raft together. Some of the junior officers pushed forward to stop him, he threatened them with his hatchet, and was cut down by a sabre. Backed up against the mast, the officers and a number of passengers were soon fending off the knives and sabres of the lower ranks in a hideous, slithering, floundering, blind man's buff of a battle. Sixty-five men died, and there was scarcely one of the survivors who remained unwounded.

The third day dawned on a calm sea and a raft strewn with the dead and the exhausted, famished living. One or two tried to fish with improvised lines, but these caught under the raft. Then they tried to use bayonets as harpoons, but the dogfish had more strength than the fishermen and dragged the weapons out of their grasp. Some men tried to chew on their swordbelts, their clothing, the leather of their filthy hats. But it was no use. In the end, 'those whom death had spared in the disastrous night . . . threw themselves on the dead bodies with which the raft covered, cut them up in slices, which some even that instant devoured'. Some passengers, said Savigny, 'at first refused to touch the horrible food; but at last, yielding to a want still more pressing than that of humanity, we saw in this frightful repast the only deplorable means of prolonging existence; and I proposed, I acknowledge it, to dry these bleeding limbs, in order to render them a little more supportable to the taste. Some, however, had still courage enough to abstain from it, and to them a larger quantity of wine was granted.'[6]

On the morning of July 8, the fourth day, some of the junior officers found an ounce of gunpowder, a tinderbox and flint, and began trying to set alight some pieces of dry rag. They staved in a cask, lined it with damp cloths to prevent it from bursting into flames, rested a keg inside to hold the smouldering rags, and placed a hearthstone on top. On it they cooked some human flesh, and this time everyone ate it. In the evening, they contrived to catch and cook some flying fish. But then the fire went out. It could not be lit again.[7]

By the sixth day, hunger and thirst, exposure to the African sun, insanity, and 'executions' for wine-stealing had reduced the number on the raft to twenty-eight. 'Out of this number,' said Savigny, 'fifteen alone appeared able to exist for some days longer; all the others, covered with large wounds, had wholly lost their reason. However, they had a share in our rations, and might, before their death, consume forty bottles of wine; those forty bottles of wine were to us of inestimable value. We held a council; to put the sick on half rations was to delay their death by a few moments; to leave them without provisions was to put them to a slow death. After a long deliberation, we resolved to throw them into the sea. This mode, however repugnant to our feelings, would procure to the survivors provisions for six days, at the rate of three quarts of wine a day. . . . Three seamen and a soldier took upon themselves this cruel execution. We averted our eyes, and shed tears of blood over the fate of these unhappy creatures'.[8]

One week later, the fifteen survivors were saved by the brig *Argus*, but five of them died soon after reaching land.

Savigny and the engineer Corréard tried and failed to win compensation from the government. Having provoked a major political scandal by their revelation of the ineptitude and cowardice of the royalist captain of *La Méduse*, they were instead hounded and harassed, fined, and sacked from government service. Their response was to write, not a report, but a book. It was published at the end of 1817, and proved a runaway success. One man who read it was Théodore Géricault, and the result was that splendid example of Romantic art, the vast canvas of the 'Raft of the Medusa' (see illustration no. 17).

Cannibalism in Europe, Africa—and America. The New World had its share of solitary eccentrics like Jeremiah Johnson, the mountain man who wandered the unexplored West in the early nineteenth century, living off the land and the livers of Crow Indians (247 of them). But the land could be as dangerous as the sea for those who were not acquainted with the way of the wilds. When America began to expand across Indian and Mexican territory to the west coast of the continent, there were few trails through the high mountains and inhospitable plains and many of the settlers who attempted to blaze new ones paid for the attempt with their lives.

In August 1846 a party of twenty-three vehicles, carrying twenty-six men, three of them elderly, fourteen women, and forty-four children under eighteen, began to battle through the Wasatch mountains of Utah on a so-called short cut, or cut-off, route to California. Led by George Donner, the party struggled at a rate of little more than a mile a day, man-handling boulders, hacking at vegetation, shovelling, clearing a path for the wagons, until at last they emerged on an open plain—eighty waterless miles of scorching, blinding white salt desert. They cut grass, filled every vessel they had with water, and ventured on. Some of their thirst-crazed cattle stampeded and were lost. Soon, the animals drawing the wagons lay down and would not move. But some of the men pressed forward driving the unyoked draught animals before them to where there was water, and then back to the stranded women and children.

The Donner party survived the salt desert and crept on through Indian country. One man had already died, two more were murdered as tempers grew short, another was accidentally shot, and a fifth was left behind to die when his strength failed. One of the murderers was banished from the company, sent to ride alone. One man pushed ahead to Sutter's Fort and returned with food and two Indian helpers. But by now it was mid-October and down from the Gulf of Alaska swept the first of the storms that batter the Pacific coast in winter. It caught the Donner party just short of the Sierra Nevada summit.

Some of the party found an abandoned cabin and succeeded in building additional huts by what is now known as Donner Lake. Those who lagged behind, including the Donners themselves, made a camp of shanties covered with wagon canvas and buffalo robes five miles back down the trail. The oxen and horses strayed away and vanished. Relentlessly the huge fluffy snowflakes swirled down. Christmas came and went.

Having contrived some makeshift snowshoes, ten men, two boys and five women set out from the camp on the trail in an attempt to reach the summit. Two turned back. The others fought on through the blizzards. One man went mad. Four others died. It had been five days since any of the group had eaten. But they ate now. Later, another man went mad and killed the two Indians of the party. Thirty-three days after they had left the camp on the trail, one man, one boy, and five women stumbled into an Indian camp—and safety.

When rescue parties broke through to the cabin by the lake and to the trail camp, they found there, too, the grim evidence of cannibalism. Without this recourse, none of the Donner party would have survived. As it was, some of the children died even as they were being carried down the mountains on the backs of their rescuers. But half the party lived to see California.[9] In the village of San Juan Bautista there still stands the sedately pretty house in which one family, the Breens, settled down and built a new life after the icy hell of the Sierra Nevada.

Light relief is rare in the annals of cannibalism, but one enterprising lady in the 1830s succeeded in turning her dreadful sufferings at the hands of cannibals into something very close to farce. A contemporary London broadsheet conveniently summed up the first part of her story:

> The Stirling Castle on May 16th
> From Sydney she set sail,
> The crew consisting of twenty,
> With a sweet and pleasant gale.
> Likewise Captain Fraser of the ship,
> On board he had his wife,
> And now, how dreadful for to tell,
> The sacrifice of human life.
>
> Part of the crew got in one boat,
> Thinking their lives to save,
> But in a moment they were dash'd
> Beneath the foaming waves.
> And Mrs Fraser in another boat,
> Far advanc'd in pregnant state,
> Gave birth unto a lovely babe.
> How shocking to relate.
>
> And when they reach'd THE FATAL SHORE,
> Its name is call'd Wide Bay,
> The savages soon them espied,
> Rush'd down and siez'd [*sic*] their prey,
> And bore their victims in the boat,
> Into their savage den,
> To describe the feelings of those poor souls
> Is past the art of man.
>
> This female still was doom'd to see,
> A deed more dark and drear,
> Her husband pierc'd was to the heart,
> By a savage with his spear.
> She flew unto his dying frame,
> And the spear she did pull out,
> And like a frantic maniac,
> Distracted flew about . . .[10]

'Distracted' was an improbable adjective to apply to Eliza

Fraser, a strong-minded woman of thirty-seven with fine eyes, a commanding nose, and an air of resolute calm. Even when, clad only in a sou'wester hat and a figleaf of flowering sea-grapes, she was dragged off to the nearest tribal settlement, she still did her best to maintain her dignity. As her biographer justly remarked, if circumstances had been different she would have been in her element teaching needlework and hygiene to the flat-nosed, mop-haired, feather-bedecked Kabi women. As it was, she had a difficult, frightening, and thoroughly uncomfortable time, learning to climb trees, raid wild bees' nests, grub for roots, and dive for lily bulbs. She was beaten, burned with firesticks, used as target practice by children learning to throw boomerangs, and bitten by every abominable insect on Australia's Pacific coast. But she was not eaten, nor offered human flesh to eat—unlike another member of the crew, who had been appropriated by a different branch of the tribe. John Baxter, a nephew of the deceased Captain Fraser, said that he saw a father strike his son for taking, unbidden, a piece of fish. 'I afterwards saw the boy dead, and they put part of the flesh to the fire and afterwards ate it. They offered me the heart and part of the liver'—a sardonic gesture that implied Baxter would be the better for some strength and courage—'and then dragged me about by the hair when I refused.'

Mrs Fraser's miseries lasted for about six weeks, after which she was rescued by an army lieutenant who was having a few days' holiday at sea in a ship manned by a convict crew. One of the convicts knew the natives and literally talked Mrs Fraser out of the encampment and into the rescue boat.

Back in Sydney, Mrs Fraser became something of a celebrity. She was installed at the home of a high government official, attended numerous tea parties and picnics, dined out on her experiences, and profited by about £400 ($1000) subscribed for her benefit by the local worthies. On February 25, 1837, six months after her rescue, Mrs Fraser set sail for England as a passenger in the *Mediterranean Packet*, whose captain was one Alexander John Greene.

In July she reached Liverpool and threw herself on the mercy of anyone in authority who would listen. She was in great financial distress, she said, and required assistance to go to London. At the Parish Office, she 'recapitulated the details of her shipwreck in the Stirling Castle and subsequent privations and sufferings. In reply to some questions put to her respecting the savages with whom she professed to have been so long domiciled, she detailed a few particulars, compared with which the marvels witnessed by the renowned Mr Lemuel Gulliver would be very commonplace matters indeed.' But Liverpool was unproductive, and Mrs Fraser contrived to find her own way to London—where she requested the Colonial Office to subsidise her. The Colonial Office also proved unhelpful.

Not so the Lord Mayor of London. A public subscription was launched, the press turned out in force, and Mrs Fraser was soon the talk of the town. The Lord Mayor's fund brought in £553 ($1382.50), quite a substantial sum in days when a fair living wage was £2 ($5) a week.

But Mrs Fraser, in the end, received only £50 ($125), most of the rest being put in trust for the three children she had left behind in Orkney when she set off for Australia. The Lord Mayor, to his extreme embarrassment, had discovered not only that she had left Sydney considerably the richer for her distressing experiences—but as the newly wed wife of Alexander John Greene, captain of the *Mediterranean Packet.*

Some time after, London was edified by the sight of an advertising man in Hyde Park bearing a large poster decorated with a garish painting of savages with bows and arrows, the corpses of some white men and women in the process of being carved up, and other savages spitroasting pieces of them over a huge fire. The legend read: '*Stirling Castle* wrecked off the coast of New Holland, Botany Bay, all killed and eaten by savages: Only survivor a woman: To be seen: 6d admission.'

Was it Eliza sitting in the booth while her captain raked in the sixpences, or an impostor cashing in on her fame? Whichever it was, twenty-two years after her adventures on the Fatal Shore, Mrs Fraser died prosaically enough in a carriage accident in Melbourne, Australia, where she and her second husband had finally settled and lived a blameless life.[11]

In the intervening years, the civilised world had become almost blasé about cannibals. Mrs Fraser's experiences would by now have appeared very tame indeed in comparison with the revelations of the missionaries who had marched off, armoured in faith, innocence, and fortitude, into the darkest corners of the darkest continents. Scarcely a month passed without the public being told bloodcurdling tales about the habits of newly discovered heathen tribes, and asked to subscribe to their salvation. The trouble was that though God's mercy might be sufficient reward for the missionary, it was not so for the printer. Bibles had to be paid for, and the more benighted the heathen, the more freely did the money flow from the churchgoers of Europe and America. Genuinely appalled though they were by the customs of the tribes they had gone to convert, the missionaries still had a subconscious eye on the collection plate when they compiled their reports for home.

The tone of missionary endeavour was admirably conveyed by this 1836 appeal on behalf of the Fijians:

Men and Brethren, To your sympathy this Appeal is made, and your help is implored on behalf of a most interesting but deeply depraved people, the inhabitants of the group of islands called FEEGEE, little known to the civilised world except for the extreme danger to which vessels touching at them are exposed, from the murderous propensities of the islanders, and for the horrid CANNIBALISM to which they are addicted. . . .

In FEEGEE, cannibalism is not an occasional but a constant practice; not indulged in from a species of horrid revenge, but from an absolute preference for human flesh over all other food.

It is on behalf of this cannibal race that we appeal to you. Let all the horrors of a CANNIBAL FEAST be present to your minds while you read. . . . Pity CANNIBAL FEEGEE, and do so quickly. Come, then, ye Christians, and teach the poor, idolatrous, war-loving, man-devouring FEEGEEANS better things. . . .

We spare you the details of a cannibal feast: the previous murders, the mode of *cooking* human beings, the assembled crowd of all ranks, all ages, both sexes, Chiefs and people, men, women, and *children*, anticipating the feast with horrid glee. The actual feast. The attendants bringing into the circle BAKED HUMAN BEINGS—not one, not two, nor ten but twenty, thirty, forty, fifty at a single feast! . . . The writer of this APPEAL has himself conversed with persons who have seen forty and fifty eaten at a single sitting—eaten without anything like disgust; eaten indeed with a high relish! . . .[12]

It was all splendidly emotive, just the thing to titillate the imagination of the stay-at-home, to send a pleasurable tingle down the spine—and to loosen the purse-strings.

The nineteenth-century missionaries were extraordinary people but scarcely ideal witnesses. They were separated from their potential flocks not only by their religious beliefs and their Victorian ethos, but by a five-thousand-year gap in human understanding. Most of them were constitutionally incapable of even attempting to enter into the lives or minds of the tribals—fortunately, perhaps, for the emotional consequences would have been traumatic. Instead, they preserved their detachment, and (however unwittingly) admitted defeat, by taking on the role of a kindly father dealing with recalcitrant children.

What they saw, they could report on truthfully if without comprehension. But a great many of their most horrific tales were prefaced by the words: 'It is said'. Correctly interpreted, this meant: 'I think it is said', for the language difficulty was acute during the early encounters between missionaries and newly discovered tribes. Further, the missionaries were not as yet aware that in closed societies the puzzled native nearly always answers his interlocutor's questions by telling him what he thinks he wants to hear. Nor did they recognise that converts, *plus royaliste que le roi*, revelled in testifying against those who remained unenlightened. In a word, the missionaries had problems.

It must be admitted, however, that few of the tribes who were marked down for conversion were conspicuous for their charm. Until the arrival of the Europeans, for example, the only animals indigenous to Fiji were rats, and cannibalism had probably developed to satisfy a genuine need for flesh food (besides acting as a simple method of population control). But what the missionaries found so repulsive about the Fijians' cannibalism was the joviality with which they indulged it. In one case, reported by a Methodist missionary named Jaggar in 1844, 'the men doomed to death were made to dig a hole in the earth for the purpose of making a native oven, and were then required to cut firewood *to roast their own bodies*. They were then directed to go and wash, and afterwards to make a cup of banana leaf. This, from opening a vein in each man, was soon filled with blood. This blood was then drunk, *in the presence of the sufferers*, by the Kamba people.

'Seru, the Bau chief, then had their arms and legs cut off, cooked and eaten, some of the flesh being presented to them. He then ordered a fish-hook to be put into their tongues, which were then drawn out as far as possible before being cut off. These were roasted and eaten, to the taunts of "We are eating your tongues!" As life in the victims was still not extinct, an incision was made in the side of each man, and his bowels taken out. This soon terminated their sufferings in this world.'[13] The Reverend Mr Jaggar heard this gory saga from a convert who had refused to stay and watch it.

Two years later, the Reverend John Watsford—substituting short, snappy sentences for his colleague's italics, but equally dependent on hearsay—wrote: 'We do not, and we cannot, tell you all that we know of Feegeean cruelty and crime. Every fresh act seems to rise above the last. A chief at Rakeraki had a box in which he kept human flesh. Legs and arms were salted for him and thus preserved in this box. If he saw anyone, even if of his friends, who was fatter than the rest, he had him—or her—killed at once, and part roasted and part preserved. His people declared that he eats human flesh every day. At Bau, the people preserve human flesh and chew it as some chew tobacco.'[14]

Fijians clearly enjoyed human flesh for its own sake. Even when pigs and poultry were introduced to the islands, they continued to prefer long pig (*puaka balava*) to real pig (*puaka dina*). But gluttony was not quite the whole story. The violence of their pursuit and preparation of victims may have represented hooliganism in an extreme form; nevertheless, the heads of their victims were duly turned over to the priests for use in religious ceremonies, and some of those who died were killed specifically because of the need for building sacrifices not dissimilar to those of the ancient Near East and mediaeval Europe (see pages 29–30), especially when canoes—more important than buildings to islanders—were under construction.

It is, of course, unfair to condemn missionaries for being men of their time, the product of hundreds of years of a particular kind of conditioning process. However much their blindness may irritate and their rectitude jar, they suffered the most acute discomforts and dangers for what they believed in. Unfortunately, the obverse of faith is credulity. They went to their far-flung missions prepared to believe the worst, and because of it heard, and believed, the worst. It was the missionaries who were largely responsible for codifying the traditions of primitive tribes into the doctrine of what Rudyard Kipling later defined as The White Man's Burden:*

> Take up the White Man's burden—
> 　Send forth the best ye breed—
> Go bind your sons to exile
> 　To serve your captives' need;
> To wait in heavy harness,
> 　On fluttered folk and wild—
> Your new-caught, sullen peoples,
> 　Half-devil and half-child. . . .
>
> Take up the White Man's burden—
> 　And reap his old reward:
> The blame of those ye better,
> 　The hate of those ye guard—
> The cry of hosts ye humour
> 　(Ah, slowly!) toward the light:—
> 'Why brought ye us from bondage,
> 　Our loved Egyptian night?'[15]

In other words, a doctrine of pained paternal despotism.

As the nineteenth-century scramble for empire intensified, the number of 'new-caught, sullen peoples' increased, and colonial administrators and diplomats, travellers and traders, began to vie with the missionaries in publishing grisly tales to divert the reading public. Every continent (except Europe), every chain of islands, produced its crop of ritual cannibals.

In Samoa, it was usually only enemies who were eaten, as a

* When he was suggesting that it was time for America to take up the burden in the Philippines.

final satisfaction of revenge. The worst insult that could be paid to a Samoan was to talk of roasting him—which meant that missionaries had to guard their tongues and leave hellfire out of their sermons. In the Marquesas islands, north-east of Tahiti, revenge was also the main reason for cannibalism, although one doctor later argued that the suppression of cannibalism was responsible for the depopulation of the islands, as it deprived the people of an important source of protein. In the islands of the New Hebrides, the tribes ate enemies and sometimes exchanged non-inimical corpses; a case of exophagy, of never eating members of one's own tribe.[16]

The aborigines of Australia—who maintained their Stone Age way of life until well into the twentieth century—ate human flesh for a great number of reasons. It was a sacrificial ritual, it was good magic, a symbol of revenge, a sign of respect for the dead; it gave strength and courage, and some tribes are said to have believed that it was what led women to conceive. The life of the dead man passed into the woman's body from which it was born again.[17]

Sensitive, emotional, often gentle, the Australian aborigine differed greatly from the Maori of New Zealand, whose wars and cannibalism were marked by the same jaunty ferociousness as those of the Fijians. Absorbing an enemy's strength was, again, the main motive, although one authority declared that a prolonged diet of vegetable food tended to encourage the despatch of raiding parties in search of stray humans to brighten up the menu. Certainly, a New Zealand chief who was imported to London in 1818 and lived there for some years confessed that what he missed most about home 'was the feast of human flesh, the feast of victory. He was weary of eating English beef. . . . The flesh of women and children was to him and his fellow-countrymen the most delicious, while certain Maoris prefer that of a man of fifty, and that of a black rather than that of a white. His countrymen, Touai said, never ate the flesh raw, and preserved the fat of the rump for the purpose of dressing their sweet potatoes.' Touai also remarked that missionaries who feared they might be popped in a cooking cauldron really had very little to worry about. A hungry Maori would be more likely to go to a neighbouring tribe for his dinner, since black men had a much more agreeable flavour than white. Nevertheless, the Maoris did manage to force a white man down occasionally. When they killed a certain Captain Grant during the course of 'Heke's war', they dried and ate his flesh in an attempt to reduce the *mana*, or supernatural powers, of his surviving troops.[18]

In Sumatra, ritual cannibalism took on the trappings of a judicial system. The Batak tribe ate anyone who had committed adultery with one of their sovereign's wives, who was a traitor, a spy, a deserter, or a member of an attacking war party. The victim's relatives had to supply salt and lime for dressing the flesh; this participation in the punishment ruled out any possibility of a subsequent vendetta.[19]

China, racked and torn by the ambitions of the imperial powers, saw a despairing revival of the old belief in the strength-giving properties of flesh and blood. In Kwang-si and Yunnan, the southerly provinces bordering on Indo-China, there were reports that the heart and brains of a Catholic missionary and of a celebrated robber had been extracted and eaten. In the 1890s, it was said that 'no Chinese soldier in Tonking during the late war lost an opportunity to eat the flesh of a fallen French foe, believing that human flesh, especially that of foreign warriors, is the best possible stimulant for a man's courage'. In 1901, the inhabitants of one area of Kwang-si boiled and ate a Chinese officer who had been sent (unsuccessfully) to pacify them.[20]

In a country where filial piety was regarded as one of the cardinal virtues, sons and daughters were sometimes known to give their own flesh or blood to their parents. In the 1870s, two cases were reported in Chinese newspapers, one in which a son cut a piece of flesh from his arm to make soup for his ailing mother (who recovered), and the other concerning a girl who placed a piece of her own flesh in her dying father's medicine. He, too, recovered. When he went to his ancestors ten years later, the girl pined away and died. The deputy governor of Honan province then petitioned the emperor to erect a triumphal arch to her memory, and the petition was granted.[21]

By way of contrast, there was an early Women's Lib. group in China in the 1870s which made magical use of the blood of unborn infants. It was incorporated in a charm against husbands by a 'set of young unmarried women, comprising a sisterhood who are sworn never to marry. If forced by their parents to do so, they then employ this charm to destroy their husbands in order to remain single and be faithful to the oaths of the sisterhood.'[22]

The British in India found themselves with a string of cannibal tribes to govern. There were the Gonds of Madhya Pradesh, the headhunting Nagas, and the Khonds of Orissa who fertilised their fields with human flesh (see page 21). There were others, also, but the British were on the whole too much concerned with what they regarded as general evils to devote much time to local ones (many of which could be expected to, and did, die out in the face of expanding law enforcement routines). Among their more urgent problems in the 1820s and '30s was that of the Thugs, a sect of religious murderers whose tentacles stretched all over central India and whose activities were seen at the time as the greatest criminal conspiracy in history. From first to last, they were estimated to have murdered a million travellers and wayfarers.

The Thugs were not cannibals, and they went to extreme lengths to avoid shedding blood—but their story has, briefly, a place here because the whole edifice of their belief was built on the supernatural power of blood. In the youth of the world there arose 'the demon of blood and seed'. As the Creator created men, so this demon destroyed them. But the goddess Kali went out, in turn, to destroy him. She struck at him with her avenging sword and his flesh was cut deep so that his blood welled out from it and splashed to the earth. Then from each drop of blood there arose another demon, armed to kill the men the Creator created. Kali struck at them, too, and from every drop of their blood rose yet another demon. Kali struck, the demons bled, other demons sprang up. At last Kali rested, and wiped the sweat from her arms with a handkerchief. Two drops of sweat fell to the earth, and from them the Creator fashioned two men. Kali said to them: 'Take my handkerchief and kill the demons of blood and seed so that no drop falls to the earth.' And the men took the handkerchief (the *rumal*) and travelled the earth, strangling the demons with it. At last, they were able to report to Kali that none re-mained. As a reward, she permitted them to keep the *rumal* and told them to use it to live. However many men they killed with it, she said, all mankind owed them a living.

For hundreds of years the Thugs operated as a secret society of whose existence everyone except the country's rulers was aware. The initiates would slip from their homes at night and disappear for a week or two, usually in the cool season when merchants and travellers took to India's dusty roads, many of them never to see home again. They were waylaid by Thug bands, murdered with the *rumal*, robbed and buried. Ironically enough, Thuggee was discovered and wiped out by the British only a few years before its operations would in any case have been brought to an end by the coming of the railroads and the telegraph.[23]

Europeans in Africa were deeply offended to discover that here, in what they saw as the heartland of unregenerate cannibalism, they themselves were thought to be cannibals. When Mungo Park, one of the first great modern explorers of the Dark Continent, encountered a *coffle* (or chain) of slaves destined for sale to the highest bidder, 'they viewed me at first with looks of horror, and repeatedly asked if my country-men were cannibals'. This was in 1797, when the slave trade to America was still in full flow, and there was 'a deeply rooted idea that the whites purchase negroes for the purpose of devouring them, or of selling them to others, that they may be devoured hereafter, [which] naturally makes the slaves contemplate a journey towards the coast with great terror'.[24]

What shocked Europeans most in Africa was the report that human flesh was sold in the markets as freely as if it were beef or mutton. In 1700 a traveller named Barbot said that on the west coast all prisoners of war, unless they could be disposed of alive for a greater profit, were fattened up and then sold to butchers for slaughter, while in the late nineteenth century it was stated in a Sierra Leone newspaper, 'on the authority of Mr Priddy, a missionary of the Countess of Huntingdon's Connection in that colony, not that *he had heard of*, but *that he had seen* hampers of dried human flesh carried about on men's backs, to be sold for eating purposes, in the progress of a recent civil war between the Soosoo and Tisnney tribes'.[25]

The motives for cannibalism in Africa were numerous. In many cases it may have arisen from a basic need for protein food, but there were undoubtedly tribes such as the Mambila who ate human flesh for the very simple reason that they liked it. Some Nigerian tribes claimed that human flesh was by far the most succulent of meats, though monkey was almost as good. The palms, fingers and toes made the best eating,* but the Bafum-Bansaw had a technique for improving the rest of the carcase by pumping palm oil into it and leaving it to marinate. Generally, tribes who ate human flesh for other than religious reasons avoided making inroads into their own villages. Most were like the Bondjo, who lived at the confluence of the rivers Congo and Ubangui and bought slaves from neighbouring tribes when they ran out of prisoners of war.[26]

Sacrificial and ceremonial cannibalism was almost universal in some parts of West Africa, and judicial cannibalism or blood-drinking was also common. But the economic cannibalism of the Bobos of the western Sudan struck something of a new note. There was one story published in the 1880s of a man who went on a business trip, leaving his wife with a Bobo friend. When he returned home, his friend handed over to him not his wife but the sum of 60,000 cowries (shells used as money). The friend explained that the woman had fallen ill and begun to lose weight; and as he did not want her husband to lose money on her, he had killed her and sold her in the market before she became too thin to fetch a good price.[27]

In the Americas, too, there were reports of tribal cannibalism, though these became rarer as the nineteenth century progressed and the landscape filled up with immigrants. The Dakota Indians, for example, were said to be cannibal only 'when a warrior, after slaying a foe, eats, porcupine-like, the heart or liver, with the idea of increasing his own courage'. But in the Rockies, near Fort Halkett, there was a tribe known as the Dueldeli-ottiné (men of blood) to whom famine was so routine that they had become quite accustomed to endophagy,

* The Fijians would have disagreed here. They preferred the heart, thighs, and upper arms.

to eating parents, children and friends who had died of hunger. The Eskimos, similarly, were sometimes reduced to cannibalism, but looked back on it with shame and concealed it like a crime. In South America, however, there were still a great number of tribes who continued in their prehistoric belief in the virtues of flesh, blood and spirit. The women of the Chavantes tribe on the river Uruguay, for example, ate the bodies of their children in order to re-absorb their souls, particularly in the case of very young mothers who were thought to have given away some of their own soul-stuff to their children too soon for their health.[28]

But the slaves who had been brought from the west coast of Africa to labour in the southern states, the Caribbean and Brazil, reintroduced cannibalism to areas from which it had virtually disappeared. African traditions overlaid with the proselytising of Catholicism created that hypnotic, secretive cult known as voodoo.

Voodoo, as might have been expected, went down well with the Victorians. It had all the right ingredients—blood, sinister rituals, the living dead (zombies), and, for good measure, a few 'nameless horrors'. It was particularly strong in Haiti, which had thrown off the French yoke in the early nineteenth century to become an independent republic. 'In general,' remarked Her Britannic Majesty's consul-general there in the 1860s, 'when incidents are spoken of in society in Hayti relating to the Vaudoux worship, Haytian gentlemen endeavour to turn the conversation, or they say you have been imposed upon, or the events have been exaggerated.' Nevertheless, although a white cock or a white kid was the usual victim in voodoo sacrifices, there were undoubtedly occasions when only a 'goat-without-horns' (a girl child) would do.

The consul-general was suspicious of most of the stories he heard, even in court, because 'the French procedure is observed in all trials in Hayti, and to an Englishman the procedure, as practised in that republic, is contrary to the first principles of justice. The prisoners were bullied, cajoled, crossquestioned, in order to force avowals, in fact, to make them state in open court what they were said to have confessed in their preliminary examinations. I can never forget the manner in which the youngest female prisoner turned to the public prosecutor and said, "Yes, I did confess what you assert, but remember how cruelly I was beaten before I said a word". . . . That prisoners are tortured to make them confess is known to be a common practice in Hayti.'[29] Despite his cynicism, however, Sir Spenser St John could not resist describing one trial at which he had been present.

Near Port-au-Prince there lived a man called Congo Pellé who 'was anxious to improve his position without any exertion on his own part'. He consulted his sister Jeanne and certain of her voodoo friends, and it was decided that their niece Claircine, twelve years of age, should be sacrificed. The child was duly kidnapped and on New Year's Eve a large party assembled at Jeanne's house for the occasion. The child was thrown to the ground and ceremonially strangled by one of the 'papaloi' (priests), Floréal. 'Then Jeanne handed him a large knife, with which he cut off Claircine's head, the assistants catching the blood in a jar; then Floréal is said to have inserted an instrument under the child's skin, and detached it from the body. Having succeeded in flaying their victim, the flesh was cut from the bones, and placed in large wooden dishes; the entrails and skin being buried near to the cottage. The whole party then started for Floréal's house, carrying the remains of their victim with them. On their arrival Jeanne rang a little bell, and a procession was formed, the head borne aloft, and a sacred song sung. Then preparations were made for a feast.'

Peering through some chinks in the wall, a woman and girl sleeping next door saw what happened next, and watched 'Jeanne cooking the flesh with congo beans, small and rather bitter, whilst Floréal put the head into a pot with yams to make some soup. Whilst the others were engaged in the kitchen, one of the women present, Roséide Sumera, urged by the fearful appetite of a cannibal, cut from the child's palm a piece of flesh and ate it raw (this I heard her avow in open court).

'The cooking over, portions of the prepared dish were handed round, of which all present partook; and the soup being ready, it was divided among the assistants, who deliberately drank it. The night was passed in dancing, drinking and debauchery. In the morning the remains of the flesh were warmed up, and the two witnesses who had watched the proceedings were invited to join in the repast: the young woman confessed that she had accepted the invitation, but the girl did not.' This girl, in fact, was next on the sacrificial list but was saved during the course of a police search for the missing Claircine.

Fourteen people were arrested and eight of them brought to trial. Jeanne said that 'she had only been practising what had been taught her by her mother as the religion of her ancestors. "Why should I be put to death for observing our ancient customs?" They were all found guilty of sorcery, torture, and murder, and condemned to death.' Death by target practice, for the firing squads of five soldiers to each two prisoners were so inefficient that it took them fully half an hour to complete their work. In the morning, three of the graves were found empty. The bodies of the two voodoo priests and the priestess had disappeared.

For years after, remarked Spenser St John laconically, 'congo beans were forbidden at our table'.[30]

With all this going on in the real-life world, fictional cannibals and vampires like Sweeney Todd and Count Dracula faced some stiff competition in the bookshops. But horror fiction had been firmly established since the late eighteenth century, an offshoot of that passion for the picturesque (especially the Gothick) that had offered such a welcome change of mood from the humdrum tenor of everyday existence. The 'picturesque' was not concerned with beauty but with dramatic effect, poetic melancholy, anything that could burst the bonds that constrained the imagination of a highly formalised society. The yearning for excitement found sanctuary in the mediaeval or Gothic past, in anything that demonstrated the triumph of time over human endeavour. Like cobwebs, dungeons, and skeletons, for example.

Among the earliest exponents of the Gothick* style, in literature as in architecture, was Horace Walpole, whose home at Strawberry Hill was a fantasy of gilded pinnacles and painted glass, a monument of Gothick gimcrackery that

* The terminal 'k' distinguishes the eighteenth-century version from the fourteenth-century original.

was greatly admired by some (not all) fashionable Georgians. Overcome by his surroundings, no doubt, Walpole dreamed one night in 1764 that he was in a mouldering mediaeval castle. Resting on the banister of its great staircase was a gigantic, disembodied, armoured hand. Next morning, Walpole sat down and began to write *The Castle of Otranto*, a mildly hair-raising piece of nonsense that had a resounding success and was soon being slavishly copied by other, less stylish writers.

Haunted castles, vaults, apparitions, ruins, ivy and owls, appeared with monotonous frequency for the next half century, notably in such works as Ann Radcliffe's *The Mysteries of Udolpho*, Matthew Lewis's *The Monk*, and *Melmoth the Wanderer* by Charles Robert Maturin, who admitted to being quite in love with bells rung by unseen hands, daggers encrusted with long-shed blood, sinister doors behind still more sinister tapestries, mad nuns, headless spectres, and all the paraphernalia of romantic spookery.[31] In the 1790s there were several translations into English of the German poet Gottfried Bürger's ballad *Lenore*, which had been borrowed from folk legend and richly embellished with charnel horrors, and Bürger's dead lover returning to carry off his betrothed had its echo in Goethe's *The Bride of Corinth* (1797), the work that was to make vampirism respectable (in the literary sense). In Goethe's ballad, based on the classical story of Phlegon of Trales but incorporating more recent Hungarian vampire beliefs, it is the girl who dies and reappears, 'driven forth from the grave to seek again what was missed, to love again the man who was lost, to suck his heart's blood'.

Lurid though it all was, most Gothick poetry and fiction was oddly genteel. Even works of contemporary 'realism', such as Richardson's *Clarissa* and Diderot's *La Religieuse*, to some extent masked their brutality and prurience with a thick layer of unctuous morality. But when the Marquis de Sade emerged on the literary scene, clandestine editions of his works pouring from the presses, brutality increased and morality diminished.

De Sade, it is salutary to note, carefully combed the reports of travellers and explorers for any primitive sexual customs that could be used to prove the 'naturalness' of his own peculiar erotic fantasies. The link between the kiss and the bite, between blood and sexuality, is by no means an abnormal feature of sexual psychology, but de Sade carried it to extremes. His Comte de Gernade in *Justine, ou les malheurs de la vertu* (1791) watched the blood flow from his victims with the orgasmic avidity of a new Gilles de Rais (whom de Sade rather admired), and the characters in *Juliette* included the necrophiliac Cordelli, and the Muscovite giant Minski, whose favourite dish was human flesh and whose furniture was made of human bones.*

Life in the nineteenth century was no less harsh than it had ever been, but it was a harshness in which blood moved out of the average man's existence and into the pages of literature. Byron's *The Giaour* (1813) called down a true vampirish curse:

> But first, on earth as Vampire sent,
> Thy corse shall from its tomb be rent:
> Then ghastly haunt thy native place,
> And suck the blood of all thy race;
> Then from thy daughter, sister, wife,
> At midnight drain the stream of life;
> Yet loathe the banquet, which perforce
> Must feed thy livid living corse. . . .

Byron was also partly responsible for one of the most successful vampire yarns until *Dracula*. In 1816 he and some friends were gathered in Geneva and, inspired by reading German ghost stories, decided to try their own hands at the genre. The results were Mary Shelley's *Frankenstein* and a sketched-out 'tale of terror' by Byron which was expanded by one of the other guests, Dr John Polidori, into *The Vampire*. This, published in 1819 (mistakenly under Byron's name), concerned the exploits of a young libertine Lord Ruthven, who died in Greece, became a vampire, but returned to London for the balls and ridottos of the fashionable 'season', where his dead grey eye cast something of a damper on the proceedings. Establishing a supernatural ascendancy

* Restif de la Bretonne reported that Danton, responsible for much of the blood-letting during the French Revolution, read *Justine* for kicks—a thought to conjure with![32]

over a young man named Aubrey, he permits the youth to accompany him on his travels through Europe. These are packed with incident, and at last it dawns even on the obtuse Aubrey that his mentor may have something to do with the trail of blood-drained beauties the travellers leave in their wake. He hastens back to London, but too late! The sinister nobleman has bewitched his sister. Dying—from a burst blood vessel—Aubrey tells all, and his sister's guardians hasten off to save her. Alas! 'Lord Ruthven had disappeared, and Aubrey's sister had glutted the thirst of a Vampyre!' The mortality rate in this kind of fiction was always extremely high, and heroes and heroines who did not go so far as to die almost invariably went mad—in which the reader had every sympathy with them.

Polidori's tale was soon translated into French and German, and little more than a year after publication was adapted for the stage, first as a play and then as an opera. In Paris, people began to complain that there was scarcely a theatre free of vampires, and by 1824 a distinguished French Academician was driven to speak out against the current trend towards blood and thunder. 'Abominate,' he exclaimed, 'this literature of cannibals, which feeds on scraps of human flesh and gulps the blood of women and children. . . . Abominate . . . that cynical, even infernal poetry that seems to have been instigated by Satan himself to stir up crime, showing it ever sublime and triumphant, to discourage virtue by portraying it always feeble, pusillanimous and oppressed.'[33] The glorification of violence had its critics long before the days of television.

But the theme was too much of a challenge for authors and poets to be able to renounce it. Prosper Mérimée, in his *La Guzla*, a collection of so-called 'Illyrian tales', had some slight justification for including a few stories on the vampire theme, but Petrus Borel, who called himself The Lycanthrope (or werewolf), would—if he could—have penned his macabre tales with a hearse-plume on a winding-sheet. Gautier and Dumas in, respectively, *La morte amoureuse* and *Le Vampire*, merely indulged the current fashion for the 'indescribably voluptuous' vampire's kiss, but Baudelaire's *Les Fleurs du Mal* was the subject of an obscenity trial in 1857 after which

six of the poems—including *Les Metamorphoses du Vampire*—
were banned in the interests of public decency.[34]

Healthier, in a way, were the penny-part shockers that
poured from the presses in the 1840s and 50s, among them
such gems as *Varney the Vampire, or The Feast of Blood*—868
lurid pages of it, each part ending with a cliffhanger that would
have put Pearl White to shame. Gorgeous half-clad girls were
faced with a fate *worse* that a fate worse than death, while the
vampire licked his lips in anticipation of dinner. 'Blood!—raw
blood, reeking and hot, bubbling and juicy from the veins of
some gasping victim'. And there was Tom Prest's tale of
Sweeney Todd, the demon barber of Fleet Street, first published under the improbable title *The String of Pearls: or The
Sailor's Gift. A Romance of Peculiar Interest.* Sweeney Todd
jettisoned his plumpest customers through a revolving trap-
door into the basement, where their throat-cut corpses were
stripped and robbed, carved up, and then handed over to Mrs
Lovett who kept a cookshop next door that was much frequented by lawyers, their clerks and apprentices. Mrs Lovett's
meat pies were famous. On one unfortunate occasion when
Sweeney's labours had come to naught and mutton had to be
used, the customers complained bitterly over the deterioration
in quality. But the day came when all was revealed. And it was
revealed just when the hungry habitués were tucking into a
fresh batch of pies, talking and laughing 'as they smacked
their lips and sucked in all the golopshious gravy of the pies,
which by the way appeared to be all delicious veal that time'.
The author did not shirk the duty of describing customer-
reaction to the news.

In 1858, the temperance movement excelled itself by producing a teetotal tract on the vampire theme—*The Vampyre,
by the wife of a medical man*. The hero was a dipsomaniac and
the villain, a personification of 'The Vampyre Inn'. The work
ran to twenty-seven chapters. 'They fly,' screamed the hero.
'They bite—they suck my blood—I die. That hideous "Vampyre"! Its eyes pierce me thro'—they are red—they are blood-
shot. Tear it from my pillow. I dare not lie down. It bites—I
die! Give me brandy—brandy—more brandy!'[35] At least vampires made a change from pink elephants.

Robert Louis Stevenson, in 1886, created in *Dr Jekyll and*

Mr Hyde a variant on the werewolf theme, but the epitome of the Victorian taste for gorgeous gore was Bram Stoker's *Dracula* (1897), which the author attributed to a night of indigestion. Author, actor, and man-about-town, Stoker researched extensively into vampire lore. He also confused later historians of the horrific by giving his anti-hero a name with an apparently feminine -a ending. In Munich in 1958, however, a number of learned philologists attending the Sixth Congress of Onomastic Sciences solemnly concluded that Stoker's Dracula could be identified with Vlad the Impaler, sometimes called Vlad Dracula, 'son of the dragon'. It is generally agreed that Stoker's novel succeeded because it satisfied the sexual hang-ups of the Victorian age, although the pundits remain curiously reticent about why it should have maintained its cinematic appeal in the present era of permissiveness. In fact, it is a combination of sex and thinly veiled sadism that is—and, it is to be hoped, will remain—acceptable only in fiction. Stoker was, however, very good at it. Consider Jonathan Harker, the innocent young English traveller who fell asleep in a forbidden part of Count Dracula's Transylvanian castle. Awaking to find three mysterious ladies bending over him, he watched them under his eyelashes 'in an agony of delightful anticipation'. One of them 'went down on her knees and bent over me, simply gloating. There was a deliberate voluptuousness which was both thrilling and repulsive, and as she arched her neck she actually licked her lips like an animal, till I could see in the moonlight the moisture shining on the scarlet lips and on the red tongue as it lapped the white sharp teeth.'

The sexual shiver alternated with the sadistic shudder. Sweet, virginal Lucy Westenra had been turned by Dracula into a vampire, and one fateful night lay in her coffin replete with blood. Three (no less) of her former suitors came upon this hideous scene. Said one of them: 'She seemed like a nightmare of Lucy as she lay there; the pointed teeth, the bloodstained, voluptuous'—that word again—'mouth, which it made one shudder to see, the whole carnal and unspirited appearance seeming like a devilish mockery of Lucy's sweet purity.' The suitors felt it their duty to release her from this terrible thrall, took a stake, and drove it into her breast. 'The thing in the coffin writhed; and a hideous, blood-curdling screech came from the opened red lips. The body shook and quivered and twisted in wild contortions; the sharp white teeth champed together till the lips were cut, and the mouth was smeared with a crimson foam. But Arthur never faltered . . . as his untrembling arm rose and fell, driving deeper and deeper the mercy-bearing stake.' Arthur was apparently unaware that the authorities recommended only a single strike (see page 124). 'And then the writhing and quivering of the body became less, and the teeth ceased to champ, and the face to quiver. Finally it lay still. The terrible task was over.' And the reader's stomach could stop churning. When *Dracula* was adapted for the stage in the 1920s, there were nurses constantly on duty in the theatre foyer.

Bram Stoker did not pretend to be a literary lion, and when he doused his readers in blood it was done in the name of entertainment. But some of his contemporaries—*fin-de-siècle* Decadents such as Huysmans and Swinburne, D'Annunzio and Lorrain—used the same morbid clichés to express their own exasperated sensuality, and to shock. It was Lorrain who summed up the atmosphere of the movement, 'heavy with scents of blood and carrion, heavy with the fragrance of flowers and incense'.[36] The association between blood and flowers was characteristic of the fake mysticism of the Decadents, but otherwise they were the narcissistic heirs of thousands of years of blood fixations, and of a century that had begun (in effect if not in date) with the French Revolution and was ending under the unamused eye of a stout old lady in black bombazine. The Decadents embraced all the bloodied horrors, real and fictional, of the past, and turned them into a precious but unmistakably rude gesture towards the present.

CHAPTER EIGHT

Survival Kits

AT THE beginning of the twentieth century, that soft-hearted cynic Hilaire Belloc composed a few verses relating to one of the great talking points of the time.

> Behold, my child, the Nordic Man,
> And be as like him as you can,
> His legs are long, his mind is slow,
> His hair is light and made of tow.

> And next to him is the [Alpine] race,
> Oh what a broad and brutal face,
> His hair is dark, his skin is yellow,
> He is a most unpleasant fellow.

> And then the lowest race of all
> Mediterranean we call,
> His hair is crisp and even curls
> And he is saucy with the girls.

Ever since the beginning of recorded history, differences between peoples had been recognised and accepted, but it had taken the nineteenth century with its passion for classifying, its dedication to the new science and technology, its pouter-pigeon pride in Western achievement, to turn race into a philosophical concept. The old, loaded word 'blood', however, was still used as a synonym. (Indeed, it could be argued that if Wilhelm Johannsen had invented the pristine term 'genes' in 1859 instead of fifty years later the whole subject of race might subsequently have generated rather less emotional heat.)

The idea that 'pure blood' meant greatness—and its antithesis, that 'a mongrel is frequently very clever, but never

165

reliable; morally he is always a weed'[1]—was to be responsible for one of the greatest blood-lettings in history. Joseph Arthur, Comte de Gobineau, started it all in the 1850s with his *Essai sur l'inégalité des races humaines* in which, drawing on a wealth of data, he propounded a racial theory of history. He argued that races were inherently unequal, that by mixing their blood they changed character. The 'Aryans', Gobineau claimed, were superior to all others, and of the Aryans it was the Germanic tribes that were purest and most dynamic. Not unnaturally, this reasoning went down very well in Germany (less so in France), and Gobineau's theories had a deep influence on such philosophers as Nietzsche.

In 1859, only four years after Gobineau's third volume appeared, Charles Darwin rocked the scientific world with *The Origin of Species*. Adam and Eve went out of date. All men, it seemed, were not brothers after all. The idea of natural selection confirmed that some races might be superior, and the scientists of Europe and America were soon conjuring up statistics to show that no degenerate or feeble stock could ever be improved by environmental reform, and that cross-breeding would infallibly result in deterioration of the superior strain. Blood was the deciding factor—as magical a substance, still, as it had been five thousand years before.

Science thus gave its imprimatur to racism, made it desirable—almost incumbent on—WASPs to cut themselves off from social contact with Jews and Latins in Europe, with Blacks, Indians and Chinese in the United States, where colour became an instant index to blood and race.

It was an expatriate Englishman, the son-in-law of the composer Richard Wagner, who in 1899 merged the emotive themes of pure blood, nationhood, and racial supremacy, into a gospel for Nazism. Theodore Roosevelt described Houston Stewart Chamberlain as 'an influence to be reckoned with and seriously to be taken into account', and George Bernard Shaw called his book 'a masterpiece of really scientific history'.[2] But though its title seemed innocent enough and its pages were littered with scholarly references, the *Grundlagen des Neunzehnten Jahrhunderts* ('The Foundations of the Nineteenth Century') was a live match looking for a powder keg.

'The greatest mistake of all,' wrote Chamberlain, 'is the

17. "Despair and cannibalism on the raft"—one of Géricault's rejected studies for "The Raft of the Medusa."

18. The "lady vampire" in 1974. Pauline Peart in the Hammer Films
production *The Satanic Rites of Dracula*.

19. Transfusion for a vampire from *Draculas Ende, 28 Zeichnungen*, by Luis Murschetz, 1969.

assumption that our civilisation and culture are but the expression of a general progress of mankind; not a single fact
in history supports this popular belief . . . [but the] empty
phrase strikes us blind, and we lose sight of the self-evident
fact—that our civilisation and culture . . . are the works of a
definite, individual racial type.' The type in question was the
Teuton, 'intellectually, morally and physically pre-eminent
among his kinsmen. . . . If we look around, we see that the
importance of each nation as a living power today is dependent upon the proportion of genuinely Teutonic blood in its
population.'

'The richer the blood that courses invisibly through the
veins, the more luxuriant will be the blossoms of life that
spring forth', and because of this, Chamberlain wrote, Germans were nobly endowed with 'physical health and strength,
great intelligence, luxuriant imagination, untiring impulse to
create'. They were marvellously free, supremely loyal, 'sunny,
proud . . . men who fearlessly grasp the right hand of the God
to whom they pray'.[3] They were the master race.

But now that it was possible to view history in a scientific
perspective, the master race had to learn to maintain, even to
increase, the purity of its blood. From his exhaustive, if
eccentric researches, Chamberlain deduced that the world's
great races had all started life with a blend of the best available
bloods, which they had steadily refined over the centuries by
inbreeding according to the laws of 'artificial selection', by
encouraging the strong and eliminating the weak.[4]

From blood and race Chamberlain passed on to the subject
of nationhood. A nation united by purity of blood had a
'common memory, common hope, common intellectual
nourishment; it fixes firmly the existing bond of blood and
impels us to make it ever closer'. Such a nation was not to be
compared with that 'state without a nation . . . that union
of mongrels bound together only by a community of taxes
and superstitions', that soulless rabble that, lacking the fellowship of blood, could never hope to send the finest of its children
soaring heavenward 'like some strong and stately tree, nourished
by thousands and thousands of roots—no solitary individual,
but the living sum of untold souls striving for the same goal'.[5]

Chamberlain's supercharged rhetoric, embedded in well over

a thousand pages of highly selective history, was a charter for
megalomania. When Adolf Hitler, in 1924, set out his beliefs
in *Mein Kampf*, they were derived from Chamberlain, Wagner,
Nietzsche and Gobineau. Pure blood was to be the survival
kit that ensured the thousand-year Reich and German
domination of the world.

It was to be the Jews and gypsies who suffered most. Anti-
semitism reached a new pitch in the last decades of the nineteenth century and the first of the twentieth. Jews were
described as Lazarus figures, as beasts of prey; they were as
dangerous as cholera germs, as voracious as the phylloxera
louse. As Chamberlain pointed out, the Jews (who had
guarded their blood so assiduously) were the purest race in the
world, but thousands of their 'side branches are cut off and
employed to infect the Indo-Europeans with Jewish blood.
If that were to go on for a few centuries, there would be in
Europe only one single people of pure blood, that of the Jews,
all the rest would be a herd of pseudo-Hebraic mestizos, a
people beyond all doubt degenerate physically, mentally and
morally.'[6] Jewish blood threatened the pure strain of the
master race, and the Jews' own, undeniable strength—a direct
product of the purity of their blood—was a cultural and
political danger to the Teutonic states.

The ravings of the theorists and politicians; virulent scan-
dals such as the one that raged around the 'plot against
civilisation' contained in the forged *Protocols of the Elders of
Zion*; even the stridently nationalist, anti-semitic tone of the
penny-dreadful vampire tales written by authors like Hans-
Heinz Ewers; all these contributed to the success of Nazism
and the enactment of such legislation as the 1935 Law for the
Protection of German Blood, which stated: 'A marriage cannot
take place if offspring dangerous to the preservation of the
purity of German blood can be expected from it.'[7]

To protect that purity, social restriction was followed by
the sterilisation of Jews and gypsies, and then by their exter-
mination. Between 1939 and 1945, 219,000 gypsies and
5,100,000 Jews are estimated to have died in German-occupied
territories.[8] Protecting the power of blood instead of giving
the power of blood—it was just one more variant on the age-
old theme of human sacrifice.

During those same years, the British and Japanese in the more remote parts of South Asia were discovering that the practice of hunting for another kind of life-essence had not, as they had been led to believe, entirely died out. The Naga tribes on the eastern borders of Assam, for example, although they had been reclaimed from outer darkness to become ardent Baptists (at least on Sundays), found the temptation to relieve any stray Japanese soldiers of their heads quite irresistible. They were delighted to find that the British did not actively discourage this ancestral pastime. In Burma, too, there were instances of headhunting, though the motivation was different. In 1943 and 1944, long-range military penetration units, consisting mainly of Gurkhas, made a series of commando-intelligence raids along the coast of Japanese-occupied Arakan. Returning from one foray, the Gurkhas were highly incensed when their British officers raised a sceptical eyebrow over their claim to have killed a hundred Japanese. Next time they reappeared at base, they came laden with sacks of Japanese heads.[9]

The Gurkhas, in fact, had no tradition of headhunting, just a well-developed and slightly gruesome sense of humour, but in Asia the practice of counting heads (in the precise and literal sense) was at least two thousand years old. Both the Scythians and the Chinese had been expected to deliver to their commander the heads of all enemies killed in battle; as Herodotus put it, a head was 'a sort of ticket by which a soldier is admitted to his share of the loot—no head, no loot'.[10]

For many of the tribes of the Indonesian archipelago, however, headhunting held great spiritual significance. Each head contained a quantity of life-essence that could be used to give vitality to man and fertility to the fields. It was not, of course, the vaporous life-essence of the head that gave man vitality, but the solid protein contained in the body; headhunting was almost invariably accompanied by a cannibalism that could be as savage as that of Fiji. But whatever the ostensible motive of the various tribes—life-essence, revenge, justice, magic—cannibalism supplied an important item of diet, particularly in the highland areas of Borneo and New Guinea. Today, when the practice has been outlawed but no serious official attempt made to provide a substitute for the human steaks of the past, the more inaccessible tribes of New Guinea face near-starvation when their vegetables and root crops are struck by frost or drought and supplies have to be flown in over the dense, roadless rain forests. In 1972, a quarter of a million people were condemned to live on a ration of one pound of rice and one vitamin-C tablet a day. It is hardly surprising that though cannibalism has been outlawed cases continue to be reported, and the administration classifies areas inhabited by such tribes as the Hewas as forbidden territory.[11]

On the whole, however, the twentieth century has seen cannibalism more or less disappear as a feature of religious and political life, though in some cases it seems only to have gone underground. Occasionally it bursts out in response to some sudden stimulus. The Mau Mau of Kenya overlaid the darkest memories of their shamanist past with the most loathsome rituals they could devise when they called in magic to help them bring white supremacy to an end. The Indians of Brazil now and then eat one of the envoys of their destruction, a government agent. And in Canada's forested northland, some Cree and Ojibwa Indians suffer from a bizarre mental disorder technically known as the *wiitiko* psychosis, an acute anxiety state marked first by melancholy, then by a distaste for ordinary food, and finally by an obsessive desire for human flesh that ends in homicidal cannibalism.[12]

In the concrete jungle, too, there is the occasional moral misfit who provides the tabloids with an excuse for their largest headline type. Perhaps the classic twentieth-century case was that of Fritz Haarmann, the 'Hanover Vampire', who was found guilty in 1924 of biting to death at least twenty-seven young men, and converting their flesh into sausages.

Haarmann, forty-five years old, had had a miserable and sickly youth, a brief spell of glory as a soldier, and then a career as a petty criminal during which he was in and out of jail for offences ranging from larceny to indecency. In 1918, after a long stretch inside, he opened a cookshop in the old quarter of Hanover. It was much frequented because even at that time of extreme scarcity Haarmann always had good stocks of fresh meat and was prepared to undersell his competitors.

As a sideline, Haarmann became a police informer and used

to go with them to the great railroad station in the centre of Hanover, which at night, was thronged with the flotsam of a dislocated, defeated Germany, the homeless and the run-aways. In the small hours of the morning, Haarmann would officiously demand to be shown the papers of some frightened youth huddled in a waiting-room, and then, touched by the sad story the youth had to tell, would invite him home to spend the rest of the night on a comfortable mattress.

The parents of one boy who disappeared succeeded in tracing him as far as Haarmann. A policeman went to enquire, and found Haarmann in such a compromising position with another youth that he promptly arrested him for 'gross indecency'. If the policeman had not been distracted by this, he would have found the head of the missing boy hidden under a newspaper behind the oven. Haarmann did nine months for homosexuality.

Towards the end of 1919, free again, he met his evil genius (as if he needed one), Hans Grans. This handsome, vicious young parasite selected many of Haarmann's later victims— he coveted one youth's new trousers, another's flashy shirt. Many of the victims were picked up at gay cafés or drag balls; despite the laws, Hanover had a substantial homosexual element. Haarmann would take the chosen victim home, feed him lavishly, and then admire and caress him until the love-bite in the throat turned into a vampire's kiss. The dead boy's clothes—those that Grans did not want—were put up for sale in Haarmann's shop, the body was dismembered, and Haarmann sold such of the flesh as he did not eat himself. It was reported that on one occasion he even made some sausages in his kitchen, cooked them, and sat down with a customer to eat them. Bones and skulls were kept in a cupboard until they could be thrown into the river Leine, which flowed behind Haarmann's apartment.

It was these bones and skulls which led to Haarmann's undoing. Some were dredged out of the river in 1924, still bearing the marks of butchering, and a search of his rooms produced damning evidence. He was tried for twenty-seven murders, though some experts estimated that fifty would have been nearer the mark and the newspapers made the point that there could have been more still, since six hundred boys had disappeared in Hanover in 1924 alone. Haarmann was executed and Grans condemned to life imprisonment, though his sentence was later commuted to twelve years.[13]

There was a very similar case in Berlin at about the same time. A fifty-year-old former butcher named Grossmann sold hot dogs at the main railroad station there—made from the pickled and ground flesh of buxom country girls he picked up at that very same station while he was out at work. The constant stream of girls seen entering, but not leaving, his apartment finally made his neighbours suspicious and the police were called in.[14]

Perhaps with memories of these cases, Britain's minister of food during the second world war (Lord Woolton) rejected with loathing a suggestion put forward by some of his scientific advisers. Large numbers of people had volunteered to aid casualties by becoming blood donors, and the transfusion service's bank was soon overflowing. The advisers recommended that the surplus should be used to make black puddings or blood sausages for general distribution on ration. But in Lord Woolton's view, consuming blood by vein was one thing, ingesting it by mouth quite another.[15]

Odd cases of cannibalism, criminal or accidental, still crop up from time to time. In 1970 in California, for example, a man arrested in connection with a minor traffic accident—prefacing his statement with that immortal American phrase: 'I have a problem'—told a patrolman he was a cannibal. He confessed to murdering a social worker, dismembering the body, and eating the heart. In 1973, in Chile, a labourer returned home after an all-night drinking spree bearing a ten-pound cut of meat that he had been offered in the street market at a bargain price. Gratefully, as there was a meat shortage, his wife divided up the meat and sold some of it to a neighbour. This woman, however, looked closely at the skin and hair and became suspicious, and in the end the two housewives hurried along to the police station—where their suspicions were confirmed. The erring husband admitted that he had not in fact bought the meat, but had found a parcel of it lying on the ground and fuzzily thought it would be a shame to waste it. The rest of the body turned up a few days later, and a murder hunt then began.[16]

But it is hunger and desperation that have most often led to cannibalism in the twentieth century. In parts of Germany and along the banks of the Volga during the troubled years after the 1914–18 war cannibalism was rife. After Stalin's collectivisation of the Ukraine in 1929–31 there was a great famine and human flesh began to appear in the peasants' cooking pots. From September 1941 until January 1944, Leningrad was under siege and some of those who survived did so only because they forced themselves to eat the dead. At Stalingrad, too, cannibalism was reported, and again in the Ukraine in 1947 there was famine. Khrushchev described in his memoirs how one of his subordinates reported it. 'The woman had the corpse of her own child on the table,' he said, 'and was cutting it up. She was chattering away as she worked. "We've already eaten Manechka [little Maria]. Now we'll salt down Vanechka [little Ivan]. This will keep us for some time." Can you imagine? This woman had gone crazy with hunger and butchered her own children!'[17]

In the Warsaw ghetto (and others) as well as in the concentration camps of Belsen, Buchenwald and Auschwitz, human flesh was sometimes all that there was to sustain those who would not release their hold on life. On March 21, 1942 the Warsaw propaganda division of the *Generalgouvernement* curtly reported that: 'The death figure in the ghetto still hovers around 5000 per month. A few days ago, the first case of hunger-cannibalism was recorded. In a Jewish family the man and his three children died within a few days. From the flesh of the child who died last—a twelve-year-old boy—the mother ate a piece. To be sure, this could not save her either, and she herself died two days later.' In Belsen, a former British internee engaged on clearing away dead bodies gave evidence that 'as many as one in ten had a piece cut from the thigh or other part of the body. . . . On my very next visit to the mortuary I actually saw a prisoner whip out a knife, cut a portion out of the leg of a dead body and put it quickly into his mouth.'[18]

Since those days, the world has seen a number of serious famines, notably in Asia and Africa. It says much for the humanity of journalists and authors who have written about them that they have been more concerned with stressing the need for famine relief than sensationalising the shifts to which the starving have at times been driven.

Restraint, however, was cast to the winds when, in 1972, sixteen young plane-wrecked Uruguayans survived seventy days in the bitter heights of the Andes by eating the flesh of companions who had been killed in the crash and a subsequent avalanche. Swarms of reporters descended on Montevideo to attend the survivors' press conferences, and New York publishers tumbled over each other in the rush for book publication rights.

Briefly, the story that caused all this excitement was as follows. On October 12, 1972 a chartered Uruguayan Air Force plane took off from Montevideo, carrying fifteen young Rugby players (a team known as the 'Old Christians') and twenty-five of their friends and relations to Santiago in Chile for a series of friendly games. The boys were pupils or former pupils of the fashionable Stella Maris College, which is run by Irish churchmen who place a strong emphasis on the twin virtues of team spirit and Catholic piety.

After an overnight stop because of bad weather, the plane took off again on what should have been only a one-hour flight. But it went off course, and at the crest of the Andes was shaken by violent turbulence, caught in a down-draught, and finally crashed among the peaks. Thirty-two of the passengers and crew survived, but two more died during the first night, two more during the succeeding days, another nine in an avalanche that struck the fuselage on the sixteenth day of the ordeal, and three more before rescue finally came.

For the first ten days the crash victims survived on a daily ration of a few pieces of chocolate, a capful of wine, and a teaspoonful of jam. They became steadily weaker, and several of them soon realised that the time was approaching when it would be necessary to eat the dead. The subject was at last brought into the open by a third-year medical student, Roberto Canessa. There was a half-embarrassed, indecisive discussion, a struggle between reason and revulsion, and finally four members of the party left the plane and, with a piece of broken glass, laboriously sawed some fragments of flesh from one of the frozen bodies lying outside.

The crash victims passed from revulsion to acceptance, and

then to enjoyment of their new diet. A few could stomach it only when cooked, and since fuel was scarce they ate little. One young man could not bring himself to eat it at all. He died. But the others even began to develop gourmet tastes, favouring the brains and lungs they had at first discarded, relishing the piquant flavour of flesh that had begun to decay. When the rescuers at last arrived, they were horrified when one survivor, trying to identify what remained of the bodies, tossed a skull to another and said cheerfully: 'You should know who this guy is; you ate his brains.'*

Attempts to find the plane—white against white snow—had in fact been given up shortly after its disappearance, but two of the Old Christians succeeded in fighting their way down from the mountains to reach an inhabited valley and restore contact with the outside world.[20]

It was a world avid for their story, no less so because all the survivors (with the exception of one thirty-six-year-old elder statesman) were husky, handsome youths ranging in age from eighteen to twenty-six, frank, fluent, and well connected. Two of them were nephews of the President of Uruguay, one was the son of a well-known heart specialist, another of one of the country's most distinguished painters. Their social status had been of no help to them during their traumatic weeks in the Andes, but neither was it a hindrance when they returned to face the glare of world publicity. It is legitimate to conjecture whether they would have met with quite such general warmth and understanding if they had come from New York's Harlem or Glasgow's Easterhouse.

It was, of course, impossible to conceal from the rescue teams the evidences of their cannibalism, and within two or three days rumour was rife. The Church hastened to the support of its sons. On December 27, a prominent Roman Catholic theologian commented in Rome that 'if the facts took place as narrated by the survivors [whose spokesmen at that date were still busily denying the whole story], even

---

* Behavioural scientists are only just beginning to study the 'psychic numbing' effect of air crashes on the survivors, but it is clear that some people react by adopting an attitude of insensitivity that is subconsciously designed to conceal, as much from themselves as from others, the full extent of the emotional damage they have suffered.[19]

from the theological and ethical point of view the action cannot be branded as cannibalism. . . . The action is only apparently cannibalistic [!]: the necessity and the priority right to survive deprive it of any negative element.'[21]

Somewhat unnecessarily, the survivors insisted on justifying their commonsense solution to the protein problem in mystical terms. At a press conference on December 29, one said: 'If Jesus, in the Last Supper, offered his body and blood to all the disciples, he was giving us to understand that we must do the same.' Another told a news agency representative: 'We did things that in other circumstances could seem to be morbid or macabre. They were unspeakable things that could never be told [though since then, of course, they have been]. Yet what we did was really Christian. We went right back to the very source of Christianity.' A third said: 'We swallowed the little bits of flesh with the feeling that God demanded it of us. We felt like Christians.'[22]

When the full story came to be told, by a sympathetic but independent author,[23] the result was a cruel record of individual responses to stress, a factual scenario for one of those recurring Hollywood fictions about groups of people trapped in a submarine, a lighthouse, a ship, or (come to that) an aeroplane. But, clearly, what was going to linger in the survivors' nightmares was not the cannibalism but the pain-racked deaths, without anaesthesia or anodyne, that preceded it.

While the Old Christians fought their battle for survival in the heights of the Andes, a solitary German-born pilot was facing the same decisions in the wilds of the Canadian Arctic. Martin Hartwell had no one with whom to share the burden. He was also suffering from two broken ankles and a shattered kneecap.

On November 8, 1972, reluctantly and in contravention of two official flight rules, Martin Hartwell took off from Cambridge Bay carrying an English nurse and two Eskimo patients she wanted urgently taken to hospital in Yellowknife, in the North-West Territory. One was a fourteen-year-old Eskimo boy who had been diagnosed as suffering from acute appendicitis, the other his aunt who needed surgery to deliver a premature baby. Unable to get a satisfactory compass or radio bearing, the pilot came down too low and crashed into a hillside. The nurse died instantly from a fractured skull, the Eskimo woman a few hours later from a broken neck. Only the boy was uninjured (a pathologist later stated that he had been suffering from a severe ulcer, not appendicitis). Under the pilot's guidance he constructed an emergency tent and set up rabbit traps, and in the following days made four abortive attempts to reach a lake they believed to be only about three or four miles away, though it was actually twelve. The rabbit traps produced nothing, and the two survivors lived on a tiny supply of corned beef, sugar cubes, salt and soap, and ultimately on the frozen drugs they found in the nurse's medical bag and a one-inch piece of candle.

On the twentieth day there was nothing left. The boy said he would not eat the bodies of the nurse or his aunt, who had been good to him. On November 30, Hartwell noted: 'Still alive. David is going to die tomorrow and I two or three days later. No food. My legs don't carry me.' Next day, the boy was dead.

On December 2, the injured Hartwell dragged himself twelve yards to the nearest tree, hacked off the lichened lower branches, and struggled back to the tent. It took him two hours. He made a small fire and concocted a mouthful of soup from the lichens, but there was no possibility of finding enough lichens to keep him going until his ankles mended enough to allow him to look further afield.

'There was no way out but to eat human flesh and this I did,' he said. For the few days between the final decision and his rescue on December 9, he sustained himself on the flesh of the twenty-seven-year-old nurse.

The inquest jury returned a verdict of accidental death on the crash victims, and the nurse's family stated that they held no 'vindictiveness or malice' towards Hartwell for what he had done. Afterwards, however, on the basis of the jury's comments, they proceeded to sue the pilot and his employers for negligence.[24]

In striking contrast to the Andes survivors, Hartwell refused to talk to reporters. 'I have not made any public statements,' he said, 'because the authorities seem to want it that way, and I do not wish to talk about those events. I

also feel that speaking about these things will cause distress
to the relatives of the people who died.'[25]

POSTSCRIPT

TODAY, STILL buried somewhere in the recesses of man's mind, are many of the old beliefs about flesh, blood and spirit, but the public expression of them has become not much more than what *Time* magazine, in a somewhat jaundiced discussion of Dracula—'not really a monster for our times'—described as 'a soggy bit of low camp'.[1]

Except when it really happens, eating people is no longer startling or even very remarkable, just blackly humorous. Jean-Luc Godard's 1968 film *Weekend* revolved round an obsessive, aggressive Parisian couple who capped their exploits with a bout of cannibalism. The Parisian public, remarked one commentator, was just a little put out about the film. 'Aggressive? *Bien sur!* Avaricious? *Pourquoi pas?* Gluttons? *Sans doute!* But cannibals? Here there was a note of inquiry. No disbelief, mind you. Just inquiry.'[2]

Every so often the theme crops up in novels and films of the brutalist school, and in fictional-factual epics such as Henri Charrière's *Papillon*. Usually it is no more than one incident among many. But in 1973 the Hollywood film *Soylent Green* and David Sale's novel *The Love Bite* both used cannibalism to provide a gruesomely logical answer to, first, the world's food problem, and second, its population problem.

Meanwhile, in London, perfectly sane-looking people (who were not being funny at all) were distributing leaflets warning against the activities of 'a worldwide neo-Nazi apparatus sponsored and controlled by the Gehlen Bureau'. This outfit, for some unspecified reason, aimed to rid Britain of anything up to eight million inhabitants. Some British citizens had already met a secret end and were, the leaflet claimed, 'being converted for profit into leather goods, bacon and pork, man-made fibres [!], plastic wallpaper . . . soap powder, glue and

179

fertiliser, and there have been numerous indications that human brain fluid is being added to whisky and gin, and "body" to beer'. As a clincher, the leaflet reminded its readers of the current advertising slogan—'Mrs Campbell makes good soup'.[3]

So much for the body. What of the soul? Perhaps because half a million years of speculation and investigation have failed to pin the spirit down into a scientific formula, the supernatural is still alive and well and living in Occultsville. In an age to which most of the secrets of creation are thought to be an open book, this one unknown quantity exercises a powerful attraction. Astrology, dreams, witchcraft and satanism are all aspects of that single area of ignorance. So, of course, is religion.

Not so long ago, the Black Mass was something that a few cranks were prepared to pay heavily to watch—£20 ($50) was the going rate in the seedier hot spots of Paris in the 1930s, Italy in the 1950s.[4] Now it is a do-it-yourself hobby. In suburban villas and on college campuses, horned gods and moon goddesses are worshipped according to magical-sexual-religious rites of immemorial antiquity (most of them invented by a former Customs official in the 1950s).[5] There are said to be one hundred thousand avowed witches in the United States, and at least ten million others who dabble in the occult arts, on levels ranging from 'white' witchcraft to Black Masses and even blood-drinking orgies.[6] In Britain, too, the figures are gradually creeping up as 'Wicca'—the contemporary name for witchcraft—attracts new followers. The authors of the *Malleus Maleficarum* would still have found themselves on familiar ground in London in 1974 when a man described as 'high priest of the British Occult Society' was charged with 'unlawfully removing a corpse from a tomb at Highgate cemetery'.[7]

After the years of activism, drugs, and demonstrations, there is now an eerie silence on American college campuses as students turn from the material to the immaterial world. There are accredited courses on satanism in Boston, vampirism in San Francisco, witchcraft in Wisconsin. Two professors at the latter college—lecturing on the 'History of Pseudo-science and the Occult'—tactlessly allowed their scepticism to show, and non-conformism was turned inside out when some of their students wrote to the college authorities demanding that the professors be fired—for heresy.[8]

Blood mythology, too, is still firmly embedded in the human subconscious though it emerges comparatively rarely on the obvious level. Race has become a matter of genes, not blood. In England in 1974, however, there was nearly a good old-fashioned riot when an official at one blood transfusion centre refused to give blood from coloured donors to white patients. His explanation—that there were medical grounds for believing that the blood of certain coloured donors might be responsible for passing on the hepatitis virus—was rejected with scorn. The combined insult to blood and race was just as emotive in 1974 as it was a hundred years earlier.

But blood is today more often the province of horror merchants and middle-aged adolescents. There is, for example, a fashion for vampire and werewolf 'comics', though it is pleasing to note that the luscious Vampirella ('Vampi' to her friends) resorts to human blood only when she is deprived of her blood serum substitute. *Dracula* films still pour from the studios in a river of gore. Romania aims to attract American tourists with shriek-inducing displays in *son et lumière*, at the real Vlad Dracula's castles. And jet-set millionaires give birthday parties at which the guests strut around in jackboots with bats pinned to their belfries, hissing unpleasantries through joke-fangs dripping with catsup.[9]

A *very* soggy bit of low camp.

BIBLIOGRAPHY

Where the 'notes on sources' refer to an edition other than the first, the date of the quoted edition is given at the end of the entry, 'P' means paperback.

Aarne, Antti, and Thompson, Stith. *The Types of the Folktale, A Classification and Bibliography.* 2nd revision. Helsinki 1961.

[Abd al-Latif]. *Relation de l'Égypte par Abd-Allatif, Médecin arabe de Bagdad.* Paris 1810. (Translated into French, from the Arabic, by Silvestre de Sacy.)

Ackernecht, E. H. 'Primitive Autopsies and the History of Anatomy', *Bulletin of the History of Medicine* 13, 1943, pp. 334–9.

Agehananda Bharati. *The Tantric Tradition.* London 1965.

Albertus Magnus. *The Book of Secrets*, edited Michael R. Best and Frank H. Brightman. Oxford 1973. (Only part of this late thirteenth-century work was derived from the writings of Albertus.)

American Anthropologist. (Most years see one or two articles on cannibalism, headhunting, or some related subject.)

Arciniegas, German. *Latin America: A Cultural History.* London 1969.

Bainton, Roland H. *The Horizon History of Christianity.* New York 1964, Harmondsworth (as *The Penguin History of Christianity*, P) 1967.

Baring-Gould, Sabin. *Book of Were-Wolves.* London 1865.

Barnett, Bernard. 'Witchcraft, Psychopathology and Hallucinations', *British Journal of Psychiatry* III no. 474, 1965, pp. 430–45.

Baron, Salo Wittmayer. *A Social and Religious History of the Jews*, vols. 1, 2, 11. 2nd edition. New York 1967.

Basham, A. L. *The Wonder that was India.* London 1954. P 1971.

Bataille, Georges (ed.) *Le Procès de Gilles de Rais. Les documents.* Montreuil 1965.

Bayet, Jean. *Croyances et rites dans la Rome antique.* Paris 1971.

Benedetti, Jean. *Gilles de Rais. The Authentic Bluebeard.* London 1971.

Berkowitz, Leonard. 'Anti-Semitism and the Displacement of Aggression', *Journal of Abnormal and Social Psychology* 59, 1959, pp. 182–7.

Bettelheim, Bruno. *Symbolic Wounds. Puberty Rites and the Envious Male.* London 1955.

Bhatia, B. M. *Famines in India 1860–1965.* Revised edition. Bombay 1967.

[Bible]. *The Holy Bible, Revised Standard Version containing the Old and New Testaments with the Apocrypha/Deuterocanonical Books. An Ecumenical Edition.* New York, Glasgow and Toronto 1973.

Binford, Sally R. 'A structural Comparison of Disposal of the Dead in the Mousterian and the Upper Paleolithic', *South-western Journal of Anthropology* 24, 1968.

Block, Martin. *Gypsies.* London 1938.

Bodin, Jean. *De la démonomanie des sorciers.* Paris 1580.

Boguet, Henri. *Discours des Sorciers.* Lyon 1603. (Translated by E. Allen Ashwin as *An Examen of Witches.* London 1929.)

Boüinais, Lt-Col. and Paulus, A. *Le Culte des Morts dans le Céleste Empire et l'Annam comparé au Culte des Ancêtres dans l'Antiquité occidentale . . .* Paris 1893.

Brandon, S. G. F. (ed.) *A Dictionary of Comparative Religion.* London 1970.

Bretschneider, E. 'Notices of the Mediaeval Geography and History of Central and Western Asia', *Journal of the North China Branch of the Royal Asiatic Society* X, 1876.

Brewitt-Taylor, C. H. 'Human Sacrifices', *China Review* X, p. 71.

Brothwell, Don and Patricia. *Food in Antiquity. A Survey of the Diet of Early Peoples.* London 1969.

Browe, Peter. 'Die Eucharistie als Zaubermittel im Mittelalter', *Archiv für Kulturgeschichte* XX, 1930.

Burr, George Lincoln. 'The Literature of Witchcraft', *American Historical Association Papers* IV, 1889–90 part 3, pp. 235–66.

Burton, Richard F. (adapted by). *Vikram and the Vampire, or Tales of Hindu Devilry.* London 1870.

Caleb, S. *Les Messes Noires.* Paris n.d.

Caporale, Rocco, and Grumelli, Antonio (eds.) *The Culture of Unbelief.* University of California Press 1972. (Papers from a symposium at Rome in 1969.)

Carletti, Francesco. *Ragionamenti* 1594–1606. Trs. by Herbert Weinstock as *My Voyage Around the World*, New York 1964, London 1965.

Carter, Huntly. 'Cannibalism in Soviet Russia', *Medical Press and Circular* 1922 part 2, p. 496.

Chamberlain, Houston Stewart. *The Foundations of the Nineteenth Century.* 2 vols. London and New York 1911–13. (First published in German in 1899.)

Cirlot, J. E. *A Dictionary of Symbols.* London and New York 1962.

Clark, Grahame. *World Prehistory.* Cambridge 1969.

Clark, Grahame, and Piggott, Stuart. *Prehistoric Societies.* London 1965. P 1970.

Clébert, Jean-Paul. *The Gypsies.* London 1963. P 1967.

Coles, J. M., and Higgs, E. S. *The Archaeology of Early Man.* London 1969, New York 1970.

Collin de Plancy, J. A. S. *Histoire des Vampires.* Paris 1820.

Collis, Maurice. *The Land of the Great Image, being experiences of Friar Manrique in Arakan.* London 1946.

Columbus, Ferdinand. *The Life of the Admiral Christopher Columbus.* New Brunswick 1959, London 1960. (Notes refer to the London edition.)

Coon, Carleton S. [1] *The History of Man: From the First Human to Primitive Culture and Beyond.* New York 1954, London 1955. P 1967.

Coon, Carleton S. [2] *The Hunting Peoples.* London 1972.

Cordier, Henri. *Bibliotheca Sinica. Dictionnaire Bibliographique des Ouvrages relatifs à l'Empire chinois*, vol. III. 2nd edition. Paris 1904–8. (There was a supplement in 1922–24, and see Yuan T'ung-li for the continuation.)

Cottrell, Leonard. *The Horizon Book of Lost Worlds.* 2 vols, New York 1962, Harmondsworth (as *The Penguin Book of Lost Worlds*, P) 1966.

Craig, William. *Enemy at the Gates.* London 1973. (The battle of Stalingrad).

Cross, L. B. 'Blood Ritual in the Old Testament', *Modern Churchman* XXXI, pp. 295–312.

Crowley, Aleister. *Equinox* I nos. 1–10, London 1909–13; III no. 1, Detroit 1919.

Cumont, Franz. *Lux perpetua.* Paris 1949. (Roman conceptions of death and the afterlife.)

Darlington, C. D. *The Evolution of Man and Society.* London 1969, New York 1970.

Davidson, H. R. Ellis. *Gods and Myths of Northern Europe.* Harmondsworth 1964.

Dennys, N. B. *The Folk-lore of China, and its affinities with that of the Aryan and Semitic Races.* London and Hongkong 1876.

Descamps, Paul. 'Le Cannibalisme, ses Causes et ses Modalités', *L'Anthropologie* XXXV nos. 3–4, July 1925, pp. 321–44.

Diaz, Bernal. *The Conquest of New Spain.* Harmondsworth 1963.

Digby, William. *The Famine Campaign in Southern India. 1876–1878.* London 1878.

Domalain, Jean-Yves. *Panjamon.* London 1973. (Modern Sarawak.)

Douglas, Mary (ed.) *Witchcraft Confessions and Accusations.* New York 1970.

Douglas, Mary. *Natural Symbols, explorations in cosmology.* London 1973.

Dozy, Reinhart. *Spanish Islam: A History of the Moslems in Spain.* London 1913.

Drumont, Edouard. *La France Juive.* 2 vols. Paris 1886. (Strongly anti-semitic.)

Duby, Georges, and Mandrou, Robert. *A History of French Civilisation.* London 1965.

Dunstan and Hobson. 'A note on early ingredients of Racial Prejudice in West Europe', *Race* VI no. 4, London 1965, pp. 334–9.

Early Christian Writings. The Apostolic Fathers. Harmondsworth P 1968.

Eaves, A. Osborne. *Modern Vampirism.* Harrogate 1904.

Edwardes, Michael. *In the blowing out of a flame. The world of the Buddha and the world of man.* London and New York 1975.

Eichhorn, Werner. *Chinese Civilisation. An Introduction.* London 1969.

Eitner, Lorenz. *Géricault's Raft of the Medusa.* London and New York 1972.

Eliade, Mircea [1]. *The Sacred and the Profane. The Nature of Religion.* New York P 1959.

Eliade, Mircea [2]. *From Primitives to Zen. A thematic source-book of the history of religions.* Chicago 1966, London 1967.

Enjoy, Paul d'. 'Le Baiser en Europe et en Chine', *Bulletin de la Société Anthropologique,* Paris 1897, pp. 181–5.

Evans-Wentz, W.Y. [1] (ed.) *Tibetan Yoga and Secret Doctrines, or Seven Books of Wisdom of the Great Path, according to the late Lama Kazi Dawa-Samdup's English rendering.* London 1935. 2nd edition 1958.

Evans-Wentz, W.Y. [2] (ed.) *The Tibetan Book of the Great Liberation, or the method of realizing Nirvana through knowing the mind.* London, New York and Toronto 1954.

Febvre, Lucien. 'Sorcellerie: Sottise ou révolution mentale?', *Annales: Economies, sociétés, civilisations* 3, 1948, pp. 9–15.

Filliozat, J. *La Doctrine classique de la médécine indienne.* Paris 1949.

Forbes, Thomas Rogers. *The Midwife and the Witch.* New Haven 1966.

Foucault, Michael. *Madness and Civilisation: a history of insanity in the Age of Reason.* London 1966.

Frankfort, H. and H. A., and John A. Wilson, Thorkild Jacobsen, and William A. Irwin. *The Intellectual Adventure of Ancient Man. An essay on speculative thought in the ancient Near East.* Chicago 1946.

Frazer, Sir James George [1]. *The Golden Bough. A Study in Magic and Religion.* 12 vols. London 1911–15. Abridged one-volume edition 1922.

Frazer, Sir James George [2]. *Folk-lore in the Old Testament. Studies in Comparative Religion, Legend and Law.* 3 vols. London 1919.

Furst, Peter T. (ed.) *Flesh of the Gods.* London 1972. (On the ritual associated with hallucinogens).

Gardner, G. B. *Witchcraft today.* London 1954.

Gernet, Jacques. *Daily Life in China on the Eve of the Mongol Invasions 1250–1276.* London 1962, Stanford, California 1970.

Gelling, Peter, and Davidson, Hilda Ellis. *The Chariot of the Sun, and other rites and symbols of the Northern Bronze Age.* London 1969.

[Glaber] Glabri, Rodulfi. *Historiarum. Libri Quinque. Ab Anno Incarnationis DCCCC usque ad Annum MXLIV.* Latin text published under the editorship of Maurice Prou, Paris 1886. (Glaber was a gossip rather than a reliable historian).

Gomme, George Laurence. *Ethnology in Folklore.* London 1892.

Gorce, M. and Mortier, R. *Histoire générale des religions,* vols. 1 and 5. Paris 1948–51.

Grant, Kenneth. *The Magical Revival.* London 1972.

Grant, Robert M. *Augustus to Constantine: The Thrust of the Christian Movement into the Roman World.* London 1971.

Graves, Robert. *The Greek Myths.* 2 vols. Harmondsworth 1955. P 1960.

Gray, George Buchanan. *Sacrifice in the Old Testament. Its Theory and Practice.* Oxford 1925.

Grimm, Jakob. *Teutonic Mythology.* 4 vols. New York 1883–88.

Griswold, Alexander B., Chewon Kim, and Peter H. Pott. *Burma, Korea and Tibet.* London 1964.

Grousset, René. *The Rise and Splendour of the Chinese Empire.* London 1952.

Guazzo, Francesco Maria. *Compendium Maleficarum.* Milan 1608. E. A. Ashwin translation, London 1929.

Guerra, Francisco. *The Pre-Columbian Mind.* New York and London 1972.

Gusdorf, Georges. *L'expérience humaine du sacrifice.* Paris 1948.

Hamel, F. *Human Animals.* London 1915.

Harris, C. R. S. *The Heart and the Vascular System in Ancient Greek Medicine. From Alcmaeon to Galen.* Oxford 1973.

Hartmann, Franz. 'Vampires', *Borderland* III no. 3, July 1896, pp. 353–8.

Haskins, Charles Homer. *The Renaissance of the Twelfth Century.* Harvard 1927. P 1957.

Hatch, John. *The History of Britain in Africa: From the 15th Century to the Present Day.* London 1969.

Heckethorn, Charles William. *The Secret Societies of all Ages and Countries.* 2 vols. London 1875. New edition 1897.

Hemphill, R. E. 'Historical Witchcraft and Psychiatric Illness in Western Europe', *Proceedings* of the Royal Society of Medicine 59, 1966, pp. 891–902.

Herodotus. *The Histories.* Trs. Aubrey de Selincourt. Harmondsworth 1954. P 1968.

Hilberg, Raul. *The Destruction of the European Jews.* Chicago and London 1961.

Hogg, Garry. *Cannibalism and Human Sacrifice.* London 1958. P 1973. (Deals predominantly with nineteenth-century tribals.)

Holmyard, E. J. *Alchemy.* Harmondsworth 1957.

Hooke, S. H. *Middle Eastern Mythology.* Harmondsworth 1963.

Hughes, Pennethorne. *Witchcraft.* London 1952. P 1965.

Hutton, J. H. [1]. 'Presidential Address Read before the Society at the Annual Meeting held at Exeter College, Oxford, on April 19th [subject: lycanthropy]', *Folk-Lore: Transactions of the Folk-Lore Society* LII no. 2, June 1941, pp. 83–100.

Hutton, J. H. [2]. 'Presidential Address read before the Society at the Annual Meeting held at the Royal Anthropological Institute, on March 10th, 1943. The Cannibal Complex', *Folklore: Transactions of the Folk-Lore Society* LIV no. 2, June 1943.

Indians, The American Heritage Book of. Ed. Alvin M. Josephy Jr. New York 1961, London 1968.

Jacob, H. E. *Six Thousand Years of Bread. Its Holy and unholy History.* New York 1944.

Jahn, U. *Zauber mit Menschenblut und anderen Teilen des menschlichen Körpers.* Berlin 1888.

James, E. O. [1]. *Origins of Sacrifice. A Study in Comparative Religion.* London 1933.

James, E. O. [2]. *The Ancient Gods. The History and Diffusion of Religion in the Ancient Near East and the Eastern Mediterranean.* London 1960.

Jarrett-Kerr, Martin. *Patterns of Christian Acceptance. Individual Response to the Missionary Impact 1550–1950.* Oxford 1972.

Jones, Gwyn. *Kings, Beasts and Heroes.* Oxford 1972. (Beowulf and parallel works.)

Kautilya. *Arthasastra.* Ed. R. P. Kangle. 3 vols. Bombay 1960–65. (Manual of laws and administration, north-east India, *c.* 1st century A.D.)

Kenrick, Donald, and Puxon, Grattan. *The Destiny of Europe's Gypsies.* London 1972.

Kidd, Beresford James. *The Later Mediaeval Doctrine of the Eucharistic Sacrifice.* London 1898.

Kosambi, Damodar Dharmanand. *An Introduction to the study of Indian history.* Bombay 1956. (Hindu beliefs and rituals).

Krafft-Ebing, R. von. *Psychopathia Sexualis.* 12th edition Stuttgart 1902. (Deals with sadism and the vampire legend.)

Kurtz, Donna C. and Boardman, John. *Greek Burial Customs.* London 1971.

La Barre, Weston. *The Ghost Dance. Origins of Religion.* New York and London 1972.

La Harpe, M. de. *Abrégé de l'Histoire Générale des Voyages.* 21 vols. Paris 1780.

Lattimore, Owen. *Inner Asian Frontiers of China.* London and New York 1940.

Lea, Henry Charles [1]. *The History of the Inquisition in the Middle Ages.* London and New York 1888.

Lea, Henry Charles [2]. *Materials toward a History of Witchcraft.* 3 vols. arranged and edited by Arthur C. Howland. New York 1957.

Lee, Richard B. and De Vore, Irven (eds.) *Man the Hunter.* Chicago 1968.

Lévi-Strauss, Claude [1]. *Totemism.* New York 1963, Harmondsworth P 1969.

Lévi-Strauss, Claude [2]. *Mythologiques.* 4 vols. Paris 1964–71. (*Le Cru et le cuit, Du Miel aux cendres, L'Origine des manières de table,* and *L'Homme nu* are the titles of the volumes. A structuralist view of over eight hundred American Indian myths.)

Loeb, E. M. 'The Blood Sacrifice Complex', *Memoirs* of the American Anthropological Association 30, 1923.

Macfarlane, A. D. J. *Witchcraft in Tudor and Stuart England.* London and New York 1970.

McNally, Raymond T. and Florescu, Radu. *In Search of Dracula.* New York 1973.

Marshack, Alexander. *The Roots of Civilisation. The Cognitive Beginnings of Man's First Art, Symbol and Notation.* New York and London 1972.

Masters, Anthony. *The Natural History of the Vampire.* London 1972.

Masters, R. E. L. *Eros and Evil: The Sexual Psychology of Witchcraft.* New York 1962.

Midelfort, H. C. Erik. *Witch Hunting in South-western Germany, 1562–1684. The Social and Intellectual Foundations.* Stanford 1972, Oxford 1973.

Monter, E. William. 'Patterns of Witchcraft in the Jura', *Journal of Social History* 5, 1971–72, pp. 1–25.

Moorehead, Alan. *The Fatal Impact. An Account of the Invasion of the South Pacific 1767–1840.* London 1966.

Mulvaney, Derek J. *The Prehistory of Australia.* London 1969. (Australian prehistory stretches to the eighteenth century.)

Murray, Margaret. 'Child-sacrifice among European Witches', *Man* XVIII, 1918.

Nebesky-Wojkowitz, René de. *Oracles and Demons of Tibet. The Cult and Iconography of the Tibetan Protective Deities.* The Hague 1956.

Newall, Venetia (ed.) *The Witch Figure.* London 1973.

Nock, Arthur Darby. *Essays on Religion and the Ancient World.* Edited by Zeph Stewart. 2 vols. Oxford 1972.

Onians, Richard Broxton. *The Origins of European Thought about the Body, the Mind, the Soul, the World, Time and Fate.* Cambridge 1951.

[Pan Ku: *Han Shu*]. *Food and Money in Ancient China: The Earliest Economic History of China to A.D. 25.* Translated and annotated by Nancy Lee Swann. Princeton 1950.

Parker, E. H. 'Human Sacrifices', *China Review* XVIII no. 4, p. 261.

Parkes, James. *A History of the Jewish People.* Harmondsworth P 1962.

Parrinder, Geoffrey. *Witchcraft, European and African.* London 1963.

Pauthier, M. G. and Bazin, M. *Chine Moderne, ou Description historique, géographique et littéraire . . . d'après des documents chinois.* This is *Asie* t.10 in the series entitled *L'Univers, ou Histoire et Description de tous les peuples.* Paris 1853.

Pavry, J. D. C. *The Zoroastrian Doctrine of a Future Life.* 2nd edition New York 1929.

Pelikan, Jaroslav. *The Christian Tradition. A History of the Development of Doctrine.* Vol. 1 (A.D. 100–600), Chicago 1971.

Perella, Nicholas James. *The Kiss Sacred and Profane: An Interpretive History of Kiss Symbolism and Related Religio-Erotic Themes.* Berkeley and Los Angeles 1969.

Piaget, Jean. *The Child's Conception of Physical Causality.* New York 1966.

Pliny the Elder. *Natural History.* Translated by H. Rackham. London 1950. (Book VII 190 deals with popular ways of thought on the subject of death.)

Polo, Marco. *Travels.* Translated by Ronald Latham. Harmondsworth 1958. (Notes refer to the 1968 London hardbound edition.)

Posener, Georges (ed.) *A Dictionary of Egyptian Civilisation.* London 1962. New York 1961.

Prakash, Om. *Food and Drinks in Ancient India.* Delhi 1961.

Praviel, Armand. *La tragédie de 'La Méduse'.* Paris 1931.

Praz, Mario. *The Romantic Agony.* London 1933. New edition 1951.

Prest, Thomas Peckett (or Preskett). *The String of Pearls; or The Barber of Fleet Street. A Domestic Romance.* London 1850. (The part-publication title, see p. 162, was altered for this one-volume edition.)

Rachewitz, Boris de. *An Introduction to Egyptian Art.* London 1960.

Ravaisson, François. *Archives de la Bastille: Documents Inédits.* Paris 1866–1904. (Vols. 4, 5 and 6 deal with the La Voisin poison interrogations).

Read, Piers Paul. *Alive. The Story of the Andes Survivors.* New York and London 1974.

Regardie, Francis Israel. *Golden Dawn.* 4 vols. London 1937–40, Minnesota 1969. (Rites of the Order of the Golden Dawn, a twentieth-century magical cult).

Reinaud, M. (ed.) *Relation des Voyages faits par les Arabes et les Persans dans l'Inde et à la Chine dans le IXe siècle de l'Ère chrétienne.* Paris 1845.

Remy [Remigius], Nicholas. *Daemonolatreiae.* Lyon 1595. Trs., as Demonolatry, by E. A. Ashwin, London 1930.

Rhodes, Henry T. F. *The Satanic Mass.* London 1954. P 1964.

Robbins, Rossell Hope. *The Encyclopedia of Witchcraft and Demonology.* New York 1959.

Roberts, J. M. *The Mythology of the Secret Societies.* London 1972.

Ronay, Gabriel. *The Dracula Myth.* London and New York (as *The Truth about Dracula*) 1972.

Rosen, George. 'The Mentally Ill and the Community in Western and Central Europe during the Late Middle Ages and Renaissance', *Journal of the History of Medicine and Allied Sciences* XIX, 1964, pp. 377–88.

Russell, Jeffrey Burton. *Witchcraft in the Middle Ages.* Ithaca and London 1972.

Rybakov, B. A. 'Cosmogony and Mythology of the Agriculturalists of the Eneolithic', *Soviet Anthropology and Archaeology* IV nos. 3 and 4, 1965.

Ryder, Alan. *Benin and the Europeans 1485–1897.* London 1971.

Saggs, H. W. F. *Everyday Life in Babylonia and Assyria.* London and New York 1965.

Savigny, Henri, and Corréard, Alexandre. *Naufrage de la Frégate la Méduse faisant partie de l'expedition du Sénégal en 1816.* Paris 1817, 4th (enlarged) edition 1821.

Schofield, J. N. *Archaeology and the Afterlife.* London 1951.

Schulze, W. A. 'Der Vorwurf des Ritualmords gegen die Christen im Altertum und in der Neuzeit', *Zeitschrift für Kirchengeschichte* LXV, 1953–54.

Seabrook, W. B. *The Magic Island.* London 1929. (Haiti).

Segal, J. B. *The Hebrew Passover from Earliest Times to A.D. 70.* London 1963.

Seznec, J. *The Survival of the Pagan Gods.* London and Princeton 1953.

Sheldon, William. 'Brief Account of the Caraibs, who inhabited the Antilles . . . by William Sheldon Esq. of the Island of Jamaica',

Archaeologia Americana, Transactions and Collections of the American Antiquarian Society I, 1820, pp. 365–433.

Shumaker, Wayne. *The Occult Sciences in the Renaissance. A Study in Intellectual Patterns.* Berkeley and Los Angeles 1972.

Sigerist, Henry E. *A History of Medicine.* Vol. 1: *Primitive and Archaic Medicine.* New York 1951. P 1967.

Singer, Charles. *A Short History of Medicine.* London 1928.

Smith, Kirby Flower. 'An Historical Study of the Werwolf in Literature', *Publications of the Modern Language Association of America* IX 1, New Series II 1, pp. 1–42. Baltimore 1894.

Smith, Preserved. *A Short History of Christian Theophagy.* Chicago 1922.

Solecki, Ralph S. *Shanidar. The Humanity of Neanderthal Man.* New York 1971, London 1972.

Soustelle, Jacques. *Daily Life of the Aztecs on the Eve of the Spanish Conquest.* London 1961. P 1968.

Spiel, Christian. *Menschen essen Menschen. Die Welt der Kannibalen* Munich 1972.

Sprenger, Jakob, and Institoris [or Krämer], Heinrich. *Malleus Maleficarum.* Nuremberg 1485 or 86. Translated by Montague Summers, London 1928.

Starkie, Enid. *Petrus Borel, the Lycanthrope. His Life and Times.* London 1954.

Steiner, Franz. *Taboo.* London 1956. P 1967.

Stewart, T. D. 'Stone Age Skull Surgery: A General Review, with Emphasis on the New World', *Smithsonian Report for 1957*, pp. 469–491.

Strack, Herman L. *The Jew and Human Sacrifice; an Historical and Sociological Inquiry.* London and New York 1909. (Human blood and Jewish ritual.)

Summers, Montague [1]. *The History of Witchcraft and Demonology.* London 1926, New York 1956. (Summers was a believer.)

Summers, Montague [2]. *The Vampire, his kith and kin.* London 1928.

Summers, Montague [3]. *The Werewolf.* London 1933.

Summers, Montague [4]. *The Vampire in Europe.* London 1929.

[Swift, Jonathan]. *A modest proposal for preventing the children of poor people from being a Burthen to their Parents or the Country, and for making them Beneficial to the Publick.* Dublin 1728. London 1730.

Symonds, John. *The Great Beast.* London 1971. (The 'magic' of Aleister Crowley.)

Tannahill, Reay. *Food in History.* New York and London 1973.

Taylor, F. Sherwood. *The Alchemists.* London 1951.

Thomas, Keith. *Religion and the Decline of Magic.* London 1971.

Thompson, Stith. *Motif-Index of Folk-Literature.* 6 vols. 2nd edition Copenhagen and Bloomington 1955–58.

Thorndike, Lynn. *A History of Magic and Experimental Science.* 8 vols. New York 1923–58.

Trachtenberg, Joshua. *The Devil and the Jews: The Medieval Conception of the Jew and Its Relation to Modern Antisemitism.* New Haven 1943.

Trevor-Roper, H. R. *The European Witch-Craze of the 16th and 17th Centuries.* Harmondsworth and New York 1969.

Trumbull, H. Clay. *The Blood Covenant. A Primitive Rite and its Bearings on Scripture.* 3rd edition Philadelphia 1898.

Tylor, Sir Edward Burnett. *Primitive Culture.* 2 vols. London 1871. P, as *Religion in Primitive Culture*, New York 1958.

Ucko, Peter J., and Dimbleby, G. W. (eds.) *The Domestication and Exploitation of Plants and Animals.* London 1969. (Symposium papers.)

Ucko, Peter J., and Rosenfeld, Andrée. *Palaeolithic Cave Art.* London 1967. (A critical evaluation of the more widely held modern theories.)

Vaillant, George C. *The Aztecs of Mexico.* New York 1944. P 1956.

Varney, the Vampire, or The Feast of Blood. By the author of Grace Rivers; or, The Merchant's Daughter. London 1845–47. (The British Museum catalogue attributes this work to James M. Rymer, modern vampirologists to T. P. Prest.)

Vaughan, Dorothy M. *Europe and the Turk. A Pattern of Alliances 1350–1700.* Liverpool 1954.

Vicens Vives, Jaime. *An Economic History of Spain.* Princeton 1969.

Volhardt, E. *Kannibalismus.* Stuttgart 1939. (A metaphysical view.)

Vries, Arnold de. *Primitive Man and his Food.* Chicago 1952.

Waite, Arthur Edward. *The Holy Grail, its legends and symbolism. An explanatory survey of their embodiment in Romance literature and a critical study of the interpretations placed thereon.* London 1933.

Walford, Cornelius. *The Famines of the World: Past and Present.* London 1879. (A statistical study, mainly in tabular form.)

W.A.P. 'Alchemy in China', *China Review* VII, pp. 242–55.

Washburn, Sherwood L. (ed.) *Social Life of Early Man.* Chicago 1961, London 1962.

Watson, William. *China before the Han Dynasty.* London 1961.

Wedgwood, C. V. *The Thirty Years War.* London and New York 1961.

Wernert, Paul. 'L'anthropophagie rituelle et la chasse aux têtes, aux époques actuelle et paléolithique', *L'Anthropologie* 46, 1936, pp. 33–43.

Willey, Gordon R. *Introduction to American Archeology.* Vol. 1 Englewood Cliffs, New Jersey 1966.

Williams, S. Wells. 'Illustrations of men and things in China', *The Chinese Repository* X, pp. 104–8.

Wolf, Leonard. *A Dream of Dracula. In Search of the Living Dead.* New York 1973.

Yovanovitch, V. M. *La Guzla de Prosper Mérimée, étude d'histoire romantique.* Paris 1911. (Vampires).

Yuan T'ung-li. *China in Western Literature.* New Haven 1958. (A continuation of Cordier.)

Yule, Sir Henry (trs. and ed.) *The Book of Ser Marco Polo.* 3rd edn. London 1921.

Zimmer, Heinrich. *Myths and Symbols in Indian Art and Civilization.* New York 1946.

NOTES ON SOURCES

Where an abbreviated reference is given below, full details of the work referred to will be found in the bibliography.

INTRODUCTION   *Flesh, blood and spirit* pp. 1–18

1   S. Langdon: *Die neubabylonischen Königinschriften*, Leipzig 1912, pp 125–7.
2   Roux pp. 356, 358, 360–4, and Saggs, map p. 165.
3   Translation of the *Enuma elish*. E. A. Speiser in *Ancient Near Eastern Texts Relating to the Old Testament*, edited by J. B. Pritchard Princeton, NJ 1950, pp. 60–72. See also Thorkild Jacobsen in Frankfort, pp. 172–84.
4   *Deuteronomy* 12:23. Generally believed to date from *c.* 621 B.C.
5   Assuming an average life span of twenty years, and a world population numbering 500,000 at the beginning of the period and 3,000,000 at the end.
6   Coon [1] p. 87.
7   Brothwell p. 24.
8   F.M. Bergounioux, in Washburn p. 114.
9   Herodotus IV 65.
10 Coles and Higgs p. 233.
11 Sallust: *Catalina* XXII; and Dr Yung Wing, cited in Trumbull pp. 43–4.
12 Trumbull p. 38.
13 Spenser St John: *Life in the Forests of the Far East*, London 1862, vol. 1, pp. 116f.
14 Henri V. Vallois, in Washburn p. 231.
15 Herodotus IV 26.
16 Strabo: *Geography* IV 201.
17 Robert L. Carneiro of the American Museum of Natural History NY, reported in the Elmira *Sunday Telegram*, February 18 1973.
18 Tannahill pp. 19–20; and Stanley M. Garn and Walter D. Block in *American Anthropologist* 72, 1970, p. 106.
19 Edward S. Deevey: 'The Human Population', in *Scientific American* 203, 1960, pp. 194–204.
20 William T. Divale in *World Archaeology* 4, 1972, p. 222.
21 Frazer [1] pp. 293–4.

22 Whitmarsh *The World's Rough Hand*, cited in Hutton [2] p. 283.
23 Posener p. 34; Herodotus IV 64; and Grousset p. 39.
24 Grousset p. 49.
25 *Journal of the Anthropological Institute* xiii, pp. 135 and 283; F. E. Maning: *Old New Zealand*, 1900, p. 332; *Jesuits in North America*, p. xxxix and p. 250; J. L. Wilson: *Western Africa*, 1856, pp. 167f; M. E. Durham: *Tribal Origins . . . of the Balkans*, pp. 160f.
26 Reported in the London *Times*, November 30 1971.
27 *Transactions of the Society of Biblical Archaeology* vol. IV part 1; and *Proceedings* of the same, March 3 1885.
28 Theodore Roszak: *The Making of a Counter Culture: Reflections on the Technocratic Society and its Youthful Opposition*, New York 1969, London 1970, pp. 148–9.
29 See Tylor pp. 14–42 for numerous examples of primitive views of the soul.
30 The I-thou and I-it distinction, first used by Martin Buber in a discussion of twentieth-century attitudes to God (*Ich und Du*, 1923), has since been adapted to the prehistoric situation by such scholars as Frankfort.
31 c.f. correspondence columns of the London *Times Literary Supplement*, letters from Richard Boston and E. G. Sandersley, December 14 and 21 1973.
32 A misquotation, certainly, but I have been unable to find a printed version of this traditional Scots prayer.
33 Tylor, p. 16.
34 Frazer [1], p. 190.
35 William S. Laughlin, in Washburn pp. 171–2.
36 Brandon pp. 341 and 587–9.
37 Onians pp. 13 and 67–8.
38 Brandon p. 113; and Tylor pp. 14–42.
39 *Odyssey* XI 96.
40 *ibid.* XVII 539–47.
41 *Pirkê de Rabbi Eliezer* chapter LII.
42 Onians pp. 254–63.
43 *Odyssey* XI 218ff.
44 E. B. Cross in *Journal of the American Oriental Society* iv, 1834, pp. 311ff; Franz Boas in the *Report* of the British Association, 1890, p. 396; James [1] pp. 102–3; and Onians p. 156.
45 Tylor pp. 36–40.
46 Alberto C. Blanc, in Washburn pp. 126–8.
47 *ibid.* p. 126
48 Coles and Higgs pp. 232–3; and James [2] pp. 55–7.
49 Soustelle pl. 14a.
50 Hutton [2] p. 282. Headhunting is still said to be practised in some of the more remote jungle regions of south-east Asia.
51 See examples in Solecki.
52 Brothwell pp. 24–5.

1 EATING PEOPLE IS WRONG pp. 19–34.

1 These and many other examples may be found in Frazer [1] pp. 426–38.
2 Eliade [1] pp. 102–6.
3 'The Hymn of the Primeval Man', *Rig Veda* X 90. Trs. in Basham pp. 242–43.
4 'Hymn of Creation', *Rig Veda* X 129. Trs. in Basham pp. 249–50.
5 Pliny XXX 1.
6 For the Dionysos, Zagreus and Orpheus legends, see Burn p. 135; and Graves vol. I pp. 103–15 and 118–20.
7 *Exodus* 22:29–30.
8 *ibid.* 20:9–11.
9 *ibid.* 12:29.
10 James [1] p. 189.
11 *Exodus* 12:1–36.
12 Brandon p. 490.
13 *Genesis* 22:9–13.
14 *Leviticus* 7:16–17.
15 *ibid.* 27:1–8.
16 For changing Hebrew attitudes to sacrifice, see James [1] pp. 188–193 and 257–65; [2] pp. 149–51; and Baron vol. I pp. 122–3.
17 *Psalms* 50:9–13.
18 *Berakah* 17a, quoted in James [1] p. 265.
19 *Leviticus* 17:11–14.
20 Baron vol. I pp. 44 and 51.
21 See, for example, II *Samuel* 21:1–11; 3:27–30; 25:33. On the 'voice' of shed blood, *Genesis* 4:10, and other examples in Frazer [2] pp. 101–102.
22 *Genesis* 17:9–11.
23 Freud: *Totem and Taboo*, 1950; E. Roellenbleck: *Magna Mater im-alten Testament*, 1949; F. Zimmerman: 'Origin and Significance of the Jewish Rite of Circumcision', in *The Psychoanalytic Review* XXXVIII, 1951; and Bruno Bettelheim: *Symbolic Wounds. Puberty Rites and the Envious Male* 1955.
24 *Genesis* 17:9.
25 Buxtorf: *Synagoga Judaica* Cap. II.
26 Eliade [1] pp. 51 and 56–7.
27 *Joshua* 6:26.
28 I *Kings* 16:34.
29 Paul Sartori: 'Über das Bauopfer', in *Zeitschrift für Ethnologie* 30, 1938, pp. 1–54; *The Glass Palace Chronicle of the Kings of Burma* [1829], trs. Pe Maung Tin and G. H. Luce, 1925, describes how the Guardians of the Gates proved useful in time of war, p. 174; C. Doughty: *Travels in Arabia Deserta*, 1888, p. 100; S. I. Curtiss: *Primitive Semitic Religion Today*, 1902, pp. 182ff.
30 *Exodus* 24:6–8.
31 *Deuteronomy* 28:16.

32 *ibid.* 28:54–7.
33 Irwin in Frankfort p. 263; and James [2] pp. 187–93.
34 j. Killaim IX 4 32b, cited in Baron vol. II p. 312.
35 Baron vol. II p. 312
36 Griswold p. 180. A description of the intermediate stage of *Bardo* in Tibetan Buddhism, but equally applicable to the *Vedic* view.
37 From *Bundahishn*, ed. Anklesaria, trs. by R. C. Zaehner in his *The Teachings of the Magi*, 1956, pp. 145–50.

2 THE CENTURIES OF HUNGER pp. 35–55

1 Quoted in Sir E. A. Wallis Budge: *The Divine Origin of the Craft of the Herbalist*, London 1928, p. 5.
2 Quoted in Grousset p. 106.
3 From Ibn Ishaq: *Life of Muhammad*, written *c.* A.D. 770 and expanded *c.* A.D. 820 by Ibn Isham. Full MS translation by Edward Rehatsek in the library of the Royal Asiatic Society, London. This quotation is taken from the much abbreviated edition published, under the editorship of Michael Edwardes, in London, 1964. pp. 106–110.
4 Sa'id ibn Judi, quoted in Dozy p. 332.
5 Dozý pp. 331–3.
6 Geraldus Cambrensis: *Conquest of Ireland* I 4.
7 Quoted in Yule I p. 313.
8 Guibert de Nogent (1053–1124): *Gesta Dei per Francos* VII,s ummarised in G.P.R. James: *The History of Chivalry*, 1830, pp. 178–79.
9 The *Nibelungenlied*, trs. William Nanson Lettsom, New York and London 1901. 36th adventure, XXXIII–XXXVIII, pp. 340–1.
10 Hayton, in Ramusio XVII.
11 Quoted in Yule I p. 312
12 Vincent de Beauvais: *Speculum historiale*, quoted *ibid.* p. 313.
13 Cited *ibid.*
14 Cited (without source) in Stuart Legg; *The Heartland*, London 1970, p. 293.
15 Bergmann: *Nomad. Streifereien* I 14, cited in Yule I p. 313.
16 Evans-Wentz [2] pp. 138–9.
17 *Apastamba Dharma Sutra* I 6.18, cited in Prakash p. 39.
18 Herodotus III 101; and Dalton, cited in Hutton [2] p. 283.
19 Nebesky-Wojkowitz pp. 343–4.
20 Della Penna, cited in Yule I p. 312.
21 John Pian del Carpine: *History of the Mongols*. Hakluyt Society 137.
22 Graves I pp. 39–44.
23 The Greek legends may be found in many editions. For sacrificial practices, see for example Graves I n. 2 p. 42 and n. 9 p. 110.
24 Nock I pp. 101–3.
25 James [2] pp. 199, 317–18.
26 Coptic text (British Museum Oriental MS no. 7026) trs. in Sir E. A.

Wallis Budge: *Coptic Apocrypha*, London 1913, pp. 59f. and 241f.

27 Pan Ku pp. 148, 156, 183–4, 197, 200, 213.

28 In Pauthier and Bazin p. 461.

29 *ibid.*

30 *ibid.*

31 In Reinaud pp. 52 and 68.

32 Pian del Carpine (see note 21, above), p. 638.

33 Gernet p. 135.

34 Dandin, trs. in Basham p. 444.

35 Walford pp. 5–6.

36 Glaber IX 17, p. 44.

38 *Harleian Miscellany* III p. 151, quoted in Walford p. 7.

38 Abd al-Latif pp. 370–2.

39 Al-Baghdadi (1226), trs. in A. J. Arberry: 'A Baghdad Cookery-Book', in *Islamic Culture* 13, 1939, p. 34.

40 Abd al-Latif pp. 360–9.

3 THE RED ELIXIR pp. 56–74

1 Bainton II p. 40. The Definition is quoted in C. G. Coulton: *Five Centuries of Religion* I p. 104.

2 *Mark* 14: 22–4.

3 *Luke* 22:19.

4 Nock II p. 804. On the disciples, see Brandon, also *The Saints*, ed. John Coulson, New York 1958.

5 Nock II pp. 104–9, 807; James [1] pp. 267–9; Alberto C. Blanc, in Washburn p. 134.

6 I *Corinthians* 11:24–6.

7 Quoted in J. M. Neale: *History of the Holy Eastern Church*, 1850, p. 650.

8 Quoted in Jacob p. 162.

9 James [1] p. 181.

10 *John* 6:35.

11 Quoted in Jacob p. 161.

12 *Didache* II 9, in *Early Christian Writings* p. 232.

13 Parkes pp. 82–90; Jacob pp. 164–72; Baron XI pp. 167–75; Hughes p. 143.

14 Waite pp. 327ff. and 511ff.

15 Salerno Regimen, rhymed English version: *The Englishman's Doctor* by Sir John Harington, London 1608.

16 Thorndike III pp. 79–80.

17 *Chroniques de France*, 1516, f.ccii, quoted by Soane in *Notes and Queries*, February 28 1857.

18 Pliny XXVI 5; Soane *ibid*; Thorndike II p. 332; Dennys pp. 66–7.

19 Calvert and Gruner: *A Hangman's Diary* p. 63; Frazer [2] I p. 90; D. F. Rennie: *Peking*, 1865, II p. 244.

20 Roger Bacon (1267) quoted in Holmyard p. 120.

21 Holmyard pp. 96–7.
22 For the story of Gilles de Rais, see Benedetti's recent account. The trial transcript is in Bataille.
23 Ronay pp. 93–145.
24 Manrique, quoted in Collis p. 205.
25 Collis pp. 203–44; Edwardes 140–51.

4 BLOOD FOR THE GODS pp. 75–91

1 Columbus p. 78.
2 *ibid.* pp. 122–3.
3 *ibid.* p. 125.
4 *ibid.* p. 126; Hugh Popham in *The Cunarder*, 1970; Sheldon p. 426.
5 Sheldon p. 427.
6 Labat: *Nouveaux Voyages aux Isles Françoises de l'Amérique*, 1712, t.1 par. 2 p. 11.
7 La Harpe t. 15 p. 218.
8 Charles Wesley, hymn no. 534 in *The Church Hymnary, Revised Edition*, 1937.
9 Vicens Vives p. 386.
10 Diaz p. 104, 122.
11 *ibid.* pp. 120, 122–4.
12 *ibid.* pp. 137–8.
13 *ibid.* p. 183.
14 *ibid.* pp. 198–9.
15 *ibid.* p. 225.
16 *ibid.* pp. 222–3.
17 Soustelle pp. 109–10, 155, and 114–15.
18 *Indians* p. 109.
19 Diaz pp. 234–40.
20 *ibid.* pp. 386–7.
21 *ibid.* pp. 405–7.
22 Cited in *Indians* p. 105.
23 Vicens Vives p. 386.
24 Carletti pp. 66, 59.

5 THE NONCONFORMISTS pp. 92–107

1 Boguet pp. xxxiii–vii.
2 Baron I pp. 192–3.
3 Cited, with sources, in Russell pp. 89–93; Boguet p. 57.
4 Russell pp. 86–8, 93.
5 Baron XI pp. 146–7.
6 Quoted Parkes p. 82.
7 Baron XI p. 149.

8 *ibid.* p. 155.
9 Eckhardt: *Gesetze* I 114, art. 64:2a; *ibid.* II p. 268; capitulary of A.D. 775–90 for Saxony, cap. 6, trs. McNeill and Gamer p. 389; Russell p. 69; Hutton [2] p. 281.
10 Haskins p. 279.
11 Russell pp. 24, 253.
12 Sprenger and Institoris II i 15, p. 149.
13 Midelfort p. 187.
14 Sprenger and Institoris III 22, p. 243.
15 *ibid.* II i 13, p. 140.
16 *ibid.* II i 2, p. 101.
17 Remy p. 57 n.
18 Russell pp. 251, 240.
19 Sprenger and Institoris II i 3, p. 107.
20 Cardan, quoted in Boguet p. 70.
21 Boguet p. 71.
22 Sprenger and Institoris pp. 102, 229.
23 Quoted in Summers [1] p. 26.
24 Ravaisson t. 6 pp. 251, 300, 328, 334, 432.
25 Clébert pp. 102–3.
26 Parkes p. 83.
27 Robert Lindsay of Pitscottie: *The Chronicles of Scotland 1436–1603,* 2 vols, 1814.
28 *Denham Tracts,* Folklore Society 2 vols. 1892–5, I p. 155.
29 Captain Charles Johnson: *A General History . . . of the most Famous Highwaymen, Murderers, Street-Robbers, &c.,* London 1734, pp. 132–3.
30 All about Vlad in Ronay pp. 58–90.
31 William Hilton Wheeler: *Brigandage in South Italy,* 1864; *Causes Célèbres,* Paris 1840, VII p. 117.
32 *Travels and Works of Captain John Smith,* ed. Edward Arber, Edinburgh 1910, II p. 499.
33 C. Whitehead: *Lives and Exploits of English Highwaymen, Pirates and Robbers.*
34 Michel de Montaigne: 'On Cannibals', in *Essays of Montaigne* trs. Charles Cotton, 3 vols, London 1877, I pp. 258–9.
36 Quoted in F. Parkman: *The Jesuits in North America in the seventeenth century,* p. 228 n; *ibid.* xxxix; *ibid.* xl n.
37 Walford pp. 11–12.
38 Peter Mundy, quoted in Philip Woodruff: *The Founders,* London 1953 (vol. I of *The Men who ruled India*), pp. 46–7; Abdul Hamid, quoted in C. G. F. Simkin: *The Traditional Trade of Asia,* London 1968, p. 173.

6 WEREWOLVES AND VAMPIRES pp. 108–136

1 'Fulahn' in *From Strange Places,* Edinburgh 1933, pp. 135–9; Adamson: *The Empire of the Snakes*; Hutton [1] p. 91; Davidson p. 68.

2 Petronius: *The Satyricon*, trs. William Arrowsmith, New York 1960, pp. 68–9.

3 Boguet pp. 140–1.

4 Cited, with sources, in K. F. Smith pp. 34–5.

5 Nicole Belmont: *Les signes de la naissance*, Paris 1971.

6 K. F. Smith pp. 21–2; Summers [2] pp. 163–4.

7 Remy p. 263.

8 K. F. Smith p. 23.

9 Augustine of Hippo: *De civitate dei* XVIII 18.

10 Marcellus Sidetes, cited in Summers [2] p. 166.

11 Quoted in *ibid.* p. 167.

12 Herodotus IV 105.

13 Theodore of Tarsus: *Liber Poenitentialis* cap. XXVII.

14 For example, P. Saintyves: *Les Contes de Perrault et les Recits parallèles* pp. 341ff.

15 Quoted in Le Comte de Résie: *Histoire et Traité des Sciences Occultes*, Paris 1857, t. 2 pp. 513–14; Olaus Magnus: *Historia de gentibus septentrionale* XVIII 14, quoted in Remy p. 113.

16 Mandrou, in Duby and Mandrou pp. 220–3.

17 Hutton [1] pp. 89–90.

18 Bodin p. 256; Hughes p. 184; Hutton [1] p. 89. Other examples in Boguet pp. 136–54.

19 Cited in *L'Homme et l'Animal: Cent mille ans de vie commune*, ed. Jacques Boudet, Paris 1962, p. 191.

20 One version of the legend may be found in Hogg, pp. 58–63.

21 For fuller details of the Leopard Societies, see *ibid.* pp. 101–8.

22 Zopfius: *Dissertatio de Vampiris Seruiensibus*, Halle 1733, quoted in Summers [2] pp. 1–2.

23 Dom Augustin Calmet: *Dissertations sur les apparitions des anges, des démons et des esprits. Et sur les revenants et vampires de Hongrie, de Bohème, de Moravie et de Silésie*, Paris 1746, quoted in Summers [2] pp. 27–8.

24 Summers [2] p. 183.

25 *Les Lettres Juives*, 1732.

26 Quoted in Ronay pp. 18–19.

27 Quoted in Summers [2] p. 206.

28 Quoted, without source, in *ibid.* p. 208.

29 Report in *The Times*, London, January 9 1973.

30 Map, cited in Russell p. 97; William of Newburgh: *Historia Rerum Anglicarum*, ed. Thomas Sebright, Oxford 1719, V 22–3.

31 G. Willoughby-Meade: *Chinese Ghouls and Goblins*, London 1928.

32 Mathias de Giraldo: *Histoire curieuse et pittoresque des sorciers divins, magiciens, astrologues, voyants, revenants, âmes en peine, vampires, spectres, esprits malins, sorts jetés, exorcismes, etc. depuis l'antiquité jusqu'à nos jours. Revue et augmentée par Fornari*, Paris 1846. Giraldo was said to be a Dominican and former Inquisition exorcist, but his existence appears to have been as fictional as many of his tales.

33 Z. T. Pierart, quoted (approvingly) by Summers [2] pp. 195–6.
34 Quoted in Summers [2] p. 171. See full title under note 23, above.
35 W. Tebb and M. D. Vollum: *Premature Burial and how it may be prevented*, 2nd edn. London 1905; report in *The Times*, London, March 30 1974; report in the *Sunday Times*, London, March 3 1974.
36 W. G. Aitchison Robertson: 'Bier Right', *Fifth International Congress of Medicine* [Geneva 1925], 1926, pp. 192–8.
37 Allacci: *De Graecorum hodie quorundam opinationibus*, Köln 1645.
38 Tylor p. 38.
39 Summers p. 90.
40 Ronay pp. 21, 27.
41 *Yu-yang-tsa-tsu*, quoted in Basil Davidson (ed.) *The African Past: Chronicles from Antiquity to Modern Times*, London and Boston 1964. 1966 P edn. p. 121; Michael Psellus *Chronographia*, trs. by E. R. A, Sewter as *Fourteen Byzantine Rulers*, Harmondsworth 1966, VII 69; B. A. L. Cranstone, in Ucko and Dimbleby pp. 250–62; Marco Polo pp. 81–2.

7 WHO'S FOR DINNER? pp. 137–64

1 Swift p. 10.
2 *ibid*. pp. 10–12.
3 *ibid*. pp. 11–13, 17–19.
4 Eugene Tarlé: *Napoleon's Invasion of Russia 1812*, London 1942, pp. 282–3.
5 Quoted *ibid*. pp. 244, 277, 280.
6 Savigny's story was reported in full in *The Times*, London, September 17 1816, p. 2.
7 Praviel pp. 176–7.
8 *The Times*, London, September 17 1816, p. 2.
9 David Lavender: *The American Heritage Book of the American West*, New York 1965. Paperback edn. (as *The Penguin Book of the American West*), Harmondsworth 1969, pp. 257–60.
10 Contemporary broadsheet, 1837, published by J. Cartnach of Seven Dials, London.
11 For the story of Eliza Fraser, see Michael Alexander: *Mrs Fraser on the Fatal Shore*, London 1971.
12 Quoted in Hogg pp. 24–5.
13 *ibid*. p. 31.
14 *ibid*. pp. 33–4.
15 'The White Man's Burden', in Rudyard Kipling: *The Five Nations*, London 1903.
16 Turner: *Nineteen Years in Polynesia*, p. 194; cited in Delmas: *Religion des Marquisiens*, p. 149; R. Verneau: *Les races humaines*, Paris 1891, p. 171.
17 Roheim: *Australian Totemism*, London 1925, p. 391.
18 Firth: *Primitive Economics of the New Zealand Maori*; Felix May-

nard, quoted in Hogg p. 191; F. E. Maning: *Old New Zealand*, 1900, p. 332.

19 Loeb: *Sumatra*, pp. 34ff.

20 *Annales de la Propagation de la Foi* XXIX, p. 353, and XXI, p. 298; letter in *North China Mail*, quoted in Trumbull p. 364; E. H. Parker, in *China Review* February–March 1901, p. 136.

21 Shanghai *Courier and Gazette*, November 1875; *Peking Gazette*, May 1874.

22 Denny p. 68.

23 William Sleeman: *Report on the depredations committed by the Thug gangs of upper and central India*, 1842. Philip Meadows Taylor's *Confessions of a Thug*, 1839, is a fictional account by an officer who took part in the suppression of the gangs.

24 Mungo Park: *Travels in the Interior Districts of Africa*, London 1799.

25 Barbot, in A. and J. Churchill: *A Collection of Voyages and Travels*, 6 vols. 1744–6, vol. 5, p. 479; Consul Hutchinson, in *Transactions of the Ethnological Society*, New Series I, p. 338.

26 P. A. Talbot: *Southern Nigeria*, Oxford 1926; C. Maistre: *À travers l'Afrique centrale: Du Congo au Niger*, Paris 1895, pp. 24–26.

27 Mary Kingsley: *Travels in West Africa* pp. 287f; Burckhardt: *Travels in Nubia* p. 356; Dr Tautain: 'Quelques Renseignements sur les Bobo', in *Revue Ethnologique*, 1887 no. 6, pp. 230–1.

28 Richard Burton: *The City of the Saints*, 1861, p. 117; F. Michel: *Dix-huit ans chez les Sauvages*, Paris 1866, p. 374; Sollas: *Ancient Hunters*, 1924, p. 225; Sumner: *Folkways*, p. 332.

29 Sir Spenser St John: *Hayti, or The Black Republic*, London 1884, pp. 196, 201–2.

30 *ibid.* pp. 196–206.

31 *British Review*, 1818, XI, p. 37.

32 *Monsieur Nicolas, v^e époque*, quoted in Praz pp. 107–8.

33 Quoted in E. Estève: *Byron et le romantisme français*, Paris 2nd edn. 1929, p. 130.

34 For a study of morbid romanticism in nineteenth-century literature (European), see Praz. The Baudelaire obscenity trial is described in Enid Starkie: *Baudelaire*, London 1957. Paperback edn. 1971, pp. 358–82.

35 Quoted in Summers [2] p. 331.

36 Jean Lorrain's story of Narkiss, prince of Egypt, in his *Princes de nacre et de caresse*.

8 SURVIVAL KITS pp. 165–78

1 Chamberlain I p. 261.

2 Reviews quoted in Chamberlain II, page 9 of publisher's appendix.

3 Chamberlain I pp. lxviii, 257, 298, 574–5.

4 *ibid.* pp. 276–89.

5 *ibid.* pp. 297, 327, 269.

6 Speech in the Reichstag, 1895, by Deputy Ahlwardt, quoted in Hilberg pp. 10–11; Chamberlain I p. lxxxiii; *ibid.* p. 331.
7 Quoted in Kenrick and Puxon p. 71.
8 *ibid.* pp. 183–4; Hilberg p. 767.
9 I am indebted to Michael Edwardes for this information.
10 Grousset p. 39; Herodotus IV 63.
11 *Sunday Times*, London, October 22 1972; for historical details and travellers' accounts of cannibalism in Borneo and New Guinea, see Hogg pp. 125–53.
12 Ione Leigh: *In the Shadow of the Mau Mau*, London 1954; *Sunday Times Magazine*, London, October 7 1973; Seymour Parker: 'The Wiitiko Psychosis in the Context of Ojibwa Personality and Culture' in *American Anthropologist* 62, 1960, pp. 603–23.
13 Trial report in *The News of the World*, London, December 21 1924.
14 H. Söderman: *Auf der Spur des Verbrechen*, Köln-Berlin 1957.
15 Dr Magnus Pyke, reported in *The Times*, London, November 15 1969.
16 *The Times*, London, July 16 1970; *Sunday Times*, London, March 11 1973.
17 A. Anatoli (formerly Kuznetsov): *Babi Yar*, London 1970; Harrison Salisbury: *The 900 Days*, *New York* 1969; *Khrushchev Remembers*, New York 1970, London 1971.
18 Quoted in Hilberg p. 172; quoted in Lord Russell of Liverpool: *The Scourge of the Swastika*, London 1954.
19 Psychiatrist Robert Jay Lifton, reported in *Time*, January 15 1973.
20 The story of the Andes crash may be found in Read.
21 Reuter report in *The Times*, London, December 28 1972.
22 Reports in *The Times*, London, December 30 1972, and the *New York Times*, January 1 1973.
23 See note 20, above.
24 *The Times*, London July 14 1973.
25 Hartwell's story is taken from the inquest reports in the *Globe and Mail*, Toronto, March 1, 2, and 3 1973, and *The Times*, London, March 5 1973; his statement to reporters from the *Evening Standard*, London, March 1 1973.

POSTSCRIPT pp. 179–81

1 John Skow in *Time*, January 15 1973.
2 Peter Lennon in the *Sunday Times*, London, November 24 1972.
3 This leaflet, distributed in 1969, was anonymous.
4 Rhodes p. 230.
5 Gerald Gardner, until 1936 a British Customs official in Malaya.
6 *Los Angeles Herald-Examiner*, August 11 1973; *Time*, March 13 1972.
7 *The Times*, London, March 15 1974.
8 *Newsweek*, April 9 1973.
9 *Vampirella* magazine, New York; report from Bucharest in the

Elmira Star-Telegram, New York, January 30 1973; Gunther Sachs' fortieth birthday party, reported in the *Sunday Times Magazine*, London, February 1973.

INDEX